Panda3D 1.7 Game Developer's Cookbook

Over 80 recipes for developing 3D games with Panda3D, a full-scale 3D game engine

Christoph Lang

PACKT PUBLISHING

open source *
community experience distilled

BIRMINGHAM - MUMBAI

Panda3D 1.7 Game Developer's Cookbook

First published: March 2011

Production Reference: 1170311

Published by Packt Publishing Ltd.
32 Lincoln Road
Olton
Birmingham, B27 6PA, UK.

ISBN 978-1-849512-92-3

www.packtpub.com

Cover Image by Asher Wishkerman (a.wishkerman@mpic.de)

Credits

Author
Christoph Lang

Reviewers
C.G. Anderson
Paulo Barbeiro

Acquisition Editor
Usha Iyer

Development Editor
Meeta Rajani

Technical Editor
Prashant Macha

Indexer
Hemangini Bari
Tejal Daruwale

Editorial Team Leader
Mithun Sehgal

Project Team Leader
Priya Mukherji

Project Coordinator
Sneha Harkut

Proofreader
Samantha Lyon

Graphics
Nilesh Mohite

Production Coordinator
Aparna Bhagat

Cover Work
Aparna Bhagat

About the Author

Christoph Lang is a game developer currently working for Mi'pu'mi Games in Vienna. He has a BSc in Computer Science and an MSc in Game Engineering and Simulation Technology, both from UAS Technikum Wien. Christoph has a strong interest in developing and designing games as well as computer graphics and game engine design. He tries to take an active part of the game developer community by contributing code, blog posts, tweets, and of course, this book.

I would like to thank Kathi, my one love, for always being there for me. My parents, siblings, and friends for all their support. Thanks also goes to Alexander Hofmann and his team at UAS Technikum Wien for encouraging me to do this.

About the Reviewers

Cynthia "CG" Anderson (yes, CGA are really her initials) has been involved in the software industry for over 20 years, and has worn many hats—from researcher, to software designer, to UI/UX consultant, to marketing/customer insight researcher, to AI experimenter, to technical writer, to program manager, but also to avid artist, and storyteller. She's shipped multimedia titles as well as written hundreds of pages of user/developer documentation for various companies, as well as advised other past technical books during her varied history. She's seen the rapid expansion of the Internet and of the visual dimension of computing, including being involved in virtual worlds standards definition and couldn't be happier at the result. In fact, she hopes many more people will embrace open source gems like Panda3D, as well as others of equal caliber, and continue to keep not just the open source community but the whole software industry alive and vibrant with new innovations, new opportunities for storytelling, and the creation of entirely new methods for virtual world immersion. You can contact CG through her page on LinkedIn. CG resides currently in the Seattle, WA area.

Paulo Barbeiro is Brazilian, from São Paulo, graduated in Graphic Design in 2004, at Belas Artes SP College, and postgraduate in Game Development at SENAC SP. Paulo has started his professional carrier in 1999, as web developer.

Today, besides the web and mobile application development work, Paulo is involved in experimental educational projects in technology and cyber culture, at SESC SP, where he leads activities about creative code, and art-software, like interactive environments, games, and entertainment media.

www.PacktPub.com

Support files, eBooks, discount offers, and more

You might want to visit www.PacktPub.com for support files and downloads related to your book.

Did you know that Packt offers eBook versions of every book published, with PDF and ePub files available? You can upgrade to the eBook version at www.PacktPub.com and as a print book customer, you are entitled to a discount on the eBook copy. Get in touch with us at service@packtpub.com for more details.

At www.PacktPub.com, you can also read a collection of free technical articles, sign up for a range of free newsletters, and receive exclusive discounts and offers on Packt books and eBooks.

http://PacktLib.PacktPub.com

Do you need instant solutions to your IT questions? PacktLib is Packt's online digital book library. Here, you can access, read, and search across Packt's entire library of books.

Why Subscribe?

- ► Fully searchable across every book published by Packt
- ► Copy and paste, print and bookmark content
- ► On demand and accessible via web browser

Free Access for Packt account holders

If you have an account with Packt at www.PacktPub.com, you can use this to access PacktLib today and view nine entirely free books. Simply use your login credentials for immediate access.

Table of Contents

Preface

Panda3D is a free and open source game engine. It has been used successfully by hobbyists as well as big studios to create games ranging from quick prototypes to full-scale commercial MMOs. Panda3D makes it easy to use models, textures, and sounds to create impressive interactive experiences. With this book, you too will be able to leverage the full power of the Panda3D engine.

Panda3D 1.7 Game Developer's Cookbook will supply you with a set of step-by-step instructions to guide you to usable results quickly. Enabling physics, working with shader effects, and using Panda3D's networking features are only a few of the things you will learn from this book.

This book will take you through all the topics involved in developing games with Panda3D. After a quick sweep through setting up a basic scene, Panda3D 1.7 Game Developer's Cookbook will bring up topics like render-to-texture effects and performance profiling.

Focused recipes will get you closer to your game development goals step-by-step. This book covers advanced topics of game development with the industry-scale Panda3D engine. With every article you will be able to add more features and you will be guided from getting user input from gamepads and shader effects to user interfaces, adding physics, and using the engine's networking capabilities. Using these features, you will also get in touch with other languages and technologies like C++, the Cg shading language, or the Twisted server framework.

Panda3D 1.7 Game Developer's Cookbook provides a great reference for your Panda3D game development needs and helps you to deliver impressive results more quickly and with great ease.

What this book covers

Chapter 1, Setting Up Panda3D and Configuring Development Tools: Get set for working with Panda3D. Install and configure the engine as well as the development tools used throughout the book.

Chapter 2, Creating and Building Scenes: Learn about the scene management of Panda3D. This chapter will show you how to load models, animations, and terrain, and how to place them in a 3D world. You will learn how to work with virtual cameras and how to make them follow an object.

Chapter 3, Controlling the Renderer: This chapter shows, how to set attributes for controlling how a single model or an entire scene should be displayed on the screen. Work with color channels and alpha masks. Create a splitscreen mode and learn how to render on multiple displays.

Chapter 4, Scene Effects and Shaders: Lights, shadows, and particles are some of this chapter's topics. Apply shader effects to models. Take control of the advanced shader generator system of Panda3D and learn how to implement your own custom shader generator.

Chapter 5, Post-Processing and Screen Space Effects: Learn how to add polish and professional looks to your games using post-processing techniques like color grading or depth of field. This chapter also provides an implementation of a deferred rendering pipeline.

Chapter 6, 2D Elements and User Interfaces: Panda3D can also be used for 2D rendering. This chapter focuses on loading and displaying images and on how to use the GUI libraries of Panda3D.

Chapter 7, Application Control: Gain insight on Panda3D's messaging and task systems. Learn how to use messages for inter-object communication. Elegantly handle code that is run on every frame using tasks.

Chapter 8, Collision Detection and Physics: Physics and proper collision handling are important parts of a game. Panda3D gives you powerful programming libraries for controlling physics and collisions like PhysX or ODE that will be presented in this chapter.

Chapter 9, Networking: This chapter is dedicated to sending and receiving data over networks with Panda3D. Learn how to download data, synchronize game objects, and how to post high scores to a remote server.

Chapter 10, Debugging and Performance: Find performance issues and bugs in your Panda3D based games. Use the tools provided by Panda3D and the included Python runtime for fixing these problems.

Chapter 11, Input Handling: Game controllers, a keyboard, and a mouse or even the network—many input measures can be used for providing interactive experiences with Panda3D. This chapter will show you how to transparently handle input from various devices in an elegant, easy, and reusable way.

Chapter 12, Packaging and Distribution: Learn how to package your game code and assets and make them ready for redistribution. Find out how to use set-up and use the browser plugin for a seamless and nearly installation-free end-user experience.

Chapter 13, Connecting Panda3D with Content Creation Tools: Export model files from Blender and preview them with the tools provided by the engine. Learn how to write a data converter for Panda3D's model format and how to compress model data to more space-saving formats.

What you need for this book

Apart from Panda3D and the tools that come included with it, the following software is used in this book:

- ▸ NetBeans 6.8
- ▸ Visual Studio 2008
- ▸ Blender

All these tools and programs are either free software or provide free versions that can be downloaded and used without any further costs. Refer to the chapters discussing these programs for instructions on how to obtain copies and how to install them.

Who this book is for

If you are a developer with experience in Python, Panda3D, and optionally C++ and shading languages and you are looking for quick and easy method to integrate solutions to common game development problems with Panda3D, this book is for you.

Conventions

In this book, you will find a number of styles of text that distinguish between different kinds of information. Here are some examples of these styles, and an explanation of their meaning.

Code words in text are shown as follows: "Save it as `PandaSettings.vsprops` in a directory of your choice."

A block of code is set as follows:

```
from direct.showbase.ShowBase import ShowBase

class Application(ShowBase):
    def __init__(self):
        ShowBase.__init__(self)
```

When we wish to draw your attention to a particular part of a code block, the relevant lines or items are set in bold:

```
from direct.showbase.ShowBase import ShowBase

class Application(ShowBase):
    def __init__(self):
        ShowBase.__init__(self)
```

Any command-line input or output is written as follows:

```
pzip -9 model.egg
```

New terms and **important words** are shown in bold. Words that you see on the screen, in menus or dialog boxes for example, appear in the text like this: "If you can't find it this way, click **View | Property Manager** in the main menu".

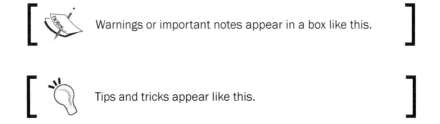

Warnings or important notes appear in a box like this.

Tips and tricks appear like this.

Reader feedback

Feedback from our readers is always welcome. Let us know what you think about this book—what you liked or may have disliked. Reader feedback is important for us to develop titles that you really get the most out of.

To send us general feedback, simply send an e-mail to feedback@packtpub.com, and mention the book title via the subject of your message.

If there is a book that you need and would like to see us publish, please send us a note in the **SUGGEST A TITLE** form on www.packtpub.com or e-mail suggest@packtpub.com.

If there is a topic that you have expertise in and you are interested in either writing or contributing to a book, see our author guide on www.packtpub.com/authors.

Customer support

Now that you are the proud owner of a Packt book, we have a number of things to help you to get the most from your purchase.

Downloading the example code

You can download the example code files for all Packt books you have purchased from your account at `http://www.PacktPub.com`. If you purchased this book elsewhere, you can visit `http://www.PacktPub.com/support` and register to have the files e-mailed directly to you.

Errata

Although we have taken every care to ensure the accuracy of our content, mistakes do happen. If you find a mistake in one of our books—maybe a mistake in the text or the code—we would be grateful if you would report this to us. By doing so, you can save other readers from frustration and help us improve subsequent versions of this book. If you find any errata, please report them by visiting `http://www.packtpub.com/support`, selecting your book, clicking on the **errata submission form** link, and entering the details of your errata. Once your errata are verified, your submission will be accepted and the errata will be uploaded on our website, or added to any list of existing errata, under the Errata section of that title. Any existing errata can be viewed by selecting your title from `http://www.packtpub.com/support`.

Piracy

Piracy of copyright material on the Internet is an ongoing problem across all media. At Packt, we take the protection of our copyright and licenses very seriously. If you come across any illegal copies of our works, in any form, on the Internet, please provide us with the location address or website name immediately so that we can pursue a remedy.

Please contact us at `copyright@packtpub.com` with a link to the suspected pirated material.

We appreciate your help in protecting our authors, and our ability to bring you valuable content.

Questions

You can contact us at `questions@packtpub.com` if you are having a problem with any aspect of the book, and we will do our best to address it.

1

Setting Up Panda3D and Configuring Development Tools

In this chapter, we will cover:

- ▶ Downloading and configuring NetBeans to work with Panda3D
- ▶ Configuring Visual Studio 2008 to work with Panda3D
- ▶ Understanding Panda3D's runtime configuration options
- ▶ Setting up the game structure
- ▶ Building Panda3D from source code

Introduction

The Panda3D game engine has initially been a closed-source project of Disney Interactive but was later opened to the community, allowing anyone to use the engine or contribute code. Development of Panda3D is now driven and coordinated in a joint effort by Disney Interactive and the Entertainment Technology Center of the Carnegie Mellon University. Together, they are adding new features, fixing bugs, and preparing new releases of the engine.

Panda3D is distributed under a version of the very liberal BSD open-source license, which allows anyone interested to download, view, alter, and redistribute the source code compiled binaries without ever having to pay any license fees. This applies to commercial projects too. So creating a game using Panda3D and selling it is no problem and will never require any amount of money to be paid.

Panda3D is a very powerful and feature-rich game engine that comes with a lot of features needed for creating modern video games. Using Python as a scripting language to interface with the low-level programming libraries makes it easy to quickly create games because this layer of abstraction neatly hides many of the complexities of handling assets, hardware resources, or graphics rendering, for example. This also allows simple games and prototypes to be created very quickly and keeps the code needed for getting things going to a minimum.

Panda3D is a complete game engine package. This means that it is not just a collection of game programming libraries with a nice Python interface, but also includes all the supplementary tools for previewing, converting, and exporting assets as well as packing game code and data for redistribution. Delivering such tools is a very important aspect of a game engine that helps with increasing the productivity of a development team.

The Panda3D engine is a very nice set of building blocks needed for creating entertainment software, scaling nicely to the needs of hobbyists, students, and professional game development teams. Panda3D is known to have been used in projects ranging from one-shot experimental prototypes to full-scale commercial MMORPG productions like Toontown Online or Pirates of the Caribbean Online.

Before you are able to start a new project and use all the powerful features provided by Panda3D to their fullest, though, you need to prepare your working environment and tools. By the end of this chapter, you will have a strong set of programming tools at hand, as well as the knowledge of how to configure Panda3D to your future projects' needs.

Downloading and configuring NetBeans to work with Panda3D

When writing code, having the right set of tools at hand and feeling comfortable when using them is very important. Panda3D uses Python for scripting and there are plenty of good integrated development environments available for this language like IDLE, Eclipse, or Eric. Of course, Python code can be written using the excellent Vim or Emacs editors too.

Tastes do differ, and every programmer has his or her own preferences when it comes to this decision. To make things easier and have a uniform working environment, however, we are going to use the free NetBeans IDE for developing Python scripts throughout this book. This choice was made out of pure preference and one of the many great alternatives might be used as well for following through the recipes in this book, but may require different steps for the initial setup and getting samples to run.

In this recipe we will install and configure the NetBeans integrated development environment to suit our needs for developing games with Panda3D using the Python programming language.

Getting ready

Before beginning, be sure to download and install Panda3D. To download the engine SDK and tools, go to www.panda3d.org/download.php:

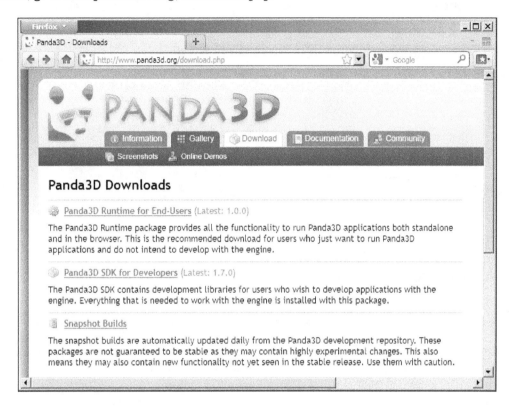

The **Panda3D Runtime for End-Users** is a prebuilt redistributable package containing a player program and a browser plugin. These can be used to easily run packaged Panda3D games. You can find more information on this topic in *Chapter 12, Packaging and Distribution*.

Under **Snapshot Builds**, you will be able to find daily builds of the latest version of the Panda3D engine. These are to be handled with care, as they are not meant for production purposes.

Finally, the link labeled **Panda3D SDK for Developers** is the one you need to follow to retrieve a copy of the Panda3D development kit and tools. This will always take you to the latest release of Panda3D, which at this time is version 1.7.0. This version was marked as unstable by the developers but has been working in a stable way for this book. This version also added a great amount of interesting features, like the web browser plugin, an advanced shader, and graphics pipeline or built-in shadow effects, which really are worth a try and will be treated in the following chapters.

Click the link that says **Panda3D SDK for Developers** to reach the page shown in the following screenshot:

Here you can select one of the SDK packages for the platforms that Panda3D is available on. This book assumes a setup of NetBeans on Windows but most of the samples should work on these alternative platforms too, as most of Panda3D's features have been ported to all of these operating systems.

To download and install the Panda3D SDK, click the **Panda3D SDK 1.7.0** link at the top of the page and download the installer package. Launch the program and follow the installation wizard, always choosing the default settings. In this and all of the following recipes we'll assume the install path to be `C:\Panda3D-1.7.0`, which is the default installation location. If you chose a different location, it might be a good idea to note the path and be prepared to adapt the presented file and folder paths to your needs!

How to do it...

Follow these steps to set up your Panda3D game development environment:

1. Point your web browser to `netbeans.org` and click the prominent **Download FREE** button:

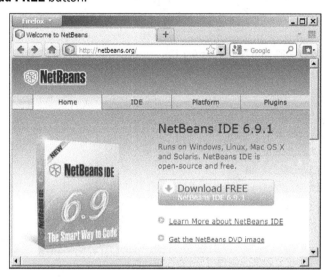

2. Ignore the big table showing all kinds of different versions on the following page and scroll down. Click the link that says **JDK with NetBeans IDE Java SE bundle**.

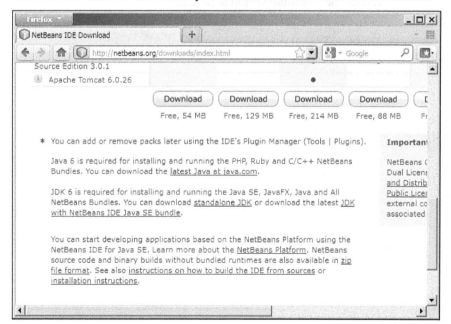

3. This will take you to the following page as shown here. Click the **Downloads** link to the right to proceed.

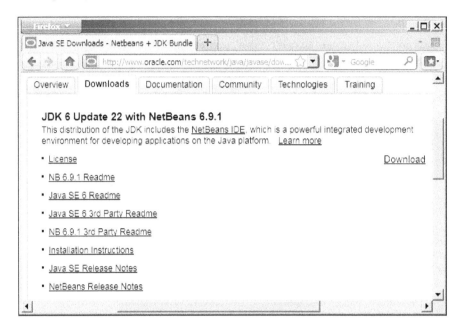

4. You will find yourself at another page, as shown in the screenshot. Select **Windows** in the **Platform** dropdown menu and tick the checkbox to agree to the license agreement. Click the **Continue** button to proceed.

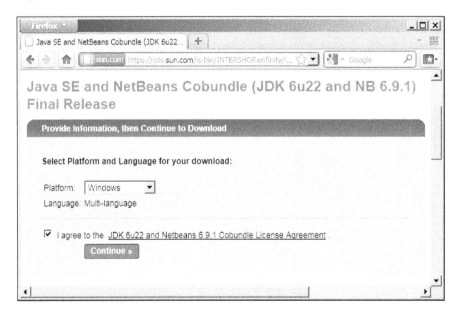

5. Follow the instructions on the next page. Click the file name to start the download.

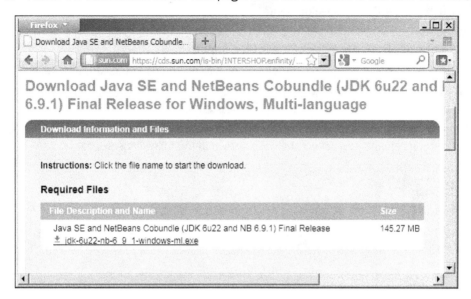

6. Launch the installer and follow the setup wizard.
7. Once installed, start the NetBeans IDE.
8. In the main toolbar click **Tools | Plugins**.
9. Select the tab that is labeled **Available Plugins**.
10. Browse the list until you find **Python** and tick the checkbox next to it:

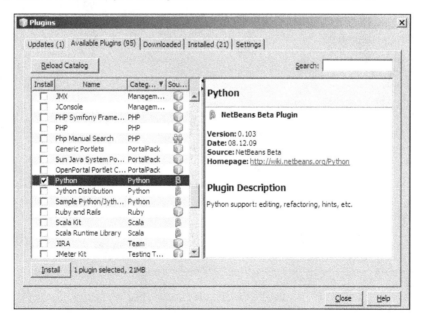

11. Click **Install**. This will start a wizard that downloads and installs the necessary features for Python development.

12. At the end of the installation wizard you will be prompted to restart the NetBeans IDE, which will finish the setup of the Python feature.

13. Once NetBeans reappears on your screen, click **Tools | Python Platforms**.

14. In the **Python Platform Manager** window, click the **New** button and browse for the file `C:\Panda3D-1.7.0\python\ppython.exe`.

15. Select Python 2.6.4 from the platforms list and click the **Make Default** button. Your settings should now reflect the ones shown in the following screenshot:

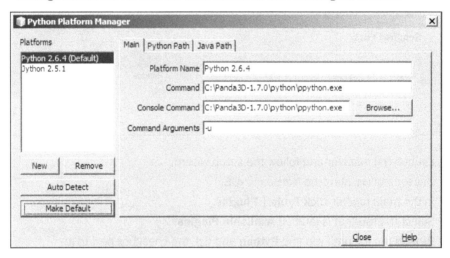

16. Finally we select the **Python Path** tab and once again, compare your settings to the screenshot:

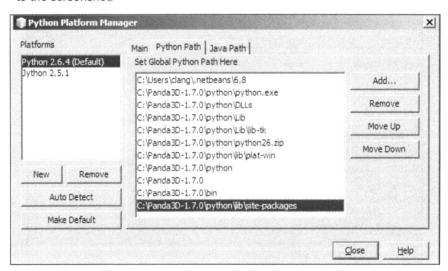

17. Click the **Close** button and you are done!

How it works...

In the preceding steps we configured NetBeans to use the Python runtime that drives the Panda3D engine and as we can see, it is very easy to install and set up our working environment for Panda3D.

There's more...

Different than other game engines, Panda3D follows an interesting approach in its internal architecture. While the more common approach is to embed a scripting runtime into the game engine's executable, Panda3D uses the Python runtime as its main executable. The engine modules handling such things as loading assets, rendering graphics, or playing sounds are implemented as native extension modules. These are loaded by Panda3D's custom Python interpreter as needed when we use them in our script code.

Essentially, the architecture of Panda3D turns the hierarchy between native code and the scripting runtime upside down. While in other game engines, native code initiates calls to the embedded scripting runtime, Panda3D shifts the direction of program flow. In Panda3D, the Python runtime is the core element of the engine that lets script code initiate calls into native programming libraries.

To understand Panda3D, it is important to understand this architectural decision. Whenever we start the ppython executable, we start up the Panda3D engine.

 If you ever get into a situation where you are compiling your own Panda3D runtime from source code, don't forget to revisit steps 13 to 17 of this recipe to configure NetBeans to use your custom runtime executable!

Configuring Visual Studio 2008 to work with Panda3D

The scripting-centric architecture of the Panda3D divides development into two sides. One of them is the application code written in Python that is created by game programmers to control the gameplay behavior of their games. On the opposite side we can find the engine modules, which are written in C++ and compiled to native modules. At runtime, the Python interpreter found that the core of Panda3D loads these modules and lets us make calls into them to control the engine and the game running on it.

This programming model combines the best of both of these programming worlds. While the performance critical parts are implemented in C++, gameplay programmers do not know any of the advanced stuff going on under the hood to get things done. Instead, they are able to use Python, an expressive and easy to learn programming language, for using Panda3D's great features. This also allows the engine developers to work on the internals of Panda3D while gameplay programmers are able to concentrate on creating interesting games.

While this split between application and gameplay code works really well, nothing keeps us from using the Panda3D programming libraries and writing application side code in C++. There's nothing wrong with coding our games in Python, and in general it is the path to follow with Panda3D. But the possibility to use C++ is there, so we shouldn't omit discussing this topic.

In this recipe we will configure Visual Studio 2008 for compiling Panda3D C++ projects on Windows. Panda3D is a cross-platform game engine and other compilers like gcc and alternative IDEs like KDevelop might as well be used for writing C++ programs that link to the Panda3D libraries but within the context of this book, we will be looking at how things are working on the Windows platform.

Getting ready

This recipe assumes that Visual Studio 2008 is already installed on your system. If not, you can download Visual C++ 2008 Express Edition from `www.microsoft.com/express/Downloads/` for free. Some restrictions apply to this free edition, but all recipes in this book are tested to work with this version of Visual Studio.

 Although technically very similar, the Express and full editions of Visual Studio do differ in several ways. Some menus, options, and functions of the full versions are not available in the free Express edition. So if you are looking for help online you should always clearly state which version you are using.

How to do it...

The following tasks will help you to configure Visual Studio 2008 for developing Panda3D projects:

1. In a text editor of your choice, create a new file and paste the following code:

```
<?xml version="1.0" encoding="Windows-1252"?>
<VisualStudioPropertySheet
    ProjectType="Visual C++"
    Version="8.00"
    Name="PandaSettings"
```

```
>
<Tool
    Name="VCCLCompilerTool"
    AdditionalIncludeDirectories="&quot;C:\Panda3D-1.7.0\
python\include&quot;;&quot;C:\Panda3D-1.7.0\include&quot;"
    />
<Tool
    Name="VCLinkerTool"
    AdditionalDependencies="libp3framework.lib libpanda.
lib libpandafx.lib libpandaexpress.lib libp3dtool.lib
libp3dtoolconfig.lib libp3pystub.lib libp3direct.lib"
    AdditionalLibraryDirectories="&quot;C:\Panda3D-1.7.0\
python\libs&quot;;&quot;C:\Panda3D-1.7.0\lib&quot;"
    />
</VisualStudioPropertySheet>
```

2. Save it as `PandaSettings.vsprops` in a directory of your choice.

3. Start Visual Studio 2008 or Visual C++ 2008 Express and create a new C++ project.

4. Open the **Property Manager**, which is located in the same pane as the **Solution Explorer** and the **Class View** by default. If you can't find it this way, click **View | Property Manager** in the main menu.

5. Right-click the item **Release | Win32** and select **Add Existing Property Sheet...** from the popup menu.

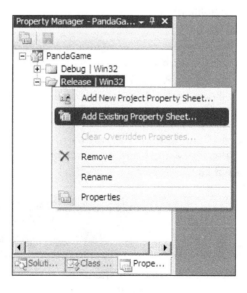

6. Locate and select the `PandaSettings.vsprops` file.

How it works...

In this recipe we set all the options for using Panda3D using a feature of Visual Studio called **Property Sheets**, which allow you to configure each build target of your project independently and in a reusable way.

Property Sheet settings are stored using XML, as you can see in the previous sample code. Let's have a look at the data stored in `PandaSettings.vsprops`:

Following the XML header and the opening tag of the property sheet, we can see two `<Tool/>` tags, the first of which is adding the required include paths to the header search paths. The second `<Tool/>` tag instructs the linker to use the listed library files when it is generating the executable, as well as where it will need to look for these files.

There's more...

You might have noticed that we only configured the release target in this recipe. The reason for this is that the recipe is aimed at the precompiled Panda3D SDK, which only includes the files needed to produce release builds.

If you want to create debug builds you will definitely need to compile Panda3D yourself and configure your debug target in the way shown in this recipe (but don't forget to modify the search paths accordingly!).

Also, you don't have to use Property Sheets to configure include directories and linked libraries. You may also right-click the project node in the project explorer, click **Properties** and then click **Configuration Properties | Properties | C++** in the tree of configuration categories to then fill in the include directories in the **Additional Include Directories** field in the right pane of the window.

To configure the linker, choose **Configuration Properties | Properties | Linker** in the same window as previously described and fill in the library file names into the **Additional Dependencies** and **Additional Library Directories** fields.

Understanding Panda3D's runtime configuration options

Panda3D allows you to configure the engine runtime using a central configuration file. This recipe will show you where to find this configuration file and will explain a selection of settings you are able to specify to tweak Panda3D's behavior.

How to do it...

You can configure the Panda3D engine with these two steps:

1. Open the file `C:\Panda3D-1.7.0\etc\Config.prc` in a text editor.
2. Edit and add settings.

How it works...

Now that you've opened Panda3D's configuration file, it is time to explain a good part of the vast array of settings the engine allows you to modify. The following table will present the names of the configuration variables, the values that can be set, as well as a short description of what part of Panda3D is influenced by the setting.

The column containing the possible values uses several notations:

- Square brackets are used to denote an interval of values. For example, [0..8] denotes an interval of integers between 0 and 8, while the notation [0.0..1.0] stands for an interval of floating point values. The interval boundaries are inclusive.

- Within intervals, the labels `MAX_INT` and `MAX_DBL` are used as placeholders for the maximum possible values for signed integer and floating point variables.

- The `prc` file format uses `#t` for true and `#f` for false for Boolean configuration flags. For example, the following line in `Config.prc` enables full screen mode:

  `fullscreen #t`

- "A valid file path" means a Unix-style file path, even on Windows. For example, the following line is used to set the application icon:

  `icon-filename /c/mygame/assets/icon.ico`

- Any other values than the ones previously described are meant to be inserted directly, without quotes. If multiple values are listed, you may use one of them at a time.

Name	Possible Values	Description
audio-volume	[0.0..1.0]	Sets the master volume of your game.
background-color	Any combination of 3 floating point numbers between 0 and 1, e.g.: 1.0 0.3 0.4	This variable sets the default background color for the render window and all render buffers in RGB format.
cursor-filename	A valid file path	Allows you to specify an image file to use as the mouse cursor.
cursor-hidden	#t, #f	If set to true, this makes the mouse cursor invisible when it is within the bounds of the game window.

Name	Possible Values	Description
disable-sticky-keys	#t, #f	If set to true, this disables the "sticky keys" feature of Windows. It's a good idea to set this to true because the sticky keys popup window will cause your game to lose focus!
fullscreen	#t, #f	Set this variable to #t if your game should switch to fullscreen mode on startup.
icon-filename	A valid file path	This variable instructs Panda3D to use the given file as its application icon.
model-path	A valid file path	The model-path variable sets one or more paths the engine will use as your search path when looking for models to load. The special symbol $THIS_PRC_DIR can be used to define directories relative to the configuration file. With $MAIN_DIR you are able to set a path relative to the directory the game's main python file resides in.
		For example, we can find these three lines in the default `Config.prc` file:
		`model-path $MAIN_DIR`
		`model-path $THIS_PRC_DIR/..`
		`model-path $THIS_PRC_DIR/../models`
		These lines add the directory containing the main Python source file and the directories containing the sample models that come with the Panda3D SDK to the engine asset search path.
show-frame-rate-meter	#t, #f	If enabled, this shows a frame rate counter in the game window.
sync-video	#t, #f	Enables and disables vertical synchronization. If this is set to true, the maximum frame rate will be equal to the refresh rate of your display device.
win-origin	Two integer values, for example, 25 20	Lets you define the position of the top left corner of the game window. When fullscreen mode is enabled, this setting has no effect.
win-size	Two integer values, for example, 640 480	Sets the window size as well as the resolution when in fullscreen mode. When going to fullscreen mode, Panda3D switches the screen resolution to the values specified in this variable. If this does not match your screen resolution, it might have an effect on the positions and sizes of your desktop icons and any open program window.

Name	Possible Values	Description
window-title	A string	This setting is used to specify the title of the game window. The string does not have to be put within quotes even if it contains spaces.

There's more...

By setting the configuration variables above, you are already able to modify the engine's runtime behavior to your liking. But Panda3D's configuration system provides a few additional features you should know about.

Listing all configuration variables

The preceding table only shows a selection of the most commonly used configuration variables. To get a list of all configuration variables available in Panda3D, insert the following import statement and method call into your application code:

```
from panda3d.core import ConfigVariableManager
ConfigVariableManager.getGlobalPtr().listVariables()
```

Loading a specific configuration file

You do not need to put all engine settings into the global configuration file shown in this recipe. Instead, you can use the following function to load settings from any given file:

```
loadPrcFile("myconfig.prc")
```

You should put this call to a global scope to make sure settings are loaded before the engine systems that are using them are initialized.

Embedding configuration data in Python code

You can also put settings directly into your Python code files. Just add something similar to the following snippet to the global scope:

```
configVars = """
win-size 1440 900
fullscreen 1
"""

loadPrcFileData("", configVars)
```

Setting up the game structure

Through the course of this recipe you will learn the steps that are necessary to set up a very basic application structure to get your application going.

Getting ready

To follow the steps of this recipe you should have finished the first recipe in this chapter to have a properly configured development environment.

How to do it...

Follow these steps to create an empty project skeleton:

1. Start NetBeans and click **File | New Project...** in the main menu.
2. Select **Python Project** and click **Next** on the first screen of the **New Project** Wizard.

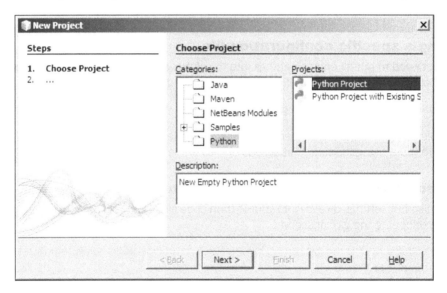

3. On the **New Python Project** screen, set the **Project Name** and choose a **Project Location**. Also select **Set as Main Project** and **Create Main File**. Set the textbox to **main.py**, and check that the right **Python Platform** is active. Click **Finish** to proceed.

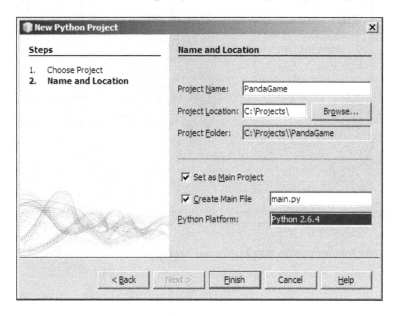

4. Right-click the **Project Name | Sources | Top Level** item in the tree view in the **Projects** tab and select **New | Empty Module**.

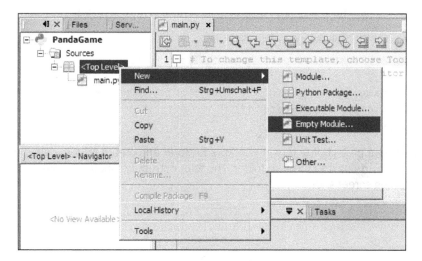

5. In the window that opens, set the **File Name** to **Application** and click **Finish**.

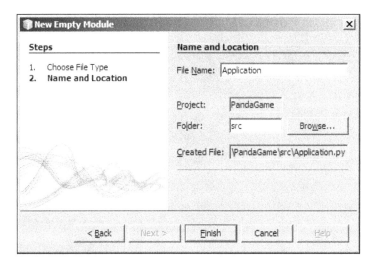

6. Paste the following code into `Application.py`:

```
from direct.showbase.ShowBase import ShowBase


class Application(ShowBase):

    def __init__(self):

        ShowBase.__init__(self)
```

7. The code that follows goes into `main.py`:

```
from Application import Application

if __name__ == "__main__":
    gameApp = Application()
    gameApp.run()
```

8. Open your project directory in Windows Explorer and create folders called `models` and `sounds` next to the `src` folder. The folder structure should resemble the following screenshot:

9. Open the `Config.prc` file as described in the prior recipe and add the following lines:

```
model-path $MAIN_DIR/../models
model-path $MAIN_DIR/../sounds
```

10. Hit _F6_ to run the application.

How it works...

First, we start by creating a new project in NetBeans. It generally is a very good idea to name the main file that will be launched by the Python runtime `main.py`, so we are already set when we want to package our code and assets for redistribution later on.

The `Application` class, derived from `ShowBase`, is added as an abstraction of our game application. We must not forget to call the constructor of `ShowBase` in the constructor of `Application` or else there won't be a window opening when launching the program.

Because we do not want code files and assets to be scattered in a mess inside one single folder, we add folders dedicated to certain asset types. Depending on the type of project we intend to create, this setup may vary and we may wish to add additional folders. What's important about that is not to forget to add these extra folders to Panda3D's search paths too in `Config.prc`, just like the `models` and `sounds` folders!

Building Panda3D from source code

When developing a game with Panda3D you may want to—and most likely will need to—compile the engine from source code. This recipe will show how to do this and show which options there are for configuring how your custom build of Panda3D is created.

Getting ready

The following instructions rely on the target system having installed Microsoft Visual Studio 2008 or Microsoft Visual C++ Express 2008. To build the DirectX 8 and 9 renderers, you also need the DirectX SDK, which can be downloaded from `msdn.microsoft.com/en-us/directx/aa937788.aspx`. If you have the Professional Edition of Visual Studio, you're set and ready to go.

For making the recipe work with the Express Edition you will need to download and install the Windows Server 2003 R2 Platform SDK, as recommended in the documentation of Panda3D. It can be obtained from the following URL: `www.microsoft.com/downloads/details.aspx?familyid=0BAF2B35-C656-4969-ACE8-E4C0C0716ADB`

How to do it...

Work through these tasks to build Panda3D from source code:

1. Go to `www.panda3d.org/download.php?platform=windows&version=1.7.0&sdk`, download the **Panda3D Complete Source Code** package and unzip the archive at a location of your choice.

2. Open the file `makepanda\makepanda.bat` in a text editor and change the line `if %PROCESSOR_ARCHITECTURE% == AMD64 goto :AMD64` to `REM if %PROCESSOR_ARCHITECTURE% == AMD64 goto :AMD64`.

3. Open a **Visual Studio 2008 Command Prompt** by clicking **Microsoft Visual Studio 2008 | Visual Studio Tools | Visual Studio Command Prompt** in the **Start** menu. If you have Visual C++ Express 2008, you can find it under **Microsoft Visual C++ Express 2008 | Visual Studio Tools | Visual Studio Command Prompt**.

4. Change to the directory you unpacked the source code to. If you enter the `dir` command and see the following directory listing (or a similar looking one) you are in the right directory:

5. Type `makepanda\makepanda.bat --everything`.

How it works...

Panda3D uses its own custom build system to produce builds from source code. In step 2, we need to modify the build system's start script to prevent it from throwing an error if the build system is using a 64-bit processor. Building 64-bit executables does not work with version 1.7.0 of Panda3D and isn't officially supported, so we force the build system to compile 32-bit executables and libraries.

In the following steps we open a **Visual Studio 2008 Command Prompt**, which guarantees that all required search paths are set properly and kick off a complete build of Panda3D. Please note that such a build, depending on the power of your machine, takes about one hour to complete!

Once the build is complete, the freshly compiled version of Panda3D can be found in the `built` subdirectory.

There's more...

Panda3D's build system allows us to configure the build using a number of command line flags. The **--everything** option we already used before will instruct the `makepanda` script to build Panda3D and all third party libraries.

The exact counterpart of the **--everything** option is **--nothing**, which will disable all third party libraries to be built.

Of course there isn't just on and off. The makepanda build script allows us to set which libraries we do and do not want to include in our build. This can be done by setting the various **--use-xxx** and **--no-xxx** flags, where xxx stands for a library to be included or left out of the resulting executable. For a full list, just issue the command `makepanda\makepanda.bat` from the top level of the unpacked source package.

The **--optimize** option allows to set the optimization level used when compiling Panda3D on a range from 1 to 4, where 1 creates a debug build and 4 enables the most aggressive optimizations, including link time code generation. If not set, this value defaults to 3, which provides a safe default while generating a very well performing build.

Lastly, we can use the **--installer** flag to generate an installer, which for example makes it easier to redistribute the custom build of the engine to other developers on a team.

2
Creating and Building Scenes

In this chapter, we will cover the following topics:

- ▸ Loading models and actors
- ▸ Loading terrain
- ▸ Loading and attaching sounds to objects
- ▸ Creating a scene using C++
- ▸ Adding an additional camera
- ▸ Inspecting and modifying the scene
- ▸ Modifying the scene graph
- ▸ Moving objects based on time
- ▸ Controlling actions using intervals
- ▸ Making animations fit to intervals
- ▸ Making objects follow a predefined path
- ▸ Making the camera smoothly follow an object
- ▸ Generating geometry at runtime
- ▸ Loading data asynchronously

Introduction

One thing that is great about games is their ability to present immersive and exciting worlds which players are able to explore over the course of their progress in the game. Be it dungeons filled with dragons and monsters or futuristic space stations, these worlds do have one thing in common they need to be built by hand by someone prior to their inclusion in a game.

In this chapter we will see how Panda3D allows us to build interesting scenes by placing and arranging static and animated objects to fill the initial void of an empty scene. Additionally, we will see how to place cameras and make our game worlds even more exciting by dynamically moving and animating objects.

Panda3D makes it very easy to quickly load some static non-animated models as well as actors that can be animated and placed to your liking to create a scene. This is one of the powerful features of the engine and, for example, makes it a very strong prototyping tool. In this recipe you will learn how to get Panda3D to load models and actors and display them on the screen.

 This book follows the naming convention used by Panda3D. Therefore the term **model** refers to a static mesh without animation data and **actor** is used for meshes that include animation data.

Getting ready

The following steps will use the application skeleton presented in the recipe *Setting up the game structure* found in *Chapter 1, Setting Up Panda3D and Configuring Development Tools*. If you're unsure about setting up a project and need a little refresher on that topic, feel free to take a step back to this topic.

How to do it...

Loading models and actors is easy. Just follow these steps:

1. Add the highlighted code to your `Application.py` file:

```python
from direct.showbase.ShowBase import ShowBase
from direct.actor.Actor import Actor
from panda3d.core import Vec3

class Application(ShowBase):
    def __init__(self):
        ShowBase.__init__(self)
        self.teapot = loader.loadModel("teapot")
        self.teapot.reparentTo(render)
        self.teapot.setPos(-5, 0, 0)

        self.pandaActor = Actor("panda", {"walk": "panda-walk"})
        self.pandaActor.reparentTo(render)
        self.pandaActor.setPos(Vec3(5, 0, 0))
        self.pandaActor.loop("walk")

        self.cam.setPos(0, -30, 6)
```

Click **Run** | **Run Project** in the main menu or press *F6* to start the application. If you followed all of the steps correctly, your scene will look like the following screenshot:

How it works...

After setting up our new project, we add new import statements for the `Actor` and `Vec3` classes we are going to use in the following code. Then the teapot model, which is included in the standard installation of Panda3D, is loaded—note that you do not need to provide a file extension!

The next line is very important. The `reparentTo()` method is used to make the calling object a child of the object given as the parameter to `reparentTo()`, which is the `render` object in this case. This allows you to build hierarchies of scene objects so that when you move a parent node, all child nodes are influenced too. For example, in a racing game you could make the wheel models child nodes of the car body model to ensure their proper position relative to the chassis. In our sample code, the teapot is a child of `render`, which is the root of the scene graph. Models and actors that are not added to the scene graph will not be drawn!

Finally, the teapot is set five units to the left of the coordinate system origin to leave some space for the big panda that is going to be loaded by the next block of code.

It is important to understand Panda3D's coordinate system, which is visualized in the following screenshot. By default, positive x (in red) points to the right, positive y (in green) points into the screen and positive z (in blue) points up.

Loading actors works a little bit different than loading models. We create a new instance of the `Actor` class and provide the name of the actor to load. The second parameter is a dictionary that maps animation names to a file containing the animation data. This parameter is optional and only necessary if animation and mesh data are stored in separate files.

After adding the panda to the scene graph and setting its position, the `walk` animation is set to play in a loop and finally, the camera is set to a position that allows it to capture our first scene.

Loading terrain

If you plan to create a game set in a non-flat outdoor environment, you will need a way to create a natural looking terrain consisting of mountains, hills, and slopes. Luckily, Panda3D comes with the `GeoMipTerrain` class that allows you to generate such an environment from a simple grayscale image called a **height map**.

Getting ready

Create a new project as described in *Setting up the game structure* and add a directory called `textures` on the same level as the `models`, `nbproject`, `sounds`, and `src` directories. Also copy the height map and terrain texture you are going to use for rendering the landscape to the `textures` directory.

Height maps can be created with specialized tools like **Terragen** or by rendering the height information of a mesh created by hand to a texture using a modeling package like Maya. A very quick solution is to generate a random landscape using a difference cloud filter found in many professional image editing programs.

The size of your height map should be 2n + 1 pixels so the engine is able to handle it efficiently. This means your height map images should be of sizes 257x257 (28 + 1) or 1025x1025 (210 + 1), for example. This image size rule is mandated by the algorithm that turns the pixels of the height map into the vertices of the terrain. If the texture image provided fails to comply with this rule, the engine will resize it, which may lead to longer loading times and undesired resulting terrains. The code we are going to write will use a texture size of 513x513 pixels.

How to do it...

Fulfill these tasks to make Panda3D load and render terrain:

1. Make sure all needed resources are in place and add the marked code to `Application.py`. The height map and color map images are assumed to be called `height.png` and `grass.png`.

```python
from direct.showbase.ShowBase import ShowBase
from panda3d.core import GeoMipTerrain

class Application(ShowBase):
    def __init__(self):
        ShowBase.__init__(self)
        self.terrain = GeoMipTerrain("terrain")
        self.terrain.setHeightfield("../textures/height.png")
        self.terrain.setColorMap("../textures/grass.png")
        self.terrain.getRoot().setSz(35)
        self.terrain.getRoot().reparentTo(render)
        self.terrain.generate()

        z = self.terrain.getElevation(256, 256) * 40
        self.cam.setPos(256, 256, z)

        self.terrain.setFocalPoint(self.cam)
        self.taskMgr.add(self.updateTerrain, "update terrain")

    def updateTerrain(self, task):
        self.terrain.update()
        return task.cont
```

2. Start your program. You should be able to see a scene similar to the following screenshot:

How it works...

After the obligatory import statement, we create a new instance of `GeoMipTerrain` and load the height map and texture. In version 1.7.0 of Panda3D, `GeoMipTerrain` seems to ignore the search paths set in the configuration. Therefore we provide the full relative paths and filenames. Additionally, we set the maximum elevation of the terrain by scaling the geometry about the z-axis with the `setSz()` method. By default, the terrain's elevation ranges between 0 and 1. Feel free to play with this value until the results suit your needs!

Next we add the terrain to the scene graph and call `generate()` to create the geometry for our landscape. We also set the camera to a position that is somewhere within the boundaries of the terrain and use `getElevation()` to sample the height map at the given position to set the camera height to be above the hills.

`GeoMipTerrain` uses **LOD (level of detail)** mapping, where items closer to the focal point are rendered in higher quality than those further away. We can also turn this off (and always get the highest quality) by calling `setBruteforce(True)` on a `GeoMipTerrain` object. To wrap things up, we add a small task to keep the terrain updated according to the focal point's position.

There's more...

`GeoMipTerrain` objects can be configured further with the following methods, which you most likely need to use as they have a great influence on rendering performance.

Block size

Geometrical mipmapping, the level of detail technique used by the terrain renderer, divides the terrain into groups of quads, which then are set to an elevation according to the information found in the height map. The method `setBlockSize()` allows you to define the number of quads to use. Clearly, a higher amount will result in increased quality and decreased performance and vice versa.

Near and far thresholds

With the `setNear()` and `setFar()` methods of `GeoMipTerrain` you are able to define two important thresholds that are used for choosing the level of rendering fidelity of the terrain. The near distance defines to which point from the focal point the highest level of detail will be used. The far distance, on the other hand, sets from which distance on the lowest detail level will be chosen.

Loading and attaching sounds to objects

In this recipe we will take a look into Panda3D's positional audio capabilities. 3D sound is a wonderful tool to immerse the player and to generate great atmosphere. Positional audio also can help the player to orientate: In a shooter, for example, it is much easier to return fire if one heard that the enemy units are attacking from behind.

Getting ready

Before starting this recipe, be sure to set up a project as described in *Setting up the game structure*. You will also need to provide a mono sound file called `loop.wav` in the `sounds` folder of your project.

How to do it...

Let's load a sound file and attach it to a model:

1. Open `Application.py` and add the highlighted code:

```
from direct.showbase.ShowBase import ShowBase
from direct.showbase.Audio3DManager import Audio3DManager

class Application(ShowBase):
    def __init__(self):
        ShowBase.__init__(self)
```

```
self.smiley = loader.loadModel("smiley")
self.smiley.reparentTo(render)

self.audio = Audio3DManager(self.sfxManagerList[0])
self.audio.attachListener(self.cam)

self.loop = self.audio.loadSfx("loop.wav")
self.loop.setLoop(True)
self.audio.attachSoundToObject(self.loop, self.smiley)
self.loop.play()

self.cam.setPos(0, -40, 0)
```

2. Hold the left mouse button and move the mouse to pan the camera, or hold down the right mouse button and use the mouse to zoom in and out of the scene. Note how the sound position changes.

How it works...

The key to positional audio in Panda3D is the `Audio3DManager` class. After adding a smiley to the scene, we initialize the `Audio3DManager` and set the camera to be the listener object. This has the effect that all sounds played using positional audio will be mixed relative to the `NodePath` we pass to `attachListener()`.

Then, the sound file is loaded, set to be a loop and attached to the smiley, so that the sound plays wherever the object is positioned in the scene. Finally we start to play the sound loop and position the camera.

 Positional audio will not work if we are using a stereo sound file. Panda3D will print a warning message in the console output if our sound is stereo, not mono.

There's more...

If you want to take the scene objects' and listener's velocity into account to achieve the Doppler effect, you need to update the listener and object positions by passing their velocity vectors to the `setListenerVelocity()` and `setSoundVelocity()` methods of `Audio3DManager`.

Creating a scene using C++

The Panda3D engine was mainly designed to be controlled by Python scripts to hide away the complexities of handling and rendering a 3D game world. This allows us to concentrate on creating game scenes and gameplay without having to think about any low-level implementation issues. Many of these have already been solved by the Panda3D developers and are implemented in a whole set of libraries written in C++. When working with Python Panda3D's API nicely wraps their functionality, but we may also use these libraries directly from our own C++ code if we prefer to use this language instead of Python.

Getting ready

If you haven't yet, please read the recipe *Configuring Visual Studio 2008 to work with Panda3D* found in Chapter 1 prior to starting this one. The following steps assume you know how to get a Panda3D project started in Visual Studio 2008 or Visual C++ Express 2008. Both editions can be used for this recipe. For the sake of readability, this recipe will refer to both of them as Visual Studio 2008.

How to do it...

These tasks will show you how to create a scene using the C++ programming language:

1. Start Visual Studio 2008 and create a new **Win32 Console Application**. Make sure to tick the **Empty project** checkbox in the project wizard.

2. Set up your project paths and settings as described in the section *Configuring Visual Studio 2008 to work with Panda3D*.

3. Right-click the **Source Files** item in the solution explorer, click **Add | New Item...**.

4. Choose the **C++ File (.cpp)** template in the **Code** category of the **Add New Item** window and add the file `main.cpp`.

5. Insert the following code to the newly created file:

    ```cpp
    #include <pandaFramework.h>
    #include <pandaSystem.h>
    #include <animControlCollection.h>
    #include <auto_bind.h>

    PandaFramework framework;

    int main(int argc, char* argv[])
    {
      framework.open_framework(argc, argv);
      WindowFramework* win = framework.open_window();
      NodePath camera = win->get_camera_group();
    ```

```
    NodePath teapot = win->load_model(framework.get_models(),
"teapot");
    teapot.reparent_to(win->get_render());
    teapot.set_pos(-5, 0, 0);

    NodePath panda = win->load_model(framework.get_models(),
"panda");
    panda.reparent_to(win->get_render());
    panda.set_pos(5, 0, 0);

    win->load_model(panda, "panda-walk");
    AnimControlCollection pandaAnims;
    auto_bind(panda.node(), pandaAnims);
    pandaAnims.loop("panda_soft", false);

    camera.set_pos(0, -30, 6);

    framework.main_loop();
    framework.close_framework();
    return 0;
}
```

6. Press *F5* to run the program. You should now be able to see the scene from the section *Loading models and actors*.

How it works...

In this recipe, we are using the `PandaFramework` class, which acts as a wrapper around Panda3D's core classes to form an application framework. To get our application started, we need to initialize our global instance of `PandaFramework` and open a window. For convenience, we also get a reference to the default camera, so we don't need to call `win->get_camera_group()` every time we want to modify the camera.

Loading the teapot and panda models and adding them to their positions within our little scene looks nearly the same as in Python, with one exception—that strange call to `framework.get_models()`. This method returns the root of scene graph, which is not rendered, but instead serves as a scratchpad area for model loading. This is passed to the `load_model()` method as the parent node that the model will be attached to and may seem a little overly verbose in this sample. In fact, we could pass `win->get_render()` as the parent node and drop the `reparent_to()` call. But in practice, where you might not add a model to the scene directly after you loaded it, the purpose of this scratch scene becomes more evident. In real world projects, hundreds of models are preloaded for the current level, with this scratchpad area removing the need to keep hundreds of `NodePath` instances around. Instead, the temporary scene is queried for the needed model, which then is reparented to its place in the rendered scene.

Loading and playing animations also works differently than what we know from Python. Instead of an explicit method for loading animation data, we use `load_model()` to load the animation and make it a child node of the panda actor. We then call `auto_bind()` to fill an `AnimControlCollection` and bind the animation data to the panda actor. Note the animation name used for starting the loop—this is the animation name found in the `panda-walk` file defined in the art tool used to create the animation.

Lastly, we set the camera position and start the main loop, from which the program will only return if the program is terminated. At this point, the `close_framework()` method is called to properly clean up.

Adding an additional camera

A great way to make scenes more interesting is to present them from multiple points of view. This can give a more cinematic feel to a game or might even be a plain necessity if you think of the TV-like replays found in most racing games.

After completing this recipe you will be able to add multiple cameras to the scene and switch between these predefined views.

Getting ready

To follow this recipe, complete the steps described in *Setting up the game structure* found in *Chapter 1* before going on.

How to do it...

Let's create a new scene and look at it from different angles:

1. Add the highlighted code to `Application.py`:

```
from direct.showbase.ShowBase import ShowBase
from direct.actor.Actor import Actor
from direct.interval.FunctionInterval import Func

class Application(ShowBase):
    def __init__(self):
        ShowBase.__init__(self)
        self.pandaActor = Actor("panda", {"walk": "panda-walk"})
        self.pandaActor.reparentTo(render)
        self.pandaActor.loop("walk")

        self.cameras = [self.cam, self.makeCamera(self.win)]
        self.cameras[1].node().getDisplayRegion(0).setActive(0)
        self.activeCam = 0
```

```
                self.cameras[0].setPos(0, -30, 6)
                self.cameras[1].setPos(30, -30, 20)
                self.cameras[1].lookAt(0, 0, 6)

                self.taskMgr.doMethodLater(5, self.toggleCam, "toggle
        camera")

            def toggleCam(self, task):
                self.cameras[self.activeCam].node().getDisplayRegion(0).
        setActive(0)
                self.activeCam = not self.activeCam
                self.cameras[self.activeCam].node().getDisplayRegion(0).
        setActive(1)
                return task.again
```

2. Press F6 to start the program. The view will toggle every 5 seconds.

How it works...

After the necessary imports and the walking panda being added to the scene, we reach the first interesting part of this recipe, where we create a list containing the default camera and a newly added one. Additionally, we turn off the new camera with `setActive(0)`, because we will use the default camera as initial point of view. We also store the index of the active camera in the `activeCam` variable.

In the following lines, the positions targets of the cameras are set. Finally, we instruct the task manager to queue the call to `toggleCam` and wait for five seconds until the method is called that switches back and forth between the cameras. The `toggleCam` method returns `task.again`, which causes it to be called again after another five seconds have passed.

In this recipe we only added one additional camera. Of course, Panda3D supports more than that and lets us create new cameras with a call to `makeCamera()`. This creates a new scene node that wraps the actual camera object so we can move it around or reparent it to an object, for example. Whenever we want to toggle between cameras, we need to get the camera objects wrapped by the scene node using the `node()` method. We can then turn cameras on and off by toggling the active state of the display region associated with each camera. This is done using the `getDisplayRegion()` and `setActive()` methods.

Inspecting and modifying the scene

Panda3D is a great engine for quickly developing prototypes of games, because creating and modifying scenes works quick and easy. But sometimes quick is not fast enough and restarting the game to see a change taking effect is a frustrating and repetitive task. This is why Panda3D provides the scene explorer, which we will use in the following recipe.

Getting ready

The following instructions are going to modify the code created in the recipe *Loading models and actors*, which can be found in this chapter.

How to do it...

The following tasks will introduce you to the features of the scene explorer:

1. Add the highlighted lines to `Application.py`:

    ```
    from panda3d.core import Vec3
    from pandac.PandaModules import loadPrcFileData

    loadPrcFileData("", "want-directtools #t")
    loadPrcFileData("", "want-tk #t")

    class Application(ShowBase):
        def __init__(self):
    ```

2. Press *F6* to start the application. Next to the game window, you will see the screenshot similar to this:

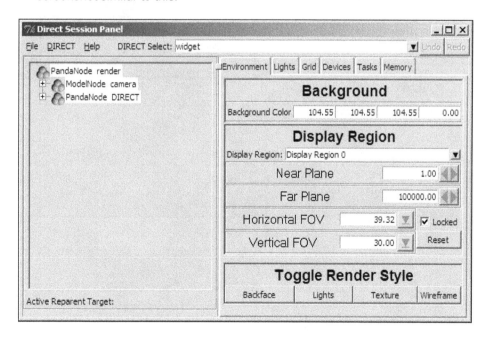

3. Push the **Wireframe** button to enable wireframe rendering.

4. Select the **Grid** tab and enable the grid:

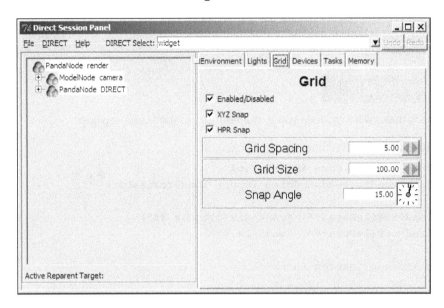

5. Go to the **Tasks** tab and push the **Update** button to watch all active tasks:

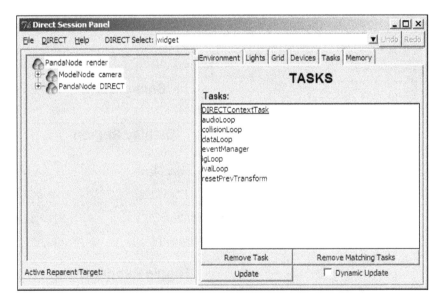

6. Expand the **PandaNode DIRECT** node in the tree view on the left side of the window. You will see the following tree:

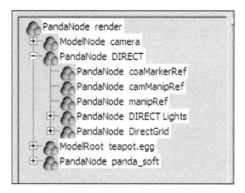

7. Right-click the **ModelRoot teapot.egg** node and click **Place** to open the **Placer Panel** enter the values from the following screenshot:

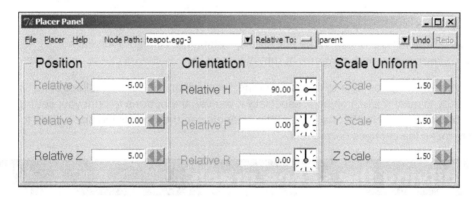

8. Click **Placer | Print** info to output your settings to Netbeans' **Output** pane:

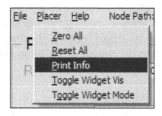

9. Close the **Placer Panel**.

10. Left-click **ModelRoot teapot.egg** in the tree view to make it the active selection.

11. Right-click **ModelRoot teapot.egg** and click **Set Color**.

12. In the **RGBA Panel**, set the following values:

13. Click the **Print to Log** button to output the color value to the **Output** pane of Netbeans.

How it works...

The scene explorer is enabled in the first step by setting the configuration flags `want-directtools` and `want-tk` at runtime using the `loadPrcFileData()` function.

Although it will never be able to replace a proper level editor, the scene explorer can come in very handy to quickly place objects, especially if you use the buttons to print your settings to the **Output** pane of Netbeans. These little snippets can then be copied and pasted to our code to make the changes permanent.

Modifying the scene graph

Today's games very often present jaw-dropping, complex scenes, and levels composed out of hundreds of single objects. So managing these object compositions can become a very challenging task without the right data structure. This is why the principle of the scene graph has become a state of the art technique in video games and computer graphics in general. A scene graph is a hierarchical tree structure that holds information about the scene models' positions, rotations, and parent-child relationships for relative positioning—among many other things.

In this recipe we will take a look at Panda3D's scene graph interfaces and will learn how to place and rotate objects within the scene and how to build a hierarchy of models and actors to allow our scene objects to be placed relative to each other.

Getting ready

Be sure to complete *Setting up the game structure* in chapter one before you start this recipe, as this project structure forms the basis for the following steps.

How to do it...

Let's see how Panda3D's scene graph works. Follow these steps to create a sample application:

1. Open `Application.py` and add the marked code:

```python
from direct.showbase.ShowBase import ShowBase
from direct.actor.Actor import Actor
from panda3d.core import Vec3

class Application(ShowBase):
    def __init__(self):
        ShowBase.__init__(self)
        self.sun = loader.loadModel("smiley")
        self.sun.reparentTo(render)
        self.sun.setScale(5)

        self.phantom = loader.loadModel("teapot")
        self.phantom.reparentTo(self.sun)
        self.phantom.setScale(0.1)
        self.phantom.setPos(0, -5, 0)
        self.phantom.hide()

        self.earth = loader.loadModel("frowney")
        self.earthCenter = render.attachNewNode("earthCenter")
        self.earth.reparentTo(self.earthCenter)
        self.earth.setPos(20, 0, 0)

        self.panda = Actor("panda", {"walk": "panda-walk"})
        self.panda.reparentTo(self.earth)
        self.panda.setScale(0.1)
        self.panda.setPos(Vec3(0.7, 0, 0.7))
        self.panda.setHpr(0, 0, 40)
        self.panda.loop("walk")

        self.moon = loader.loadModel("box")
        self.moonCenter = self.earthCenter.attachNewNode("moonCent
er")
        self.moon.reparentTo(self.moonCenter)
        self.moonCenter.setPos(self.earth.getPos())
        self.moon.setPos(0, 0, 6)
        self.cam.setPos(0, -100, 0)
```

2. Press *F6* to start the application. If you added the code properly, you will see the following scene. Hold down the left mouse button and drag your mouse to pan the camera. Keep the right mouse button pressed while moving the mouse to zoom in and out.

How it works...

If you compare the code used to create this little solar system to *Loading models and actors*, you will immediately understand how the mesh data is loaded and added to the scene. On the other hand, you just used a few new calls and some already known ones in a new fashion.

The smiley model is the sun in this little solar system, therefore we do not change its position, but scale it to five times its original size with `setScale()`.

Next comes the phantom planet that is a child of the sun, which means that all transforms of the object will happen relative to the sun. So if you decided to set the sun to a different position, this planet's position would change, too, to keep the relative position. This relationship also has an impact on the scale factor, which means that scaling the teapot model that was reparented to the sun by 0.1 really means scaling it by a factor of 0.5, because its parent object was scaled to five times its size before.

All this happens to no avail for the phantom planet, as it is disabled for rendering by the `hide()` method. A hidden model can easily be made visible again by calling the `show()` method of the object.

The earth is positioned with the help of an empty scene node you added with the line `render.attachNewNode("earthCenter")`. Using dummy objects like this one is a great way to simplify complex relative object placements!

On top of the earth, there walks a lonesome panda, which introduces another new method for modifying objects in the scene graph called `setHpr()`, which is used to make the panda lean to the side. "Hpr" in this case stands for heading, pitch, and roll. **Heading** makes the panda turn to the left and the right, **pitch** makes it lean backwards and forwards and **roll** makes it lean to the left and the right.

Finally, the moon is placed using a new dummy object attached to the earth's placement dummy, and the camera is set to capture this tiny universe in all its glory!

There's more...

Apart from the methods shown in the code sample, there are some more ways to modify the actors and models in your scene. For example, the position and rotation can be set using only one method call with `setPosHpr()`. Another way to do the same with different measures is to use `setMat()`, and provide a matrix containing transformation data. But there's even more you can do, as the following paragraphs will show!

Position

Besides `setPos()`, you can set the position of an object on each individual coordinate axis by using `setX()`, `setY()`, and `setZ()` respectively. In addition, these methods can be made using coordinates that are relative to an object by passing it as the first parameter. For example, adding the line `self.earth.setX(self.sun, 5)` in the preceding sample would position the earth five units away from the sun's coordinate origin along the x-axis.

Rotation

Just like position, rotation can be modified individually by using the methods `setH()`, `setP()`, and `setR()`.

Another way of representing rotations are quaternions, which can be set by using `setQuat()`. Quaternions are a four-dimensional extension of complex numbers, which allow you to store rotations within only four values, help to circumvent the effect of Gimbal lock (two coordinate axis becoming one after certain rotations, effectively removing one degree of freedom), and can very easily be interpolated.

Scale

The method `setScale()` used above uniformly scales geometry along all three axis. If you intend to only modify the scale of a model or an actor in your scene along one coordinate axis, you can use the methods `setSx()`, `setSy()`, and `setSz()`.

 All the methods used to set position, rotation, and scale of objects in the scene graph also provide corresponding getter methods for retrieving data!

Moving objects based on time

While there is beauty in static images, and they add much to the world of games, in modern video games, action is typically the focus. Today's games are usually very dynamic, having the player and non-player characters moving through scenes containing stacks of crates that can be tossed around, dynamic obstacles such as moving platforms, or flocks of birds that are just there to make a level more compelling.

In this recipe you will learn to make things move around in your scenes and how to use the time that has passed as a parameter for creating the illusion of movement.

Getting ready

We will be using and extending the code created in the recipe *Modifying the scene graph*, so please take a step back and follow that tip before you haven't already tried that recipe.

How to do it...

It's time to get things moving. Let's animate the scene:

1. Open `Application.py` and below the last line of code created in *Modifying the scene graph*, which is marked here, add the following lines to the source code:

   ```
   self.cam.setPos(0, -100, 0)
   self.taskMgr.add(self.update, "update")

   def update(self, task):
       self.sun.setP(task.time * 10)
       self.earth.setH(task.time * -100)
       self.earthCenter.setH(task.time * 50)
       self.moonCenter.setR(task.time * 150)
       return task.cont
   ```

2. Press *F6* to run the code and watch the planets go around.

How it works...

You just added a task to your program whose sole purpose is to set the positions and rotations of the objects found in the scene graph. The twist about this is that you are not setting these values to fixed numbers, but instead you are multiplying them with the time that has passed since the task was started, which is stored in `task.time`.

Beside the fact that you just implemented the most basic principle of animation, you also did something else! You just ensured that this little animation is progressing at the same rate, no matter how many frames per second the Panda3D's renderer is drawing.

Our `update()` method is executed every time a new frame of the scene is rendered. Depending on the speed of our system, this happens at a different frequency—a faster system is able to draw more frames per second than a slower one. If we just moved our objects by a fixed amount per frame, the animation speed would be bound to the frame rate. In a game, this would lead to the undesired effect of gameplay being not stable and unpredictable, because any occasion of the frame rate dropping or increasing would cause the game to change its pace.

By multiplying with the time that has passed, we make our animation independent of the current frame rate. Take the rotation of the sun in our code as an example. On a system that takes 0.5 seconds to render a frame, the sun is rotated by 0.5 * 10 units per frame. Now let's think about what happens if we ran the code on a system that takes one second to produce one frame—the rotation rate is multiplied by the time that has passed so that the sun is rotated 10 units per frame.

If we now compare what happens within one second on our slow and fast systems, we can see that the faster one will render two frames instead of only one. More importantly, though, the sun rotates at the same rate of 10 units per second, no matter how fast or slow the system is able to execute our code.

There's more...

Panda3D provides some additional methods for measuring how much time has passed.

For tasks, there's `task.frame` for getting the number of frames that have passed since the creation of the task.

Another way of accessing time values is the `globalClock` object, which can be accessed globally from any point within a Panda3D application. By calling `globalClock.getDt()` you can retrieve the time that has passed since the last frame, and the method `getFrameTime()` of the `globalClock` object returns the time since the program was started. Don't be afraid to experiment and replace `task.time` in the sample code with one of these methods and watch the results!

Controlling actions using intervals

The gameplay of many great video games is defined by certain movement patterns as well as their speed and timing. For example, each of the ghosts in Pac-Man has its own and unique way of hunting the player. Another great sample for gameplay-defining movement patterns can be found in Half-Life, where a Headcrab, the simplest type of enemy, tries to attack directly from the front, while fighting Marines is harder as they are taking cover and try to flank the player.

Without the proper tools, defining such action sequences can be a very time-consuming and tedious task that often requires an experienced animator or games designer to make them seem natural and compelling. But with Panda3D and its intervals system, this won't be a problem for you after reading and working through the following recipe.

Getting ready

The following code and steps build on top of *Setting up the game structure* found in the *Chapter 1, Setting Up Panda3D and Configuring Development Tools*. Please complete this recipe before you proceed!

How to do it...

Complete these steps to get a running sample of Panda3D's intervals:

1. Add the highlighted lines to the file `Application.py`:

```
from direct.showbase.ShowBase import ShowBase
from direct.showbase.RandomNumGen import RandomNumGen
from direct.actor.Actor import Actor
from panda3d.core import Vec3
from direct.interval.IntervalGlobal import *

class Application(ShowBase):
    def __init__(self):
        ShowBase.__init__(self)
        self.panda = Actor("panda", {"walk": "panda-walk"})
        self.panda.reparentTo(render)
        self.panda.setHpr(-90, 0, 0)
        self.panda.loop("walk")

        self.walkIval1 = self.panda.posInterval(2, Vec3(-8, 0, 0),
startPos = Vec3(8, 0, 0))
        self.walkIval2 = self.panda.posInterval(2, Vec3(8, 0, 0),
startPos = Vec3(-8, 0, 0))
        self.turnIval1 = self.panda.hprInterval(0.5, Vec3(90, 0,
0), startHpr = Vec3(-90, 0, 0))
        self.turnIval2 = self.panda.hprInterval(0.5, Vec3(-90, 0,
0), startHpr = Vec3(90, 0, 0))
        self.colorIval = Func(self.randomColor)
        self.pandaWalk = Sequence(self.walkIval1, self.turnIval1,
self.colorIval, self.walkIval2, self.turnIval2, self.colorIval)
        self.pandaWalk.loop()

        self.cam.setPos(0, -50, 6)
```

```
def randomColor(self):
    rand = RandomNumGen(globalClock.getFrameTime())
    self.panda.setColorScale(rand.random(), rand.random(),
rand.random(), 255)
```

2. Start the program by hitting *F6*. If your code is correct, you will see a panda walk from one side of the window to the other and back, changing its color every time it turns:

How it works...

Right after loading and adding the panda actor to the scene, we define four intervals that make the panda walk from one side to the other. The first two are position intervals that move an object from one point to the other, and the other two intervals are interpolating between two rotation values, all of which are getting passed similar parameters: The first value is the time we want the action to take until it is completed, followed by the final and starting positions.

Then we add a function interval. We cannot pass a time value to this kind of interval because it executes immediately. All the constructor of Func takes is the method to execute upon activation. Here we use the randomColor() method, which changes the panda's color tint to a random value.

Finally, all these intervals are put into a `Sequence` object. We use this to ensure that the intervals we defined before are executed in the order passed to the constructor of `Sequence`. We are creating a chain of actions. Our `Sequence` makes the panda walk from one side to the other, turn around, change its color, walk back to where it started, turn around again, and finally change its color yet another time. We start the sequence as a loop, set the camera, and the panda is on its way!

There's more...

Panda3D's interval system is very powerful and important and therefore deserves some more discussion, in order to give you a better understanding of its reach and power.

Lerp intervals

In the sample code above, we used shortcuts to directly create intervals for the panda actor. These shortcuts create instances of `LerpPosInterval` and `LerpHprInterval`, respectively. We can create instances of these classes directly, but we must not forget to pass the model or actor `NodePath` we want to modify as the first parameter of the constructor! There are even more very commonly used interpolation interval types: `LerpQuatInterval` lets us move objects from one rotation to another one using quaternions. `LerpScaleInterval` interpolates between two scale factors of a scene object. `LerpColorInterval` and `LerpColorScaleInterval` can be used to crossfade object colors. While the first one overrides the target object's initial color, `LerpColorScaleInterval` multiplies colors and tints models and actors in the given colors.

Also there are interval types that modify two or more object properties at the same time: `LerpPosHprInterval`, for example, interpolates the position and rotation at the same time, while `LerpHprScaleInterval` is used to rotate and scale. To top it off, a `LerpPosHprScaleInterval` does all of the aforementioned in parallel.

Lerp function interval

You can use a `LerpFunc` to continuously call a function or method over a given period of time, allowing you to, for example, change a parameter slightly with each iteration. The following code snippet shows how to use an interpolation function interval:

```
def someFunc(t):
    print t

fn = LerpFunc(someFunc, fromData=0, toData=1, duration=10)
fn.start()
```

This brief snippet creates a `LerpFunc` that calls `someFunc()` over the course of ten seconds while passing values ranging from zero to one, which then will be printed to the console.

Interpolation easing

Passing in the `blendType` parameter to the constructor when creating a new `LerpFunc` can be used to modify the starting and stopping behaviors of interpolation intervals to be more smooth: 'noBlend', which is the default value, causes the interval to make a hard start and stop. Setting the `blendType` parameter to 'easeIn' makes the animation accelerate until it reaches its full speed. Passing 'easeOut' has the effect of making the interpolation decelerate smoothly before coming to a stop. If you intend to create a smooth animation without any sudden starting or stopping, set the `blendType` parameter to 'easeInOut'.

Sequences and Parallels

This recipe already has shown how to use the `Sequence` class to chain intervals, but sometimes you really want to coordinate actions so that they happen at the same time. This is what you can use objects of the type `Parallel` for—creation works analogous to `Sequence`, but all intervals you added will play in parallel once this interval has started.

 Sequences and Parallels can be nested within each other. Use this fact for creating very complex action patterns with great ease!

Wait interval

Panda3D features a special kind of interval called `Wait`. The only thing it does is to wait for the specified amount of time you pass to its constructor. Note that the `Wait` class is designed to be used in conjunction with a `Sequence` or `Parallel`.

Making animations fit to intervals

Intervals are a very powerful feature of Panda3D, which you can see in the recipe *Controlling actions using intervals*. In this recipe you will go one step beyond and see how to efficiently control animations when used in conjunction with intervals.

Getting ready

If you haven't already, please read how to use intervals in *Controlling actions using intervals* and follow the steps of that recipe.

How to do it...

This recipe consists of the following tasks:

1. Open `Application.py`.
2. Delete the line `self.panda.loop("walk")`.

3. Find the following part of the code:

```
self.pandaWalk = Sequence(self.walkIval1, self.turnIval1, self.
colorIval, self.walkIval2, self.turnIval2,
self.colorIval)
self.pandaWalk.loop()
```

4. Replace it with the following code:

```
self.pandaAnim = ActorInterval(self.panda, "walk", loop = 1,
duration = 5)
self.pandaMove = Sequence(self.walkIval1, self.turnIval1, self.
colorIval, self.walkIval2, self.turnIval2, self.colorIval)
self.pandaWalk = Parallel(self.pandaAnim, self.pandaMove)
self.pandaWalk.loop()
```

How it works...

The panda is moving just like before, but now an `ActorInterval` we create in the highlighted line of the code controls animation playback. We set the animation to loop and to play over the duration of five seconds. Finally, the animation-controlling `ActorInterval` and the `Sequence` of transformations are made part of a `Parallel` that plays the two intervals at the same time.

There's more...

The actor interval constructor can take a range of optional parameters besides `loop` and `duration` that were already presented in the sample code. Let's take a look at what else you can do with `ActorInterval`:

Instead of `duration`, you can use `startTime` and `endTime` to define more precisely when to start and stop playing the animation.

The `playrate` parameter lets you set the animation playback speed. Also note that if `playrate` is a negative value, the animation is played backwards.

You can specify a sub range of the animation to be played by setting `startFrame` and `endFrame`. Also, if you want to loop an animation range, set `constrainedLoop` to one instead of `loop`.

In the following line of code, all these options have been applied to our sample code to loop the first second of the walk animation at a very low rate:

```
self.pandaAnim = ActorInterval(self.panda, "walk", startTime = 0,
endTime = 1, playrate = 0.1, constrainedLoop = 1, duration = 5)
```

Making objects follow a predefined path

In this recipe we will see how to move a model along a line, typically referred to as a path, stored in Panda3D's model format. This can come in very handy for setting paths of non-player characters inside a level. Another common use of this is to attach the camera to a path and make it fly through the game world smoothly.

Getting ready

To follow this recipe you first have to set up a project as described in *Setting up the game structure*. In addition, you need to create a curve in Maya or Blender and export it to Panda3D's .egg file format. In case you don't have these tools or do not know how to work with them, here's a sample curve you can paste into a text editor and save it as path.egg:

```
<CoordinateSystem> { Z-up }
<Group> Curve {
  <VertexPool> Curve {
    <Vertex> 0 {
      -2.66117048264 -0.964361846447 0.0 1.0
    }
    <Vertex> 1 {
      1.8930850029 -0.948404431343 0.0 1.0
    }
    <Vertex> 2 {
      10.3484048843 1.0 0.0 1.0
    }
    <Vertex> 3 {
      -3.6957449913 0.0 0.0 1.0
    }
  }
  <NURBSCurve> {
    <Order> { 4 }
    <Knots> { 0.0 0.0 0.0 0.0 1.0 1.0 1.0 1.0 }
    <VertexRef> { 0 1 2 3   <Ref> { Curve }}
  }
}
```

How to do it...

Making objects follow a predefined path can be done like the following:

1. Copy the file containing the curve to the `models` directory of your project and make sure it is named `path.egg`.

2. Copy the following code to `Application.py`:

```python
from direct.showbase.ShowBase import ShowBase
from direct.actor.Actor import Actor
from direct.directutil.Mopath import Mopath
from direct.interval.IntervalGlobal import *

class Application(ShowBase):
    def __init__(self):
        ShowBase.__init__(self)

        self.smiley = self.loader.loadModel("smiley")
        self.smiley.reparentTo(render)

        self.mopath = Mopath()
        self.mopath.loadFile("path.egg")

        self.ival = MopathInterval(self.mopath, self.smiley,
duration = 10)
        self.ival.loop()

        self.cam.setPos(0, -20, 0)
```

3. Press *F6* to start the program. The smiley model will follow the path.

How it works...

All it takes for you to use predefined paths is to create a `Mopath` object and load the file containing the curve you want your object to follow. Then you pass the `Mopath` object to a `MopathInterval` that is responsible for interpolating the model position along the path over the specified duration. That's it—it's that easy!

Making the camera smoothly follow an object

In this recipe you will learn how to program a simple camera system that follows an object smoothly, without giving the impression of being glued to the back of the target.

Getting ready

See the recipe *Setting up the game structure* to create the basic application framework for the following steps.

How to do it...

Let's build a third person camera system:

1. Add this code to `Application.py`:

```
from direct.showbase.ShowBase import ShowBase
from direct.actor.Actor import Actor
from panda3d.core import Vec3
from direct.interval.IntervalGlobal import *
from FollowCam import FollowCam

class Application(ShowBase):
    def __init__(self):
        ShowBase.__init__(self)

        self.world = loader.loadModel("environment")
        self.world.reparentTo(render)
        self.world.setScale(0.5)
        self.world.setPos(-8, 80, 0)

        self.panda = Actor("panda", {"walk": "panda-walk"})
        self.panda.reparentTo(render)
        self.panda.setHpr(270, 0, 0)
        self.panda.loop("walk")

        self.walkIval1 = self.panda.posInterval(2, Vec3(-8, -8,
0), startPos = Vec3(8, -8, 0))
        self.walkIval2 = self.panda.posInterval(2, Vec3(-8, 8, 0),
startPos = Vec3(-8, -8, 0))
        self.walkIval3 = self.panda.posInterval(2, Vec3(8, 8, 0),
startPos = Vec3(-8, 8, 0))
        self.walkIval4 = self.panda.posInterval(2, Vec3(8, -8, 0),
startPos = Vec3(8, 8, 0))

        self.turnIval1 = self.panda.hprInterval(0.5, Vec3(180, 0,
0), startHpr = Vec3(270, 0, 0))
        self.turnIval2 = self.panda.hprInterval(0.5, Vec3(90, 0,
0), startHpr = Vec3(180, 0, 0))
        self.turnIval3 = self.panda.hprInterval(0.5, Vec3(0, 0,
0), startHpr = Vec3(90, 0, 0))
```

```
        self.turnIval4 = self.panda.hprInterval(0.5, Vec3(-90, 0,
0), startHpr = Vec3(0, 0, 0))

        self.pandaWalk = Sequence(self.walkIval1, self.turnIval1,
                                  self.walkIval2, self.turnIval2,
                                  self.walkIval3, self.turnIval3,
                                  self.walkIval4, self.turnIval4)
        self.pandaWalk.loop()
        self.followCam = FollowCam(self.cam, self.panda)
```

2. Add a new file to the project. Call it `FollowCam.py`.

3. Copy the following code to the file you just created:

```python
from direct.showbase.ShowBase import ShowBase
from panda3d.core import Vec3

class FollowCam():
    def __init__(self, camera, target):
        self.dummy = render.attachNewNode("cam" + target.
getName())
        self.turnRate = 2.2
        self.camera = camera
        self.target = target
        taskMgr.add(self.updateCamera, "updateCamera" + target.
getName())

    def updateCamera(self, task):
        self.dummy.setPos(self.target.getPos())
        heading = self.clampAngle(self.dummy.getH())

        turnDiff = self.target.getH() - heading
        turnDiff = self.clampAngle(turnDiff)

        dt = globalClock.getDt()
        turn = turnDiff * dt
        self.dummy.setH(heading + turn * self.turnRate)

        self.camera.setPos(self.dummy.getPos())
        self.camera.setY(self.dummy, 40)
        self.camera.setZ(self.dummy, 10)
        self.camera.lookAt(self.target.getPos() + Vec3(0, 0, 7))

        return task.cont
```

```
def clampAngle(self, angle):
    while angle < -180:
        angle = angle + 360

    while angle > 180:
        angle = angle - 360

    return angle
```

4. Press *F6* to start the application. You should be able to see a panda walking in circles while the camera follows it:

How it works...

We use the constructor of our `Application` class to set up the scene containing the walking panda and the background scenery. In the last line we create a new instance of our `FollowCam`, which contains the camera tracking code that is the core of this recipe.

To make the `FollowCam` work correctly and to be able to have multiple cameras follow different objects, we have to pass the camera we want to be updated and its target to the constructor, where we set up a few things we need for updating the camera. For example, we add a task that will call the `updateCamera()` method each frame. Additionally, the target's name is appended to both the dummy object's and the task's names to avoid name clashes in the case where we need to use more than one `FollowCam` instance. The dummy object is an invisible helper object that will help us to position the camera, as you will see in the following paragraphs.

The `updateCamera()` method is where all the work is happening: We move the dummy to our target's current position and get its current heading. The heading angle (in degrees) is clamped to the range of values from 180 to 180. We do this to avoid the camera getting stuck or continuing to turn because of the ambiguous nature of angles.

In the next steps, we calculate the difference between the target's heading and that of our dummy object, which is also clamped to avoid the undesired results described in the previous paragraph. In the following lines we can find the explanation for the camera's smooth turning—every frame, the dummy object's heading converges towards the heading of the camera target just a little bit. This is intentional; as it is multiplied by the time it took to complete the last frame. Additionally, we can also influence how fast the camera turns by adjusting `turnRate`.

In the final steps, the camera is first moved to the position of the dummy and then pushed away again along the dummy's local axis to its final position. After setting the camera's `lookAt()` target, we are done!

There's more...

In this version, the camera only supports smooth turning for objects that only change their heading. Other rotation axes can be added rather easily, as they work exactly the same as the one presented in this recipe!

Generating geometry at runtime

In some cases, Panda3D's model loading capabilities might not be enough for your needs. Maybe you want to procedurally generate new geometry at runtime or maybe you decided to drop the native file model file format of Panda3D in favor of your own custom data file layout. For all these cases where you need to glue together vertices by hand in order to form a model, the engine provides an API that you will learn about in this recipe.

Getting ready

As a prerequisite to the following steps, please create a new project as described in the recipe *Setting up the game structure*. This recipe can be found in the *Chapter 1*.

You will also need a texture image. Preferably it should be rectangular and in the best case be in a 2n format (64x64, 128x128, 256x256, and so on.). This recipe will use a crate texture in PNG format.

Lastly, add a directory called `textures` to your project and be sure it is in Panda3D's search path. This works analogous to what you did for the `models` and `sounds` directories.

How to do it...

Follow these steps to learn how to create geometry on the fly:

1. Copy your texture image to the `textures` directory. Name it `crate.png`.

2. Open `Application.py`. Insert the following code:

```
from direct.showbase.ShowBase import ShowBase
from panda3d.core import *

vertices = [Vec3(1, 0, 1), Vec3(-1, 0, 1), Vec3(-1, 0, -1),
Vec3(1, 0, -1)]
texcoords = [Vec2(1, 1), Vec2(0, 1), Vec2(0, 0), Vec2(1, 0)]

class Application(ShowBase):
    def __init__(self):
        ShowBase.__init__(self)

        format = GeomVertexFormat.getV3t2()
        geomData = GeomVertexData("box", format, Geom.UHStatic)
        vertexWriter = GeomVertexWriter(geomData, "vertex")
        uvWriter = GeomVertexWriter(geomData, "texcoord")

        for pos, tex in zip(vertices, texcoords):
            vertexWriter.addData3f(pos)
            uvWriter.addData2f(tex)

        triangles = GeomTriangles(Geom.UHStatic)
        triangles.addVertices(0, 1, 2)
        triangles.closePrimitive()
        triangles.addVertices(2, 3, 0)
        triangles.closePrimitive()

        geom = Geom(geomData)
        geom.addPrimitive(triangles)
        node = GeomNode("box")
        node.addGeom(geom)
        box = render.attachNewNode(node)
        texture = loader.loadTexture("crate.png")
        box.setTexture(texture)

        self.cam.setPos(0, -5, 0)
```

3. Start the program. A quad with your texture on it should be rendered to the Panda3D window:

How it works...

Let's take a look at what this code is doing! We begin by creating a format descriptor for one of Panda3D's built in vertex data layouts. There are several of these layouts, which also can be completely customized, which describe what kind of data will be stored for each point in space that forms the mesh. In this particular case, we are using the getV3t2() method to get a descriptor for a vertex layout that stores the vertex position in space using three floating point values and the texture coordinate using two float values.

We then move on to create a GeomVertexData object, which uses the format we just requested. We also pass the Geom.UHStatic flag, which signals the underlying rendering systems that the vertex data will not change, which allows them to enable some optimizations. Additionally, we create two GeomVertexWriter objects—one for writing to the "vertex" channel, which stores the positions of the points that form the mesh, and the other one for writing to the "texcoord" channel of the point data we are adding to geomData in the loop that follows.

What we have so far is a cloud of seemingly random points—at least to the engine. To correct this issue, we need to connect the points to form primitives, which in this case are triangles. We create a new instance of GeomTriangles, using the Geom.UHStatic flag again to hint that the primitives will not be changed after they are defined. Then we create two triangles by passing indices to the proper points in the vertices list. After each triangle, we need to call the closePrimitive() method to mark the primitive as complete and start a new one.

At this point we have a collection of points in space, stored in a `GeomVertexData` object and a `GeomTriangles` primitive that holds the information necessary to connect the dots and form a mesh. To get the model to the screen, we need to create a new `Geom`, and add the point data and the triangle primitives. Because a model can in fact consist of multiple `Geom` objects, which also can't be added directly to the scene graph, we add it to a `GeomNode`. Finally, we attach the `GeomNode` to the scene graph, load and apply the texture and set the camera a bit back to be able to see our creation.

There's more...

There's a lot more to say about Panda3D's procedural geometry feature than what you just saw, so take your time and keep on reading to discover what else you can do to generate geometry at runtime.

Built in vertex formats

You already saw the built in `GeomVertexFormat.getV3t2()` format, but there are several more ready to use formats available:

- `getV3()`: Vertices store position only
- `getV3c4()`: Vertex position and a RGBA color value
- `getV3c4t2()`: Position, color, and texture coordinates
- `getV3n3()`: Position and normal vector
- `getV3n3c4()`: Position, normal, and RGBA color
- `getV3n3c4t2()`: This is the most extensive format. Contains position, normal, color, and texture coordinates
- `getV3n3t2()`: Position, normal vector, and texture coordinates.

There's also a packed color format, which you can use by replacing `c4` in the previous methods with `cp`. In this format, colors are stored into one 32-bit integer value. The best way to define color values for this format is in hexadecimal, because it lets you easily recognize the RGBA components of the color. For example, the value 0xFF0000FF is full red.

Custom vertex formats

Apart from the built-in vertex formats, Panda3D allows you to be much more flexible by defining your own custom formats. The key parts to this are the `GeomVertexArrayFormat` and `GeomVertexFormat` classes, which are used in the following way:

```
arrayFmt = GeomVertexArrayFormat()
arrayFmt.addColumn(InternalName.make("normal"), 3, Geom.NTFloat32,
Geom.CVector)
fmt = GeomVertexFormat()
fmt.addArray(arrayFmt)
fmt = GeomVertexFormat.registerFormat(fmt)
```

In the beginning, you need to describe your vertex array data layout by adding columns. The first parameter is the channel that Panda3D is going to use the data for. Very commonly used channels are `"vertex"`, `"color"`, `"normal"`, `"texcoord"`, `"tangent"`, and `"binormal"`.

The second and third parameters are the number of components and data type the channel is using. In this sample, the normal data is composed out of three 32-bit floating point values. Legal values for the third parameter include `NTFloat32`, `NTUint*`, where `*` is one of 8, 16, or 32, describing an unsigned integer of the according bit width as well as `NTPackedDcba` and `NTPackedDabc`, used for packed index and color data.

The third parameter influences how the data is going to be treated internally—for example, if and how it will be transformed if a matrix is applied to the data in the column. Possible values include:

- ▸ `CPoint`: Point data in 3D space, most often used for the `"vertex"` channel.
- ▸ `CVector`: A vector giving a direction in space. Use this for normals, tangents, and binormals.
- ▸ `CTexcoord`: The data in the column contains the coordinates of texture sample points.
- ▸ `CColor`: The data is to be treated as color values.
- ▸ `CIndex`: The column contains table indices.
- ▸ `COther`: Arbitrary data values.

Points and texture coordinates are transformed as points, resulting in new positions if they are involved in a matrix multiplication. Vectors of course are following different rules when being transformed, because they describe directions, not positions! It would go too far to go into the details here, but lots of material on vector math and linear algebra are freely available on Wikipedia and other websites.

Primitive types

Panda3D supports all the standard primitive types commonly known in computer graphics: Triangles, triangle strips, triangle fans, lines, line strips, and points. The according classes used to describe these primitives are `GeomTriangles`, `GeomTristrips`, `GeomTrifans`, `GeomLines`, `GeomLinestrips`, and `GeomPoints`.

See also

Loading models and actors, Modifying the scene graph.

Loading data asynchronously

Panda3D really makes it very easy to load and use assets like models, actors, textures, and sounds. But there is a problem with the default behavior of the asset loader—it blocks the execution of the engine.

This is not a problem if all data is loaded before the player is allowed to see the game world, but if models and other assets are to be loaded while the game is running, we are facing a serious problem because the frame rate will drop dramatically for a moment. This will cause game execution to stop for a short moment in a sudden and unpredictable way that breaks gameplay.

To avoid getting into such problems, Panda3D offers the ability to load data through a background thread. This is a very useful feature if game assets are loaded on the fly, such as the popular use case with seamless streaming in game worlds. It is also a great way to reduce initial loading times. The main level geometry and everything visible from the starting position is loaded before the player enters the world and the rest of it is loaded afterwards, often depending on the position in the game world.

Getting ready

For this recipe you will need to set up the basic framework described in *Setting up the game structure*.

How to do it...

Follow these steps to create a sample application that demonstrates asynchronous data loading:

1. Add the following code to `Application.py`:

```
from direct.showbase.ShowBase import ShowBase
from direct.actor.Actor import Actor
from panda3d.core import Vec3

class Application(ShowBase):
    def __init__(self):
        ShowBase.__init__(self)
        self.cam.setPos(0, -30, 6)
        taskMgr.doMethodLater(3, self.load, "load", extraArgs =
["teapot", Vec3(-5, 0, 0), self.modelLoaded])
        taskMgr.doMethodLater(5, self.load, "load", extraArgs =
["panda", Vec3(5, 0, 0), self.actorLoaded])

    def load(self, name, pos, cb):
        loader.loadModel(name, callback = cb, extraArgs = [pos])
```

```
def modelLoaded(self, model, pos):
    model.reparentTo(render)
    model.setPos(pos)

def actorLoaded(self, model, pos):
    self.panda = Actor(model, {"walk": "panda-walk"})
    self.panda.reparentTo(render)
    self.panda.setPos(pos)
    self.panda.loop("walk")
```

2. Press *F6* to run the application. You will see a delay before the teapot and the panda appear in the window.

How it works...

The previous code enqueues calls to the `load()` method using `doMethodLater()` so you can see the objects pop up as soon as they are loaded. The list passed to the `extraArgs` parameter will be used as parameters for the call to `load()`.

The call to `loadModel()` within the load method is very important, because instead of just passing the name of the model to load, you also set the callback parameter to one of the `modelLoaded()` and `actorLoaded()` methods, depending on what the cb parameter of `load()` contains.

As soon as a call to `loadModel()` uses the callback parameter, the request to load the data is handed off to a background thread. When the required asset has finished loading, the callback function is called and the loaded asset is passed as the first parameter, as you can see in the `modelLoaded()` and `actorLoaded()` methods.

3
Controlling the Renderer

In this chapter, we will cover

- ▸ Changing a model's render attributes
- ▸ Adding an alpha mask to a texture
- ▸ Creating a splitscreen mode
- ▸ Controlling the rendering order
- ▸ Using multiple displays

Introduction

Panda3D consists of many subsystems that work together to form the engine as a whole. One of these systems is the renderer, which is responsible for bringing the models and actors we place in our scenes to the screen.

With video games being such a visual medium, it is very important to understand how the rendering subsystem can be controlled and configured to suit our needs. In this chapter, we will take a look at this engine system and the interfaces Panda3D provides that allow us to modify the renderer's behavior.

Changing a model's render attributes

One of the big strengths of Panda3D is its nice and clever programming interface that allows us to quickly put together scenes by loading and placing models and actors. Getting something rendered onto the screen works amazingly fast and easy.

Beyond this simple programming interface lies a very advanced renderer that takes the information from the current scene graph and draws the models and actors found in there to the screen. The way this rendering subsystem draws geometry can be changed by setting some render attributes, which we will explore in this recipe.

Getting ready

This recipe requires a project setup as described in *Setting up the game structure* found in *Chapter 1, Setting Up Panda3D and Configuring Development Tools*. Please revisit these instructions before proceeding with this tip.

How to do it...

Let's see how Panda3D allows you to change render attributes:

1. Open `Application.py` and replace its content with the following code:

```
from direct.showbase.ShowBase import ShowBase
from direct.actor.Actor import Actor
from panda3d.core import *
from pandac.PandaModules import loadPrcFileData

loadPrcFileData("", "multisamples 8")

class Application(ShowBase):
  def __init__(self):
      ShowBase.__init__(self)

      self.pandas = []

      for i in range(4):
          panda = Actor("panda", {"walk": "panda-walk"})
          panda.reparentTo(render)
          panda.loop("walk")
          panda.setX(-10.5 + i * 7)
          self.pandas.append(panda)

      render.setAntialias(AntialiasAttrib.MAuto)

      mask = ColorWriteAttrib.CRed
      mask |= ColorWriteAttrib.CBlue
      mask |= ColorWriteAttrib.CAlpha
      self.pandas[0].setAttrib(ColorWriteAttrib.make(mask))
      self.pandas[1].setRenderMode(RenderModeAttrib.MWireframe, 1)
      self.pandas[2].setColorScale(0.5, 0.5, 0.5, 0.5)
      self.pandas[3].setColor(0.5, 0.5, 0.5, 0.5)
```

```
self.smiley = loader.loadModel("smiley")
self.smiley.reparentTo(render)
self.smiley.setDepthWrite(False)
self.smiley.setDepthTest(False)
self.smiley.setPos(5, 20, 3)
self.smiley.setScale(3)

self.cam.setPos(0, -40, 6)
```

2. Press *F6* to start the application. You should now see the following scene:

How it works...

We start to compose this sample scene by loading and adding four pandas to the scene and setting them to walk in lockstep.

Then we set the whole scene graph to use Anti-aliasing. Note that the `setAntialias()` method on its own does not enable edge smoothing. We either need to add the statement `multisamples 8` to the `Config.prc` file or use the `loadPrcFileData()` function to configure Panda3D to use antialiasing like we do in the sample code. This configuration option also controls the quality level to use for antialiasing, where a higher number means higher quality. In our code, we use eight samples, but other values can be used too. The number of samples must be a power of two. Feel free to try other quality settings! However, note that the given value only requests the given quality level from the graphics driver. If a multisampling mode is not supported, the closest matching quality setting will be chosen. If the graphics hardware doesn't support multisampling antialiasing at all, the setting is ignored.

The next feature of the renderer we use is a color write mask, which allows us to enable or disable drawing to the color and alpha channels of the screen buffer. We do this by creating a bit mask, adding the color channels that we wish to enable using bitwise OR operations. We turn off writing new color values to the green color channel, which explains the look of the panda on the outer left side of the scene. After the renderer clears the screen with the grey background color, the green color channel is static and cannot be changed anymore. As a result, the red and blue color channels are combined with the fixed value of the green color channel. In the end, this gives us a slightly pink and green panda.

The other three pandas get a different treatment: For the one second from the left, we enable the wireframe render mode, which can be useful for quickly visualizing the complexity of the geometry being rendered. The two pandas on the right show the difference between `setColorScale()` and `setColor()`. While the first method tints the second panda from right by multiplying the specified color with the original color, the latter method overrides the original color of the rightmost panda.

Lastly, we add the smiley model to the scene and set its position behind the four pandas, which should cause the model to be hidden. But because we disable writing to the depth buffer and depth testing, the position along the y-axis is completely ignored. So whatever is rendered last will be drawn over the pixels that already are in the color buffer. This feature may be used to ensure overlays like ammo and health meters to be always drawn on top of the rest of the scene, for example.

Adding an alpha mask to a texture

A very common technique in computer graphics called alpha blending is used to make whole objects, or only parts of them, appear translucent. In this recipe you will learn how to add an additional texture layer, an alpha mask, which controls the opacity of an object.

Getting ready

This recipe uses *Setting up the game structure* found in *Chapter 1* as a starting point on which the rest of the sample will be built. Please revisit this recipe to set things up before proceeding.

Analogous to the models and sounds directories, you need to add a directory called `textures` and add it to Panda3D's asset search path.

You will need two texture images—one that contains the color information and an additional grayscale texture that controls opacity. The color texture will simply be mapped onto our model, while the grayscale image will be used to determine the translucency of each color texture pixel. The whiter the pixel in the grayscale opacity map, the more opaque it will be rendered. Gray and black pixels cause the according parts of the color map to be rendered more translucent. This example uses the following two textures:

How to do it...

Complete these tasks to create the sample application:

1. Copy your texture files to the `textures` directory and rename the color texture to `texture.png` and the grayscale texture to `mask.png`.

2. Copy the following code to `Application.py`:

```python
from direct.showbase.ShowBase import ShowBase
from panda3d.core import *


class Application(ShowBase):
  def __init__(self):
      ShowBase.__init__(self)
      self.box = self.buildCube(2)
      tex = loader.loadTexture("texture.png", "mask.png")
      self.box.setTexture(tex)
      self.box.setTransparency(TransparencyAttrib.MAlpha, 1)
      self.box.setTwoSided(1)
      self.cam.setPos(10, -10, 10)
      self.cam.lookAt(0, 0, 0)

  def buildCube(self, size):
      center = render.attachNewNode("cubeCenter")
      cm = CardMaker("plane")
      cm.setFrame(-size, size, -size, size)
      front = center.attachNewNode(cm.generate())
      front.setY(-size)
      back = center.attachNewNode(cm.generate())
      back.setY(size)
      back.setH(180)
      left = center.attachNewNode(cm.generate())
      left.setX(-size)
```

```
left.setH(270)
right = center.attachNewNode(cm.generate())
right.setX(size)
right.setH(90)
top = center.attachNewNode(cm.generate())
top.setZ(size)
top.setP(270)
btm = center.attachNewNode(cm.generate())
btm.setZ(-size)
btm.setP(90)
return center
```

3. Press the *F6* key to start the program. You will see the following output:

How it works...

First, we use the `CardMaker` class, which is used for generating quad geometry at runtime, and the `buildCube()` method to build a cube from four quads.

After the geometry is set, the following four lines of code are responsible for producing the final image. First we use `loadTexture()` to load the color image together with the grayscale alpha texture, whose filename is passed in the second parameter. The transparency values are encoded in the mask texture using shades of gray—a value closer to white means more opaque, while darker shades mean more transparent, as can be seen in the previous sample mask. We are working with PNG textures here, but Panda3D supports some other image file formats like JPEG, TGA, and DDS too.

The next line of code applies the texture data we just loaded to the cube, followed by a call to `setTransparency()` that enables alpha blending. Without this, the mask texture would simply be ignored!

Finally, we need to mark the cube as two-sided geometry. Otherwise we wouldn't be able to see the backsides of the cube through the transparent parts of its faces, due to a technique called **backface culling**. Per default, the renderer discards all triangles facing away from the camera, because they are on the backside of the object and can't be seen anyway. This gives a nice performance boost as usually a lot of geometry can be discarded and doesn't have to be rendered. While this optimization works fine for opaque objects, it can't be used for transparent ones because we can actually see the backside of the rendered object.

Creating a splitscreen mode

Although online multiplayer games have become more and more mainstream and successful over the course of the last few years, there still are games being released that feature great local multiplayer modes. Games like Mario Kart are the proof that splitscreen multiplayer is far from dead and can be great fun. This is the reason why this recipe will show you how to create a splitscreen mode for your games!

Getting ready

Follow the steps found in *Setting up the game structure* in *Chapter 1* before proceeding with this recipe to have the base for the following sample code.

How to do it...

Let's get to work by implementing a splitscreen mode:

1. Open the file Application.py and add the following code:

```python
from direct.showbase.ShowBase import ShowBase
from direct.actor.Actor import Actor
from panda3d.core import Vec4

class Application(ShowBase):
    def __init__(self):
        ShowBase.__init__(self)
        self.pandaActor = Actor("panda", {"walk": "panda-walk"})
        self.pandaActor.reparentTo(render)
        self.pandaActor.loop("walk")

        self.cam.node().getDisplayRegion(0).setActive(0)

        cameras = [self.makeCamera(self.win), self.makeCamera(self.win)]
        self.makeRegion(cameras[0], Vec4(0, 0.5, 0, 1), Vec4(0, 1, 0, 1))
        self.makeRegion(cameras[1], Vec4(0.5, 1, 0, 1), Vec4(1, 0, 0, 1))
```

```
            cameras[0].setPos(0, -30, 6)
            cameras[1].setPos(-30, 0, 6)
            cameras[1].lookAt(0, 0, 6)

    def makeRegion(self, cam, dimensions, color):
        region = cam.node().getDisplayRegion(0)
        region.setDimensions(dimensions.getX(), dimensions.getY(),
    dimensions.getZ(), dimensions.getW())
        region.setClearColor(color)
        region.setClearColorActive(True)
        aspect = float(region.getPixelWidth()) / float(region.
    getPixelHeight())
        cam.node().getLens().setAspectRatio(aspect)
```

2. Press *F6* to run the program. If your code is correct, you will see this:

How it works...

The first thing we do after adding the panda actor to the scene is disable the default camera. We drop it in favor of two new ones, neatly stored in the `cameras` list, which we will use for our splitscreen mode.

Splitting the screen into two halves is done using a feature of Panda3D called **display regions**. Display regions allow us to define an arbitrary area within the game window. We then are able to redirect the output of a camera to such a region. In our sample code, we use the `makeRegion()` method to create a new display region.

To create a new display region in `makeRegion()` we must resize the default display region of the camera given by the first parameter. The default display region has the same dimensions as the window, but can easily by resized using the `setDimensions()` method. The position and size of display regions is defined in a resolution independent way: The parameters passed to `setDimensions()` denote the positions of the left, right, bottom, and top sides of a rectangle within the window, where the origin of this coordinate system is at the bottom left of the window. Values may range from 0 to 1, so for example in our code we pass 0, 0.5, 0, and 1. This means that the left side of the display region is at the left edge of the window, the right side is at the middle of the window, the bottom edge of the rectangle is at the bottom of the window, and the top border is thus defined to be at the top of the window. We use a four-component vector to store these values, storing the coordinates of the left, right, bottom, and top edges of a display region in the **x**, **y**, **z**, and **w** components of the vector.

To help better distinguishing between the two display regions, we also set their background colors, before the last line, the `makeRegion()` method sets the aspect ratio of the camera according to the size of the new display region. This prevents the scene from being displayed, warped, and squeezed.

Controlling the rendering order

To be able to render with good performance and display effects like transparency correctly, Panda3D automatically sorts the scene geometry and puts it into "cull bins", so vertices that share the same texture, for example, are sent to the graphics card in one batch.

Panda3D allows you to change the rendering order manually, to achieve custom scene sorting, which is what you will learn in this recipe.

Getting ready

This recipe requires the base code created in *Setting up the game structure* found in *Chapter 1*, to which the following sample code will be added.

How to do it...

Let's get started with this recipe's tasks:

1. Add the following code to `Application.py`:

    ```
    from direct.showbase.ShowBase import ShowBase
    from direct.actor.Actor import Actor

    class Application(ShowBase):
        def __init__(self):
            ShowBase.__init__(self)
            self.panda = Actor("panda", {"walk": "panda-walk"})
            self.panda.reparentTo(render)
            self.panda.loop("walk")
            self.panda.setBin("fixed", 40, 0)

            self.teapot = loader.loadModel("teapot")
            self.teapot.reparentTo(render)
    ```

```
self.teapot.setBin("fixed", 40, 1)
self.teapot.setDepthTest(False)
self.teapot.setDepthWrite(False)

self.smiley = loader.loadModel("smiley")
self.smiley.reparentTo(render)
self.smiley.setPos(0, 50, 6)
self.smiley.setScale(30)
self.smiley.setBin("background", 10)
self.smiley.setDepthTest(False)
self.smiley.setDepthWrite(False)

self.cam.setPos(0, -30, 6)
```

2. Start the application using the *F6* key to see the following scene:

How it works...

The quintessential parts of this recipe are the highlighted lines in the sample code. The setBin() method adds the affected scene node to the specified cull bin. The panda and the teapot are added to the "fixed" bin, which is rendered in the order given by the third parameter. To illustrate the results of manually ordering scene objects, we turned off depth writes and depth testing for the teapot. Normally, the teapot would appear between the panda's feet, but using the third parameter we force the panda to be drawn first, followed by the teapot. Because we do not use the depth buffer for rendering the teapot and we requested that drawing order, the teapot is drawn in front of the panda.

The same principle applies to the "background" bin. With a priority value of 10 it is drawn before the "fixed" bin, which causes the smiley to be overdrawn by the panda and the teapot.

At this point we can see the principle of multiple bins unravel itself. Panda3D's rendering subsystem always processes these bins from lowest to highest priority. Summing up, this creates the following render order for our sample code:

1. The "background" bin has a priority value of 10—the lowest in our scene. Therefore, the smiley model it contains is rendered first.

2. Next comes the "fixed" bin with a priority of 40. This bin allows us to manually control the render order of the contained models and actors based on another priority value. The scene object with the lowest priority value is rendered first. This means that the panda is rendered next.

3. The teapot is in the "fixed" bin and has a sub-priority value of 1. This is the highest value for all objects in the scene, causing it to be the last object to be rendered.

There's more...

The sample code only showed you a part of Panda3D's scene sorting features, so let's take a deeper look!

Cull bin types

If we take a look at the BinType enumeration found in Panda3D's API, we can see five different types of cull bins:

▶ BTUnsorted: An unsorted bin just sends geometry to the graphics card in the order it is encountered while traversing the scene graph.

▶ BTStateSorted: A state sorted cull bin sorts geometry by material, texture, and shader, among others, to minimize the switching of render states to increase drawing performance.

▶ BTBackToFront: This type of cull bin will cause the parts of a model that are the furthest away from the point of view to be drawn first. This is necessary for drawing semi-transparent models, for example: Because we need to properly blend the colors of the translucent parts of a model and the colors of the surfaces behind these see-through parts. For further information on this topic, read up on alpha blending.

▶ BTFrontToBack: This is the reversal of BTBackToFront. Geometry that is nearer to the camera is drawn first.

▶ BTFixed: The order of rendering is completely user defined and needs to be specified as the third parameter of the setBin() method. Objects with lower order values are drawn first.

Default cull bins

By default, Panda3D creates the following bins ready to be used by your code. Bins with a lower priority value are processed first.

Name	Type	Priority
background	BTFixed	10
opaque	BTStateSorted	20
transparent	BTBackToFront	30
fixed	BTFixed	40
unsorted	BTUnsorted	50
gui-popup	BTUnsorted	60

Adding a cull bin at runtime

It's very easy to add new cull bins at runtime. Consider the following code snippet:

```
from panda3d.core import CullBinManager
cbm = CullBinManager.getGlobalPtr()
cbm.addBin("mybin", CullBinManager.BTFixed, 80)
```

All you need to do is import the `CullBinManager` class, get the global singleton instance, and pass the new bin's name, type, and order value to the `addBin()` method. The bin type is one out of the types presented previously. The order value can be any positive or negative integer, but should not interfere with the priorities of the default cull bins.

Adding a cull bin using the configuration file

You can also add custom cull bins using the `Config.prc` file. All you need to do is add lines similar to the ones shown in the following code:

```
cull-bin nameA 80 unsorted
cull-bin nameB 90 state_sorted
cull-bin nameC 100 back_to_front
cull-bin nameD 110 front_to_back
cull-bin nameE 120 fixed
```

As you might have guessed already, the arguments to the `cull-bin` variable are the bin's name, the sort order, and the cull bin's type. Different to the names of the bin types shown in the preceding sections, this uses a slightly different naming convention.

Using multiple displays

Spanning the render view across multiple monitors can greatly enhance player immersion. In a racing game, for example, it's great to not only be able to see out of the car's front window, but also have the side windows available in two extra monitors.

In this short recipe you will learn how to configure Panda3D to use multiple displays and render across two monitors. While the sample assumes two display devices to be used, you can easily follow the principles presented in the following section to use three, four, or even more display devices.

Getting ready

This recipe requires the base code from _Setting up the game structure_ to be present before proceeding. Please revisit this article found in _Chapter 1_ if you haven't read it yet.

Naturally, you will need two monitors for this recipe, which have to use the same resolution to properly display the sample code's output.

How to do it...

Follow these steps to create an application that takes advantage of a multi-monitor setup:

1. Open `Application.py` and copy the following code:

```python
from direct.showbase.ShowBase import ShowBase
from direct.actor.Actor import Actor
from pandac.PandaModules import loadPrcFileData

loadPrcFileData("", "win-origin 0 0")
loadPrcFileData("", "win-size 2880 900")
loadPrcFileData("", "undecorated 1")

class Application(ShowBase):
    def __init__(self):
        ShowBase.__init__(self)

        self.pandas = []

        for i in range(8):
            panda = Actor("panda", {"walk": "panda-walk"})
            panda.reparentTo(render)
            panda.loop("walk")
            panda.setX(-28 + i * 8)
            self.pandas.append(panda)

        self.cam.setPos(0, -40, 6)
```

2. Press *F6* to run the code. You will now see the following scene across your monitors:

3. The sample uses a borderless window without controls, so use *Alt+F4* to quit.

How it works...

The entire necessary configuration is done in the three highlighted lines of the previous source code. First, the window origin is set to the top left corner of the first display. Then we set the window size to 2880 by 900 pixels. This makes the window span across two monitors with a resolution of 1440 by 900 pixels. For displays with a different size, just multiply the horizontal resolution of your display by two and use the original vertical resolution. The last configuration option makes the window borderless and removes the controls for minimizing, maximizing, and closing the window. Panda3D provides no native fullscreen rendering mode for multiple displays. But using these settings, we are able to make the application window fill both screens and make it appear as if it were set to fullscreen mode.

The same effect can be achieved by adding the following lines shown to your `Config.prc` file.

```
win-origin 0 0
win-size 2880 900
undecorated 1
```

4

Scene Effects and Shaders

In this chapter, we will cover:

- ▶ Adding lights and shadows
- ▶ Using light ramps
- ▶ Creating particle effects
- ▶ Animating textures
- ▶ Adding ribbon trails to an object
- ▶ Creating a flashlight effect
- ▶ Making objects reflect the scene
- ▶ Adding a custom shader generator
- ▶ Applying a custom Cg shader

Introduction

While brilliant gameplay is the key to a fun and successful game, it is essential to deliver beautiful visuals to provide a pleasing experience and immerse the player in the game world. The looks of many modern productions are massively dominated by all sorts of visual magic to create the jaw-dropping visual density that is soaked up by players with joy and makes them feel connected to the action and the gameplay they are experiencing.

The appearance of your game matters a lot to its reception by players. Therefore it is important to know how to leverage your technology to get the best possible looks out of it. This is why this chapter will show you how Panda3D allows you to create great looking games using lights, shaders, and particles.

Adding lights and shadows

Lights and shadows are very important techniques for producing a great presentation. Proper scene lighting sets the mood and also adds depth to an otherwise flat-looking scene, while shadows add more realism, and more importantly, root the shadow-casting objects to the ground, destroying the impression of models floating in mid-air.

This recipe will show you how to add lights to your game scenes and make objects cast shadows to boost your visuals.

Getting ready

You need to create the setup presented in *Setting up the game structure* found in *Chapter 1, Setting Up Panda3D and Configuring Development Tools* before proceeding, as this recipe continues and builds upon this base code.

How to do it...

This recipe consists of these tasks:

1. Add the following code to `Application.py`:

```
from direct.showbase.ShowBase import ShowBase
from direct.actor.Actor import Actor
from panda3d.core import *

class Application(ShowBase):
    def __init__(self):
        ShowBase.__init__(self)

        self.panda = Actor("panda", {"walk": "panda-walk"})
        self.panda.reparentTo(render)
        self.panda.loop("walk")

        cm = CardMaker("plane")
        cm.setFrame(-10, 10, -10, 10)
        plane = render.attachNewNode(cm.generate())
        plane.setP(270)

        self.cam.setPos(0, -40, 6)

        ambLight = AmbientLight("ambient")
        ambLight.setColor(Vec4(0.2, 0.1, 0.1, 1.0))
        ambNode = render.attachNewNode(ambLight)
        render.setLight(ambNode)
```

```
dirLight = DirectionalLight("directional")
dirLight.setColor(Vec4(0.1, 0.4, 0.1, 1.0))
dirNode = render.attachNewNode(dirLight)
dirNode.setHpr(60, 0, 90)
render.setLight(dirNode)

pntLight = PointLight("point")
pntLight.setColor(Vec4(0.8, 0.8, 0.8, 1.0))
pntNode = render.attachNewNode(pntLight)
pntNode.setPos(0, 0, 15)
self.panda.setLight(pntNode)

sptLight = Spotlight("spot")
sptLens = PerspectiveLens()
sptLight.setLens(sptLens)
sptLight.setColor(Vec4(1.0, 0.0, 0.0, 1.0))
sptLight.setShadowCaster(True)
sptNode = render.attachNewNode(sptLight)
sptNode.setPos(-10, -10, 20)
sptNode.lookAt(self.panda)
render.setLight(sptNode)

render.setShaderAuto()
```

2. Start the program with the *F6* key. You will see the following scene:

How it works...

As we can see when starting our program, the panda is lit by multiple lights, casting shadows onto itself and the ground plane. Let's see how we achieved this effect.

After setting up the scene containing our panda and a ground plane, one of each possible light type is added to the scene. The general pattern we follow is to create new light instances before adding them to the scene using the `attachNewNode()` method. Finally, the light is turned on with `setLight()`, which causes the calling object and all of its children in the scene graph to receive light. We use this to make the point light only affect the panda but not the ground plane.

Shadows are very simple to enable and disable by using the `setShadowCaster()` method, as we can see in the code that initializes the spotlight.

The line `render.setShaderAuto()` enables the shader generator, which causes the lighting to be calculated pixel perfect. Additionally, for using shadows, the shader generator needs to be enabled. If this line is removed, lighting will look coarser and no shadows will be visible at all.

 Watch the amount of lights you are adding to your scene! Every light that contributes to the scene adds additional computation cost, which will hit you if you intend to use hundreds of lights in a scene! Always try to detect the nearest lights in the level to use for lighting and disable the rest to save performance.

There's more...

In the sample code, we add several types of lights with different properties, which may need some further explanation.

Ambient light sets the base tone of a scene. It has no position or direction—the light color is just added to all surface colors in the scene, which avoids unlit parts of the scene to appear completely black. You shouldn't set the ambient color to very high intensities. This will decrease the effect of other lights and make the scene appear flat and washed out.

Directional lights do not have a position, as only their orientation counts. This light type is generally used to simulate sunlight—it comes from a general direction and affects all light-receiving objects equally.

A point light illuminates the scene from a point of origin from which light spreads towards all directions. You can think of it as a (very abstract) light bulb.

Spotlights, just like the headlights of a car or a flashlight, create a cone of light that originates from a given position and points towards a direction. The way the light spreads is determined by a lens, just like the viewing frustum of a camera.

Using light ramps

The lighting system of Panda3D allows you to pull off some additional tricks to create some dramatic effects with scene lights. In this recipe, you will learn how to use light ramps to modify the lights affect on the models and actors in your game scenes.

Getting ready

In this recipe we will extend the code created in *Adding lights and shadows* found in this chapter. Please review this recipe before proceeding if you haven't done so yet.

How to do it...

Light ramps can be used like this:

1. Open `Application.py` and add and modify the existing code as highlighted:

```
from direct.showbase.ShowBase import ShowBase
from direct.actor.Actor import Actor
from panda3d.core import *
from direct.interval.IntervalGlobal import *

class Application(ShowBase):
    def __init__(self):
        ShowBase.__init__(self)

        self.panda = Actor("panda", {"walk": "panda-walk"})
        self.panda.reparentTo(render)
        self.panda.loop("walk")

        cm = CardMaker("plane")
        cm.setFrame(-10, 10, -10, 10)
        plane = render.attachNewNode(cm.generate())
        plane.setP(270)

        self.cam.setPos(0, -40, 6)

        ambLight = AmbientLight("ambient")
        ambLight.setColor(Vec4(0.3, 0.2, 0.2, 1.0))
        ambNode = render.attachNewNode(ambLight)
        render.setLight(ambNode)

        dirLight = DirectionalLight("directional")
        dirLight.setColor(Vec4(0.3, 0.9, 0.3, 1.0))
        dirNode = render.attachNewNode(dirLight)
        dirNode.setHpr(60, 0, 90)
        render.setLight(dirNode)
```

```
        pntLight = PointLight("point")
        pntLight.setColor(Vec4(3.9, 3.9, 3.8, 1.0))
        pntNode = render.attachNewNode(pntLight)
        pntNode.setPos(0, 0, 15)
        self.panda.setLight(pntNode)

        sptLight = Spotlight("spot")
        sptLens = PerspectiveLens()
        sptLight.setLens(sptLens)
        sptLight.setColor(Vec4(1.0, 0.4, 0.4, 1.0))
        sptLight.setShadowCaster(True)
        sptNode = render.attachNewNode(sptLight)
        sptNode.setPos(-10, -10, 20)
        sptNode.lookAt(self.panda)
        render.setLight(sptNode)

        render.setShaderAuto()

        self.activeRamp = 0
        toggle = Func(self.toggleRamp)
        switcher = Sequence(toggle, Wait(3))
        switcher.loop()

    def toggleRamp(self):
        if self.activeRamp == 0:
            render.setAttrib(LightRampAttrib.makeDefault())
        elif self.activeRamp == 1:
            render.setAttrib(LightRampAttrib.makeHdr0())
        elif self.activeRamp == 2:
            render.setAttrib(LightRampAttrib.makeHdr1())
        elif self.activeRamp == 3:
            render.setAttrib(LightRampAttrib.makeHdr2())
        elif self.activeRamp == 4:
            render.setAttrib(LightRampAttrib.
makeSingleThreshold(0.1, 0.3))
        elif self.activeRamp == 5:
            render.setAttrib(LightRampAttrib.
makeDoubleThreshold(0, 0.1, 0.3, 0.8))

        self.activeRamp += 1
        if self.activeRamp > 5:
            self.activeRamp = 0
```

2. Press *F6* to start the sample and see it switch through the available light ramps as shown in this screenshot:

How it works...

The original lighting equation that is used by Panda3D to calculate the final screen color of a lit pixel limits color intensities to values within a range from zero to one. By using light ramps we are able to go beyond these limits or even define our own ones to create dramatic effects just like the ones we can see in the sample program.

In the sample code, we increase the lighting intensity and add a method that switches between the available light ramps, beginning with LightRampAttrib.makeDefault() which sets the default clamping thresholds for the lighting calculations.

Then, the high dynamic range ramps are enabled one after another. These light ramps allow you to have a higher range of color intensities that go beyond the standard range between zero and one. These high intensities are then mapped back into the displayable range, allocating different amounts of values within it to displaying brightness.

By using makeHdr0(), we allocate a quarter of the displayable range to brightness values that are greater than one. With makeHdr1() it is a third and with makeHdr2() we are causing Panda3D to use half of the color range for overly bright values. This doesn't come without any side effects, though. By increasing the range used for high intensities, we are decreasing the range of color intensities available for displaying colors that are within the limits of 0 and 1, thus losing contrast and making the scene look grey and washed out.

Finally, with the `makeSingleThreshold()` and `makeDoubleThreshold()` methods, we are able to create very interesting lighting effects. With a single threshold, lighting values below the given limit will be ignored, while anything that exceeds the threshold will be set to the intensity given in the second parameter of the method.

The double threshold system works analogous to the single threshold, but lighting intensity will be normalized to two possible values, depending on which of the two thresholds was exceeded.

Creating particle effects

Ranging from dust kicked up by an out of control race car spinning out into a run-off area over smoke that ascends from a battlefield to sparks spraying from a magic wand, particles are a great tool for adding life and visual fidelity to the graphics of a game. Therefore, this recipe will show you how to create a simple particle effect.

Getting ready

This recipe is based upon the project setup presented in *Setting up the game structure*. Please follow this recipe, found in *Chapter 1*, before proceeding.

How to do it...

Let's try the following Panda3D's particle effect system:

1. Open the file `Application.py` and add the following code:

```
from direct.showbase.ShowBase import ShowBase
from panda3d.core import *
from direct.particles.Particles import Particles
from direct.particles.ParticleEffect import ParticleEffect

class Application(ShowBase):
    def __init__(self):
        ShowBase.__init__(self)

        self.enableParticles()

        particles = Particles()
        particles.setPoolSize(1000)
        particles.setBirthRate(0.1)
        particles.setLitterSize(10)
        particles.setLitterSpread(3)
        particles.setFactory("PointParticleFactory")
        particles.setRenderer("GeomParticleRenderer")
        particles.setEmitter("SphereVolumeEmitter")
```

```
smiley = loader.loadModel("smiley")
smiley.setScale(0.1)
particles.getRenderer().setGeomNode(smiley.node())
particles.enable()

self.effect = ParticleEffect("peffect", particles)
self.effect.reparentTo(render)
self.effect.enable()

self.cam.setPos(0, -10, 0)
```

2. Press *F6* to launch the program and see the following output:

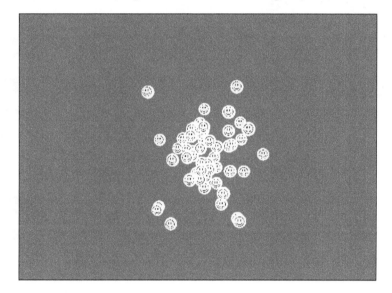

How it works...

We placed a simple particle emitter into our sample scene. It spawns new particles, represented by the smiley model, and makes them move to all directions. Let's see what we had to do to create this effect.

In the first line of our `Application` class' constructor, we enable tracking and updating of particles. After this is done, we can start setting up a particle system.

First, we set the pool size to 1000. This is the maximum amount of particles that are allowed to exist at the same time. Then we set up how many and how often particles are spawned with calls to `setBirthRate()`, `setLitterSize()`, and `setLitterSpread()`, where the last of these methods defines the maximum deviation from the litter size. With our setup, this means the particle system will spawn ten particles each 0.1 seconds with a variation of ±3 particles.

Next, we set up the particle system to use the point factory, want our particles rendered as geoms, and set the particles to be emitted within a spherical volume.

Finally, we load and attach the smiley model to the particle system renderer and add the new `ParticleEffect` that uses our settings to the scene.

There's more...

As you already may have noticed in the code sample, Panda3D allows you to choose between various factories, renderers, and emitters for your particle systems.

Particle Factories

Panda3D comes with two particle factory types: `PointParticleFactory` and `ZSpinParticleFactory`. While the former factory creates particles as points without orientation, the latter is responsible for the creation of particles that spin about their Z-axis.

Particle Renderers

The way particles emitted from a specific system are drawn depends on which particle renderer is set.

The `GeomParticleRenderer` allows you to assign a `GeomNode` to the particle system that is used to draw each of the particles, as shown in this recipe's sample code.

If you use the `PointParticleRenderer`, the `LineParticleRenderer` or the `SparkleParticleRenderer`, particles are rendered as points, lines, or little stars, respectively.

This leaves the `SpriteParticleRenderer`, which allows you to assign a texture image that is used as on-screen representation for your particles.

Particle Emitters

The `SphereVolumeEmitter` used in this recipe's code defines a sphere-shaped volume within the particles are emitted with a velocity that goes from the center of the sphere to the hull of the volume.

With a `BoxVolumeEmitter`, particles are spawned inside a box without any velocity.

A `DiscVolumeEmitter` works similar to the `SphereVolumeEmitter`, with the difference of using a flat, disc-shaped bounding volume.

`PointEmitter`, `RectangleEmitter`, and `SphereSurfaceEmitter` spawn particles from a single point, within a rectangle and on the outer hull of a sphere, without assigning any velocity to the newly created particles.

The `RingEmitter` and `TangentRingEmitter` emitters both create new particles on a ring. Particles spawned by a `RingEmitter` move on an axis that points from the center of the ring to the outside, whereas the `TangentRingEmitter` gives particles an initial velocity with a direction that is tangential to the ring that forms the emitter's bounding volume.

Animating textures

Many great effects found in games can be achieved using very simple measures. The effect you will learn about in this recipe falls into this category. Animated textures are used very often to create the illusion of a flowing lava stream, waves on a lake, or details like a transparent plasma container mounted onto an alien gun.

This recipe will teach you how to put a texture onto an object and animate its position, scale, and rotation.

Getting ready

Please make sure you completed the recipe *Setting up the game structure* found in *Chapter 1* before proceeding with the following steps. Also be sure to add a folder called `textures` to the project's folder structure and add it to Panda3D's content search paths, and have a texture file in PNG format at hand that can be used for this sample.

How to do it...

Follow these steps to complete this recipe:

1. Copy your texture file to the `textures` directory and rename it to `texture.png`.

2. Open `Application.py` and add the following code:

```python
from direct.showbase.ShowBase import ShowBase
from panda3d.core import *
from math import *

class Application(ShowBase):
    def __init__(self):
        ShowBase.__init__(self)
        cm = CardMaker("plane")
        cm.setFrame(-3, 3, -3, 3)

        self.plane = render.attachNewNode(cm.generate())
        tex = loader.loadTexture("texture.png")
        self.plane.setTexture(tex)

        self.cam.setPos(0, -12, 0)
        taskMgr.add(self.animate, "texanim")
```

```
def animate(self, task):
    texStage = TextureStage.getDefault()

    offset = self.plane.getTexOffset(texStage)
    offset.setY(offset.getY() - 0.005)
    self.plane.setTexOffset(texStage, offset)

    scale = sin(offset.getY()) * 2
    self.plane.setTexScale(texStage, scale, scale)

    rotate = sin(offset.getY()) * 80
    self.plane.setTexRotate(texStage, rotate)
    return task.cont
```

3. Press *F6* to run the program. The texture will be zoomed in and out while it is being rotated:

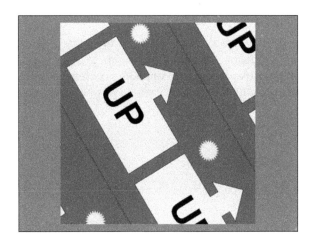

How it works...

We begin this sample by adding a textured quad to the scene using the `CardMaker` class and kicking off the task that will call the `animate()` method on every frame at runtime.

Texture stages are used to handle the properties of textures that are mapped onto an object. In our sample, there is only one texture map applied to the geometry, so we use the `getDefault()` method to get a reference to the default `TextureStage` that holds all necessary data for the next operations.

We then use the methods `setTexOffset()`, `setTexScale()`, and `setTexRotate()` to apply transformation, scaling, and rotation to the texture coordinates. This means that we need to think "in reverse" to get the proper results. To move the texture up, we need to decrease the offset along the y-axis as shown in the code. The same applies to scaling and rotation—bigger values mean that the texture will appear smaller, and turning the coordinate system to the right means that the texture will rotate to the left.

We are using a sinus function for animating the rotation and scale of the texture. This makes these two properties go back and forth, which means we are zooming in and out of the texture while it is rotated to the left and then to the right. We also apply a transformation to the texture that makes it go upwards.

Used together, all these animated properties twist and turn the texture a lot. Experiment and try adding and removing the modifications to the texture offset, scale, and rotation to find new and interesting effects!

Adding ribbon trails to an object

This recipe will show you how to implement a ribbon trail effect that is often used for emphasizing high-speed movements such as sword slashes, very fast vehicles passing by or, as you will see after finishing this recipe, the fastest running panda in the world.

Getting ready

Follow the instructions of *Setting up the game structure* found in *Chapter 1* before you proceed to create a basic project setup.

How to do it...

The following steps are necessary for implementing the ribbon trail effect:

1. Add a new file called `Ribbon.py` to the project and add the following code:

```python
from direct.task import Task
from direct.task.TaskManagerGlobal import taskMgr
from panda3d.core import *

class RibbonNode():
    def __init__(self, pos, damping):
        self.pos = Vec3(pos)
        self.damping = damping
        self.delta = Vec3()

    def update(self, pos):
        self.delta = (pos - self.pos) * self.damping
        self.pos += self.delta
```

```
class Ribbon():
    def __init__(self, parent, color, thickness, length, damping):

        self.parent = parent
        self.length = length
        self.thickness = thickness
        self.color = color

        self.lineGen = MeshDrawer()
        self.lineGen.setBudget(100)
        genNode = self.lineGen.getRoot()
        genNode.reparentTo(render)
        genNode.setTwoSided(True)
        genNode.setTransparency(True)

        pos = parent.getPos(render)

        self.trailPoints = []
        for i in range(length):
            self.trailPoints.append(RibbonNode(pos, damping))

        taskMgr.add(self.trail, "update trail")

    def getRoot(self):
        return self.lineGen.getRoot()

    def trail(self, task):
        pos = self.parent.getPos(render)
        self.trailPoints[0].update(pos)

        for i in range(1, self.length):
            self.trailPoints[i].update(self.trailPoints[i -
1].pos)

        self.lineGen.begin(base.cam, render)
        color = Vec4(self.color)
        thickness = self.thickness

        for i in range(self.length - 1):
            p1 = self.trailPoints[i].pos
            p2 = self.trailPoints[i + 1].pos

            startColor = Vec4(color)
            endColor = Vec4(color)
```

```
            endColor.setW(color.getW() - 0.2)
            color = Vec4(endColor)
            self.lineGen.unevenSegment(p1, p2, 0, thickness,
startColor, thickness - 0.3, endColor)
            thickness -= 0.3

        self.lineGen.end()
        return task.cont
```

2. Open `Application.py` and enter the following lines of code:

```
from direct.showbase.ShowBase import ShowBase
from direct.showbase.RandomNumGen import RandomNumGen
from direct.actor.Actor import Actor
from panda3d.core import *
from direct.interval.IntervalGlobal import *
from Ribbon import Ribbon


class Application(ShowBase):
    def __init__(self):
        ShowBase.__init__(self)
        self.panda = Actor("panda", {"walk": "panda-walk"})
        self.panda.reparentTo(render)
        self.panda.loop("walk")
        self.panda.setHpr(-90, 0, 0)

        self.ribbon = Ribbon(self.panda, Vec4(1, 1, 1, 1), 3, 10,
0.3)
        self.ribbon.getRoot().setZ(5)

        self.walkIval1 = self.panda.posInterval(1, Vec3(-12, 0,
0), startPos = Vec3(12, 0, 0))
        self.walkIval2 = self.panda.posInterval(1, Vec3(12, 0, 0),
startPos = Vec3(-12, 0, 0))
        self.turnIval1 = self.panda.hprInterval(0.1, Vec3(90, 0,
0), startHpr = Vec3(-90, 0, 0))
        self.turnIval2 = self.panda.hprInterval(0.1, Vec3(-90, 0,
0), startHpr = Vec3(90, 0, 0))
        self.pandaWalk = Sequence(self.walkIval1, self.turnIval1,
self.walkIval2, self.turnIval2)
        self.pandaWalk.loop()

        self.cam.setPos(0, -60, 6)
        self.cam.lookAt(0, 0, 6)
```

3. Press *F6* to start the program and see the panda running:

How it works...

Our code puts a trail behind our panda actor that slowly fades out. Let's take a closer look at the code that produced this effect.

In the constructor of the Ribbon class, after initializing our member variables, we set up a new `MeshDrawer`, which is a very convenient class for working with dynamically updated geometry like our ribbons. We configure it to use a budget of 100 triangles and enable transparency and double sided rendering for the generated geometry.

After this is done, we fill a list of `RibbonNodes`. Each of these nodes will then try to follow its predecessor in the list, but will be hampered by the amount of damping we specified in the constructor parameter, so our nodes are keeping some distance, between which we span some geometry using a `MeshDrawer` and `unevenSegment()` method that draws line segments with different sized ends. Not only the size of the line decreases, but we also make the alpha smaller and smaller with each segment until the trail smoothly fades out.

This leaves us with building a little test scene in our `Application` class, connecting the ribbon to the panda that is moved back and forth using intervals.

There's more

The `Ribbon` class is far from complete, but it does its job and shows nicely how the `MeshDrawer` class can help to procedurally generate and modify geometry. Some points you may want to extend, for example, are the way the alpha value and the ribbon size are controlled.

Additionally, you could experiment with different damping values and behaviors. Instead of using the same damping value for all `RibbonNode` objects in the trail, you could try to assign different values to the nodes, making the ones in the back of the trail slower, for example.

Creating a flashlight effect

This recipe will show you how to implement an effect that makes the scene look like it was lit from a small flashlight. This really nice effect can help you make your dark and creepy games even darker and creepier!

Getting ready

Follow the steps from *Setting up the game structure* in *Chapter 1* and add a directory called `textures` to the project.

Additionally, you will need a texture that represents the light point created by the flashlight, like the one shown as follows:

How to do it...

Let's get to the code behind this interesting effect:

1. Copy your texture file to the `textures` directory and rename it to `flashlight.png`.

2. Open `Application.py` and add the following code:

    ```
    from direct.showbase.ShowBase import ShowBase
    from panda3d.core import *

    class Application(ShowBase):
        def __init__(self):
            ShowBase.__init__(self)
    ```

```
self.world = loader.loadModel("environment")
self.world.reparentTo(render)
self.world.setScale(0.5)
self.world.setPos(-8, 80, 0)

self.proj = render.attachNewNode(LensNode("proj"))
lens = PerspectiveLens()
self.proj.node().setLens(lens)
self.proj.reparentTo(self.cam)
self.proj.setHpr(0, -5, 0)
self.proj.setPos(0, 10, 0)

tex = loader.loadTexture("flashlight.png")
tex.setWrapU(Texture.WMClamp)
tex.setWrapV(Texture.WMClamp)
ts = TextureStage('ts')
self.world.projectTexture(ts, tex, self.proj)

self.cam.setPos(0, -10, 10)
```

3. Press *F6* to run the application. You will see a dark scene like the one shown in the following screenshot. Only a small portion of the scene will be Lit up, just like using a flashlight in a very dark environment. Use *Left Mouse Button + Right Mouse Button* to look around.

How it works...

After loading the `environment` model into our scene, we add a new `LensNode`, that will be used to project our flashlight texture onto the scene. We also need to assign a new `PerspectiveLens` to this scene node, which defines the frustum used for projecting the texture so that the light blob appears as a small dot on near objects and becomes bigger if we point at objects that are further away. Additionally, we reparent the projector lens to the camera, move it a bit in front of it, and let it point down slightly.

Then we load the flashlight texture and set its wrap mode to `WMClamp`. This means that instead of repeating the whole texture image, only the outermost pixel color is repeated. In our case this means that we have only one light blob and everything else appears black.

To conclude our effect implementation, we use the `projectTexture()` method to put the flashlight texture image onto our `environment` model.

Making objects reflect the scene

This recipe will show you how to enable and use cube mapping to make your models and actors dynamically reflect any other game objects and the surrounding environment. This is a very useful effect for emphasizing movement by creating a glossy car paint effect in a racing game, for example.

Getting ready

This recipe requires you to have finished the steps of the recipe *Setting up the game structure* found in *Chapter 1* and will follow up to where this recipe left off.

How to do it...

These are the tasks for this recipe:

1. In the file `Application.py`, add the following code:

    ```
    from direct.showbase.ShowBase import ShowBase
    from panda3d.core import *
    from direct.interval.IntervalGlobal import *

    class Application(ShowBase):
        def __init__(self):
            ShowBase.__init__(self)

            self.world = loader.loadModel("environment")
            self.world.reparentTo(render)
            self.world.setScale(0.5)
            self.world.setPos(-8, 80, 0)
    ```

```
        self.teapot = loader.loadModel("teapot")
        self.teapot.reparentTo(render)
        self.teapot.setPos(0, 0, 10)

        cubeCams = NodePath("cubeCams")
        cubeBuffer = self.win.makeCubeMap("cubemap", 128,
cubeCams)
        cubeCams.reparentTo(self.teapot)

        tex = TextureStage.getDefault()
        self.teapot.setTexGen(tex, TexGenAttrib.MWorldCubeMap)
        self.teapot.setTexture(cubeBuffer.getTexture())

        rotate = self.teapot.hprInterval(10, Vec3(360, 0, 0),
startHpr = Vec3(0, 0, 0))
        move = self.teapot.posInterval(10, Vec3(-10, 0, 10),
startPos = Vec3(10, 0, 10))
        rotate.loop()
        move.loop()

        self.cam.setPos(0, -30, 10)
```

2. Hit the *F6* key to run the code and see the scene similar to the one shown in the following screenshot. Note how the teapot model reflects the scene:

How it works...

To render the reflections on the teapot model, we are using a technique called cube mapping. This effect renders the scene around a center point (marked by the object that uses the reflection texture) into six different textures, forming a so-called 'texture cube'. Each side of the cube is formed by a texture that stores what can be seen if we look up, down, left, right, forward, or backward from the center point. Finally, the six textures are mapped onto a model, making it appear as if it reflected its surroundings.

In the first few lines of code, we set up the scene that we are going to work with, before we add a new dummy node that will mark the center point from where the cube map will be generated.

Next we call the `makeCubeMap()` method, which initializes everything needed for rendering the teapot's surroundings into a texture with a size of 128x128 pixels, specified by the second parameter. The dummy node we pass as the third parameter to this method will act as parent node to the six cameras. These six cameras point at each direction from the center point and capture the image data that is then put into our cube map texture. This also means that our scene will be rendered six additional times, so be aware of the performance implications this brings!

Finally, we use `TexGenAttrib.MWorldCubeMap` to enable automatic and proper generation of texture coordinates on the teapot, before assigning the cube map texture by calling the `getTexture()` method on our cube map buffer.

In the closing steps, two intervals for moving and rotating the teapot are added to show off that the cube map texture is updated dynamically.

Adding a custom shader generator

Modern graphics cards and graphics APIs like Direct3D or OpenGL allow developers to program, and therefore customize, the behavior of parts of the graphics pipeline using shader programs, written in a C-like programming language. These shader programs define how vertices are being transformed, which textures are used for retrieving color values, and which final color pixels we have on the screen.

Luckily, Panda3D adds a very nice abstraction layer on top of this shader system, which is called the shader generator. As soon as you call the `setShaderAuto()` method on a node in the scene graph, the shader generator kicks in and pieces together the right shaders, depending on the render state (textures, colors, lights, and so on.) of your objects.

Sometimes the built-in shader generator and the code it creates may not suit your needs. Therefore, this recipe will explore and show how to add a custom shader generator to Panda3D.

Getting ready

This recipe requires you to modify and build the source code of Panda3D. Please take your time to review *Building Panda3D from source code* to get set before proceeding with the following steps. You can find this recipe in *Chapter 1*.

How to do it...

Complete the following steps to create a custom shader generator:

1. From the top level directory of your unpacked Panda3D source tree, navigate to the subfolder panda\src\pgraphnodes.

2. Create two new files called customShaderGenerator.h and customShaderGenerator.cxx.

3. Open customShaderGenerator.h and add the following code:

```
#ifndef CUSTOMSHADERGENERATOR_H
#define CUSTOMSHADERGENERATOR_H

#include "shaderGenerator.h"

class EXPCL_PANDA_PGRAPHNODES CustomShaderGenerator : public
ShaderGenerator {
PUBLISHED:
  CustomShaderGenerator(PT(GraphicsStateGuardianBase) gsg,
PT(GraphicsOutputBase) host);
  virtual ~CustomShaderGenerator();
  virtual CPT(RenderAttrib) synthesize_shader(const RenderState
*rs);

public:
  static TypeHandle get_class_type() {
    return _type_handle;
  }
  static void init_type() {
    ShaderGenerator::init_type();
    register_type(_type_handle, "CustomShaderGenerator",
                  ShaderGenerator::get_class_type());
  }
  virtual TypeHandle get_type() const {
    return get_class_type();
  }
  virtual TypeHandle force_init_type() {init_type(); return get_
class_type();}
```

```
  private:
    static TypeHandle _type_handle;
};

#endif
```

4. Open the file `customShaderGenerator.cxx` and add these lines of code:

```
#include "customShaderGenerator.h"

TypeHandle CustomShaderGenerator::_type_handle;

CustomShaderGenerator::CustomShaderGenerator(PT(GraphicsStateGuard
ianBase) gsg, PT(GraphicsOutputBase) host) :
  ShaderGenerator(gsg, host) {
}

CustomShaderGenerator::~CustomShaderGenerator() {
}

CPT(RenderAttrib) CustomShaderGenerator::
synthesize_shader(const RenderState *rs) {
}
```

 The last line of `customShaderGenerator.cxx` has to be blank for the code to compile properly!

5. Open `shaderGenerator.cxx` and copy and paste the method body of `synthesize_shader()` to the `synthesize_shader()` method in `customShaderGenerator.cxx`.

6. In `customShaderGenerator.cxx`, replace all occurrences of `saturate(dot(l_eye_normal.xyz, lvec.xyz))` with `saturate(0.5 * dot(l_eye_normal.xyz, lvec.xyz) + 0.5)`.

7. Open the file `lightLensNode.h`. Find the following code lines and add the highlighted code:

```
friend class GraphicsStateGuardian;
friend class ShaderGenerator;
friend class CustomShaderGenerator;
```

8. In the file `pgraphnodes_composite2.cxx`, find the line that reads `#include "shaderGenerator.cxx"` and add the line `#include "customShaderGenerator.cxx"` below it.

9. Open `config_pgraphnodes.cxx`. Below the line `#include "shaderGenerator.h"`, add the line `#include "customShaderGenerator.h"`. Also find this line of code: `ShaderGenerator::init_type();`. Add a new line below, containing `CustomShaderGenerator::init_type();`.

10. Go to the `panda\src\dxgsg9` subdirectory of the source tree.

11. In the file `dxGraphicsStateGuardian9.cxx`, add the line `#include "customShaderGenerator.h"` below the other includes. Also find and replace the following code line with the highlighted one:

    ```
    _shader_generator = new ShaderGenerator(this, _scene_setup->get_
    display_region()->get_window());
    _shader_generator = new CustomShaderGenerator(this, _scene_setup-
    >get_display_region()->get_window());
    ```

12. Repeat step 11 for the file `glGraphicsStateGuardian_src.cxx` in the `panda\src\glstuff` subdirectory.

13. Proceed through the steps of *Building Panda3D from source code* to compile your custom build of Panda3D.

How it works...

We begin implementing our custom shader generator by defining the interface of our new `CustomShaderGenerator`. We derive this class from the default shader generator and declare our own constructor, destructor, and `synthesize_shader()` implementations. The code of the `synthesize_shader()` method will later be handling the generation of the shader code.

Don't be irritated by the `PUBLISHED:` line and the `TypeHandle` code. This stuff is needed internally to register the class and methods with Python.

We then proceed to add method implementations to `customShaderGenerator.cxx`. The constructor calls its base constructor and the destructor remains empty. The real magic happens within the `synthesize_shader()` method, which we base upon the code of the original code to remain compatible with the existing render states. Unfortunately, the shader generator system is not written in a very modular way, which means we need to copy the method body of the original implementation of the method.

For the purpose of this recipe, we then change the standard Lambert lighting equation slightly by moving the range of possible results from [-1, 1] to [0, 1], making lit scenes appear brighter, as shown in the following comparison with the standard implementation to the left and our custom lighting to the right:

In step 7, we declare our `CustomShaderGenerator` class to be a friend of `LightLensNode`, because our base class needs to access some private and protected members of this class when the shader is put together.

The last steps before we can compile our custom version of Panda3D are necessary to add the new class to the build system and register it with the Python API. The most important steps in this closing part are 11 and 12, where we replace the instantiation of the standard `ShaderGenerator` class with our `CustomShaderGenerator`.

There's more...

This recipe only made very slight changes to the original implementation of the shader generator. For more extensive changes to this system, you might consider taking a close look at the `ShaderGenerator` class and its `analyze_renderstate()` method, which operates on instances of `RenderState` to determine which shader parts are then needed in `synthesize_shader()` to produce the proper shader permutation.

Applying a custom Cg shader

Shaders are one of the most powerful concepts in today's graphics programming, allowing programmers to program the graphics hardware and thus provide great flexibility for creating amazing effects.

This recipe will show you how to use shaders written in the Cg shading language with the Panda3D engine.

Getting ready

Setup your project as described in *Setting up the game structure* found in Chapter 1. Add an additional folder called `shaders` in the top-level source directory and add it to Panda3D's resource search paths.

How to do it...

Let's create a shader and apply it to a model:

1. Add the following code snippet to `Application.py`:

```python
from direct.showbase.ShowBase import ShowBase
from panda3d.core import *

class Application(ShowBase):
    def __init__(self):
        ShowBase.__init__(self)

        self.world = loader.loadModel("environment")
        self.world.reparentTo(render)
        self.world.setScale(0.5)
        self.world.setPos(-8, 80, 0)

        shader = loader.loadShader("shader.cg")
        render.setShader(shader)

        self.cam.setPos(0, -40, 10)
```

2. Create a new file called `shader.cg` in the `shaders` subdirectory and enter the code below:

```
//Cg

void vshader(uniform float4x4 mat_modelproj,
        in float4 vtx_position:POSITION,
        in float2 vtx_texcoord0:TEXCOORD0,
        out float4 l_position:POSITION,
        out float2 l_texcoord0:TEXCOORD0)
{
    l_position = mul(mat_modelproj, vtx_position);
    l_texcoord0 = vtx_texcoord0;
}

void fshader(uniform sampler2D tex_0,
        in float2 l_texcoord0:TEXCOORD0,
        out float4 o_color:COLOR0)
```

```
    {
        float4 fullColor = tex2D(tex_0, l_texcoord0);
        float3 rgb = fullColor.xyz;
        rgb *= 8;
        rgb = floor(rgb);
        rgb /= 8;
        o_color = float4(rgb, fullColor.w);
    }
```

3. Press *F6* to launch the application and see something similar to the following screenshot. The colors will appear somewhat strange, but don't worry, this is what our shader is supposed to do:

How it works...

In our Python code, loading and applying a shader doesn't require any heavy lifting. We just use the `loadShader()` method and then enable it on models and actors of our choice, as well as all their children in the scene graph using `setShader()`. One thing to note though, is that if we use such a custom shader, all render states and all the functionality of the shader generator are overridden and need to be reimplemented within the shader file.

After our Python code is set and ready, we implement the shader code. One very important thing about writing shaders can already be found in the first line, where the line `//Cg` must be found for the engine to be able to recognize the file as Cg shader code.

The vertex shader function must be called `vshader`, just as the pixel or fragment shader function needs to be called `fshader`. The names of the function parameters were not chosen arbitrarily, either. These names have to comply with the hard-coded naming convention of Panda3D, so the data provided by the engine can be used by our shader code.

Our simple vertex shader just transforms the scene vertices to their proper position on the screen and hands the texture coordinates on to the pixel shader.

In the pixel shader, we sample from the texture at the main color texture image channel using the `tex2D()` function. As a special twist, we limit color output to only 8 possible values, creating an old-school look for our scene.

5
Post-Processing and Screen Space Effects

In this chapter, we will cover:

- ▶ Adding built-in post-processing effects
- ▶ Building custom effects
- ▶ Adding a scanline and vignette effect
- ▶ Adding a color grading effect
- ▶ Adding a depth of field effect
- ▶ Building a deferred rendering pipeline

Introduction

Over the course of the years that passed in the industry, games have always pushed the envelope of what was possible in terms of presentation to impress players and one-up what had been done before. Color depth increased, sprites were replaced by polygons, which were later colored using texture images. With the rise of programmable hardware, elaborate lighting models were implemented and tricks like normal, parallax, and bump mapping surfaced to make games look even more realistic and awesome.

With the rise of seventh generation video game consoles like Xbox 360 and PlayStation 3, the graphics of video games reached a point where lit pixels and bumpy surfaces were just not enough anymore. So today, to make games look even more exciting, post-processing effects are added to create cinematic effects like depth of field or color correction.

Besides that, using render-to-texture functionality to generate intermediate textures that are processed, filtered, and then composited back into the final image, gives graphics developers very interesting capabilities when creating the final image. Just like in a painting, the on-screen image consists of various layers that ultimately form the final result.

In this chapter you will learn how to use Panda3D to render to off-screen buffers and how to create post-processing effects to generate stunning visuals for your games.

 Some of the effects presented in the following articles fall into a more advanced category. Therefore, depending on your mix of graphics hardware and driver you might not be able to see the effects working! Please keep issues such as this in mind if you plan to release your game to a broad audience, and never forget to test hardware-demanding features across varying hardware setups prior to releasing!

Adding built-in post-processing effects

Adding post-processing effects to a scene can boost a game's visuals and greatly enhance the perceived quality of a game. For example, it is very common to work with bloom, blur, and color warping effects like negative colors.

These effects are a very common sight in video games, which is the reason why the Panda3D developers added them to the engine. Instead of having to reinvent the wheel and roll your own implementation, you are provided with a set of drop-in effects for quickly adding state-of-the-art post-processing to your games.

In this recipe you will learn how to add these effects to your game and how to tweak their parameters to achieve a unique look.

Getting ready

Set up your project as in *Setting up the game structure*, found in *Chapter 1, Setting Up Panda3D and Configuring Development Tools*. Also, add the line `basic-shaders-only #f` to the file `Config.prc` in the `etc` subdirectory of your Panda3D installation. This enables the most recent shader profile required for the effects shown in this recipe.

How to do it...

Let's find out what can be done with Panda3D's built-in post-processing effects by writing some sample code:

1. Open `Application.py` and paste the following code:

```
from direct.showbase.ShowBase import ShowBase
from direct.actor.Actor import Actor
```

```python
from panda3d.core import *
from direct.filter.CommonFilters import *
from direct.interval.IntervalGlobal import *

class Application(ShowBase):
    def __init__(self):
        ShowBase.__init__(self)
        self.setupScene()
        self.setupPostFx()

    def setupScene(self):
        self.panda = Actor("panda", {"walk": "panda-walk"})
        self.panda.reparentTo(render)
        self.panda.loop("walk")

        cm = CardMaker("plane")
        cm.setFrame(-10, 10, -10, 10)
        plane = render.attachNewNode(cm.generate())
        plane.setP(270)

        self.cam.setPos(0, -40, 6)

        ambLight = AmbientLight("ambient")
        ambLight.setColor(Vec4(0.2, 0.1, 0.1, 1.0))
        ambNode = render.attachNewNode(ambLight)
        render.setLight(ambNode)

        dirLight = DirectionalLight("directional")
        dirLight.setColor(Vec4(0.1, 0.4, 0.1, 1.0))
        dirNode = render.attachNewNode(dirLight)
        dirNode.setHpr(60, 0, 90)
        render.setLight(dirNode)

        pntLight = PointLight("point")
        pntLight.setColor(Vec4(0.8, 0.8, 0.8, 1.0))
        pntNode = render.attachNewNode(pntLight)
        pntNode.setPos(0, 0, 15)
        self.panda.setLight(pntNode)

        sptLight = Spotlight("spot")
        sptLens = PerspectiveLens()
        sptLight.setLens(sptLens)
        sptLight.setColor(Vec4(1.0, 1.0, 1.0, 1.0))
        sptNode = render.attachNewNode(sptLight)
```

```
sptNode.setPos(-10, -10, 20)
sptNode.lookAt(self.panda)
render.setLight(sptNode)

render.setShaderAuto()
```

2. Below the code you just added, append the following method:

```
def setupPostFx(self):
    self.filters = CommonFilters(self.win, self.cam)

    switch = Sequence(Func(self.filters.setBloom, size =
"large"), Wait(3), Func(self.filters.delBloom),
                        Func(self.filters.setCartoonInk, 2),
Wait(3), Func(self.filters.delCartoonInk),
                        Func(self.filters.setBlurSharpen, 0),
Wait(3), Func(self.filters.delBlurSharpen),
                        Func(self.filters.setBlurSharpen, 2),
Wait(3), Func(self.filters.delBlurSharpen),
                        Func(self.filters.setInverted), Wait(3),
Func(self.filters.delInverted))
        switch.loop()
```

3. Press *F6* to start the sample and see it toggle through the effects:

How it works...

After the scene setup code from step one, we add a sequence of function intervals that toggle through the built-in effects that are managed by the `CommonFilters` class.

The first filter that will be applied causes bright parts of the screen to bleed color into the rest of the image. This creates the impression of being blinded by glaringly bright lights, and can be used to create soft halos around light sources, for example.

The bloom effect can be configured further using the following named parameters:

- `blend` controls how much each color channel contributes to the brightness of the scene. This means passing the list `[1, 0, 0, 0]` makes only red parts glow, while `[0, 0, 0, 1]` causes the bloom effect to be controlled by the alpha channel.

- `mintrigger` takes a value between 0 and 1 that sets the minimum intensity level. If this value is exceeded, the bloom effect starts to take effect.

- `maxtrigger` sets the intensity value the effect will see as maximum and apply the highest amount of the color bleeding effect.

- `desat` lets you set the amount of desaturation that is applied to the original scene color. If the value is 0, the original color will be used. The closer you set the value to 1, the nearer the color of the halos will be to white.

- `intensity` controls the maximum brightness of the bloom effect.

- `size` configures the size of the halos around bright spots in the scene. This parameter takes one of the string values `"small"`, `"medium"`, and `"large"`.

The next effect we apply to our scene is called **cartoon ink** by the Panda3D developers and causes an outline to be drawn around objects, giving them a hand-drawn, comic-like look. This is a very simple effect, therefore the `setCartoonInk()` method only takes one parameter that sets the thickness of the line in pixels.

Following that, we use `setBlurSharpen()` twice to first blur the scene and then sharpen the image. The amount of blur, respectively sharpness, applied can be controlled by the only parameter of the method. Values ranging from below one to zero cause the drawn frames to be blurred, where zero sets the maximum amount of blur. Passing one disables any effect of the filter, while any number greater than one sharpens the image that is rendered to the screen.

The last filter in our little program is the simplest to use. It takes no parameters at all and simply causes colors to appear inverted.

There's more...

The `CommonFilters` class contains some more filters, like ambient occlusion or volumetric lighting (the so-called "god rays"). You can give them a try using the `setAmbientOcclusion()` and `setVolumetricLighting()` methods. Be aware, though, that you might encounter driver and hardware compatibility issues when using these effects.

> Version 1.7.0 of Panda3D added new and great shader and effects capabilities to the engine, but some of them still might need some more testing and tweaking. If they do not work for you, you can help the entire community by reporting your problems. The more people contribute test data, the more compatibility the engine will eventually be able to provide!

Building custom effects

Panda3D comes with a handy feature that enables you to conveniently define off-screen render buffers that can be used to render scene information into one or more textures. This allows you to redirect rendering output to intermediate textures that can be used as a base for exciting visuals. Filtering and recombining the previously generated texture data then create the end results of these image-based special effects. This recipe will show you how to use this feature, as it is the basis for any image based rendering effect you are going to build using this engine.

Getting ready

Set up your project folder as in *Setting up the game structure* found in *Chapter 1*. Add a directory called `shaders` at the same level as the `src` and `models` directories. Make sure these directories are in Panda3D's asset search path.

How to do it...

Follow these steps to implement a custom post-processing effect:

1. Open `Application.py` and add the following listed code:

```
from direct.showbase.ShowBase import ShowBase
from direct.actor.Actor import Actor
from panda3d.core import *
from direct.filter.FilterManager import *

class Application(ShowBase):
    def __init__(self):
        ShowBase.__init__(self)
```

```
        self.setupScene()
        self.setupPostFx()

    def setupScene(self):
        self.panda = Actor("panda", {"walk": "panda-walk"})
        self.panda.reparentTo(render)
        self.panda.loop("walk")

        cm = CardMaker("plane")
        cm.setFrame(-10, 10, -10, 10)
        plane = render.attachNewNode(cm.generate())
        plane.setP(270)

        self.cam.setPos(0, -40, 6)

        ambLight = AmbientLight("ambient")
        ambLight.setColor(Vec4(0.2, 0.1, 0.1, 1.0))
        ambNode = render.attachNewNode(ambLight)
        render.setLight(ambNode)

        dirLight = DirectionalLight("directional")
        dirLight.setColor(Vec4(0.1, 0.4, 0.1, 1.0))
        dirNode = render.attachNewNode(dirLight)
        dirNode.setHpr(60, 0, 90)
        render.setLight(dirNode)

        pntLight = PointLight("point")
        pntLight.setColor(Vec4(0.8, 0.8, 0.8, 1.0))
        pntNode = render.attachNewNode(pntLight)
        pntNode.setPos(0, 0, 15)
        self.panda.setLight(pntNode)

        sptLight = Spotlight("spot")
        sptLens = PerspectiveLens()
        sptLight.setLens(sptLens)
        sptLight.setColor(Vec4(1.0, 1.0, 1.0, 1.0))
        sptLight.setShadowCaster(True)
        sptNode = render.attachNewNode(sptLight)
        sptNode.setPos(-10, -10, 20)
        sptNode.lookAt(self.panda)
        render.setLight(sptNode)

        render.setShaderAuto()
```

2. After you are done with that big pile of code, add another method to your `Application` class:

```
def setupPostFx(self):
    self.filterMan = FilterManager(self.win, self.cam)

    colorTex = Texture()
    finalQuad = self.filterMan.renderSceneInto(colortex =
colorTex)

    finalTex = Texture()
    interQuad = self.filterMan.renderQuadInto(colortex =
finalTex, div = 8)
    interQuad.setShader(loader.loadShader("filter.cg"))
    interQuad.setShaderInput("color", colorTex)

    finalQuad.setShader(loader.loadShader("pass.cg"))
    finalQuad.setShaderInput("color", finalTex)
```

3. Add new files called `filter.cg` and `pass.cg` to the `shaders` directory.

4. Open `filter.cg` in an editor and add the following shader code:

```
//Cg

void vshader(float4 vtx_position : POSITION,
            out float4 l_position : POSITION,
            out float2 l_texcoord : TEXCOORD0,
            uniform float4 texpad_color,
            uniform float4x4 mat_modelproj)
{
    l_position = mul(mat_modelproj, vtx_position);
    l_texcoord = (vtx_position.xz * texpad_color.xy) + texpad_
color.xy;
}

void fshader(float2 l_texcoord : TEXCOORD0,
            uniform sampler2D k_color : TEXUNIT0,
            out float4 o_color : COLOR)
{
    float4 color = tex2D(k_color, l_texcoord);
    o_color = float4(color.r * 1.8, color.g, color.b * 0.2, color.
a);
}
```

5. Next, paste the following to `pass.cg`:

```
//Cg

void vshader(float4 vtx_position : POSITION,
             out float4 l_position : POSITION,
             out float2 l_texcoord : TEXCOORD0,
             uniform float4 texpad_color,
             uniform float4x4 mat_modelproj)
{
    l_position = mul(mat_modelproj, vtx_position);
    l_texcoord = (vtx_position.xz * texpad_color.xy) + texpad_
color.xy;
}

void fshader(float2 l_texcoord : TEXCOORD0,
             uniform sampler2D k_color : TEXUNIT0,
             out float4 o_color : COLOR)
{
    o_color = tex2D(k_color, l_texcoord);
}
```

6. Everything is set. Now you can press *F6* to run the program:

How it works...

Our program implements a very basic effect, pixelizing, and tinting the final image. But in the case of this recipe, it is about the way and not the goal.

After putting together our obligatory panda scene in the `setupScene()` method, we add `setupPostFx()`, which sets up all the buffers and textures we use for creating our effect, but let's take a closer look. First a new `FilterManager` is created, which is the engine's interface for managing render targets. Then we tell the engine to render our scene into `colorTex` using the `renderSceneInto()` method. Besides the `colortex` parameter, `renderSceneInto()` also takes the parameters `depthtex` for storing scene depth and `auxtex` for rendering to an auxiliary color buffer, which can be used for storing scene normals for example. This also creates and returns a quad that fills the entire screen onto which we will render the final image.

We then use `renderQuadInto()` to add an intermediate processing step to our little pipeline. The result of this step will be stored in `finalTex`, sampled down to an eighth of its original edge lengths, thanks to the `div` parameter. We apply the `filter.cg` shader to this temporary quad, using `colorTex` as the input. The shader itself just samples from the data found in `colorTex` and gives the red color channel a boost, while the blue channel values are decreased, giving the scene a warm look.

In the last lines of `setupPostFx()`, we set `finalQuad` to use `finalTex` as the input for the `pass.cg` shader, which simply takes the color it finds in the texture and outputs it to the screen.

There's more...

To see the contents of your render buffers for debugging, just add the line `show-buffers #t` to your `Config.prc` file. You can also turn buffer visualization on by adding the line `loadPrcFileData('', 'show-buffers 1')` below the import section of `Application.py`.

Adding a scanline and vignette effect

This recipe will show you a very typical use of post-processing. You will create an effect that makes the scene feel as if it were observed through a security camera or the eye of a remote controlled robot by dropping every other line of output. Additionally, you will learn how to implement a simple vignette effect that directs the focus to the center of the screen.

After completing this article, you will see how very simple post-processing techniques can have a major impact on the look and feel of a scene.

Getting ready

We will be using the same scene and project setup as in *Building custom effects* found in this chapter. Please follow the recipe until you complete step 1 before proceeding with this one.

How to do it...

These are the tasks required for completing this recipe:

1. Open `Application.py` and add this method to the `Application` class:

```
def setupPostFx(self):
    self.filterMan = FilterManager(self.win, self.cam)

    colorTex = Texture()

    finalQuad = self.filterMan.renderSceneInto(colortex =
colorTex)
    finalQuad.setShader(loader.loadShader("scanline.cg"))
    finalQuad.setShaderInput("color", colorTex)
```

2. Add a new file called `scanline.cg` to the `shaders` directory.

3. Open `scanline.cg` in an editor and add the following code:

```
//Cg

void vshader(float4 vtx_position : POSITION,
             out float4 l_position : POSITION,
             out float2 l_texcoord : TEXCOORD0,
             uniform float4 texpad_color,
             uniform float4x4 mat_modelproj)
{
    l_position = mul(mat_modelproj, vtx_position);
    l_texcoord = (vtx_position.xz * texpad_color.xy) + texpad_
color.xy;
}

#define DRAW 4
#define DROP 2
#define DRAW_INTENSITY 1.1
#define DROP_INTENSITY 0.5

void fshader(float2 l_texcoord : TEXCOORD0,
             uniform sampler2D k_color : TEXUNIT0,
             uniform sampler2D k_line : TEXUNIT1,
             uniform float4 texpix_color,
```

```
                uniform float4 texpad_color,
                out float4 o_color : COLOR)
    {
        float4 color = tex2D(k_color, l_texcoord);

        float falloff = 1.1 - length(l_texcoord - texpad_color);
        color *= pow(falloff, 4);

        o_color = color * (int(l_texcoord.y / texpix_color.y) % DRAW +
    DROP < DRAW ? DRAW_INTENSITY : DROP_INTENSITY);
    }
```

4. In the Netbeans IDE, press *F6* to launch the sample:

How it works...

In this sample, our buffer setup is very simple. The scene is rendered into `colorTex`, which is modified and applied to the final fullscreen quad by the shader found in `scanline.cg`.

The interesting parts of this recipe can be found in the `fshader()` function of the shader file, which is the pixel shader code. Here we first read the color value at the current texture coordinate into a four-component vector.

The next two lines are responsible for the vignette effect. The `falloff` value is based on the distance of the current texture coordinate from the center of the texture, stored in `texpad_color`. The value of 1.1 from which the length is subtracted was chosen to make the final image appear a bit brighter and make the effect appear less harsh. The falloff is then raised to the power of 4, which results in a nice circular decline in intensity, moving the panda into focus.

Finally, we need to decide if the current pixel is on a scanline or not. The macros DRAW, DROP, DRAW_INTENSITY, and DROP_INTENSITY define how many lines to draw, how many lines to drop, at which intensity drawn lines are put onto the screen and the intensity of dropped lines, respectively. Whether the current pixel lies on a dropped or drawn line is decided by some simple math. We take the integral part of the current vertical texture coordinate (l_texcoords.y) divided by the normalized height of a pixel (texpix_color.y) modulo the number of lines we observe in our scanline pattern. If the result of this function is smaller than number of lines to draw the line is considered visible. If it is bigger than DRAW, the current line is discarded.

Adding a color grading effect

No matter if it is professional film production or photography, neither of these professions will release a piece of work without a serious amount of color editing in post-production. Proper color grading sets the overall tone and emotion of the final picture, making the sunrise scenes look warm, and movies that are set in an arctic environment feel as cold as ice.

These effects can also be achieved with some shader code and enable you to further tweak the look and feel of your games. Choosing the right color palette is a very important measure for setting and transporting mood and emotion in visual media, which includes video games.

It's a rather small change to put into your rendering pipeline but the results might have a big impact on how your scenes will be perceived by players.

Getting ready

This recipe builds upon the sample code presented in *Building custom effects*, the second recipe in this chapter. Follow the instructions of said recipe up to step 1 so you are ready to implement the setupPostFx() method and add the required shaders.

How to do it...

These steps will show you how to implement color grading in Panda3D:

1. Add this method to the Application class:

```
def setupPostFx(self):
    self.filterMan = FilterManager(self.win, self.cam)

    colorTex = Texture()
```

```
        finalQuad = self.filterMan.renderSceneInto(colortex =
colorTex)
        finalQuad.setShader(loader.loadShader("color.cg"))
        finalQuad.setShaderInput("color", colorTex)
```

2. Add a new text file called `color.cg` to the `shaders` directory.

3. Open `color.cg` in an editor and add the following code:

```
//Cg

void vshader(float4 vtx_position : POSITION,
             out float4 l_position : POSITION,
             out float2 l_texcoord : TEXCOORD0,
             uniform float4 texpad_color,
             uniform float4x4 mat_modelproj)
{
    l_position = mul(mat_modelproj, vtx_position);
    l_texcoord = (vtx_position.xz * texpad_color.xy) + texpad_
color.xy;
}

#define overlay_blend(base, blend) (base < 0.5 ? (2.0 * base *
blend) : (1.0 - 2.0 * (1.0 - base) * (1.0 - blend)))
#define overlay_add(base, blend) (base + blend)
#define overlay_mul(base, blend) (base * blend)

void fshader(float2 l_texcoord : TEXCOORD0,
             uniform sampler2D k_color : TEXUNIT0,
             out float4 o_color : COLOR)
{
    float gamma = 1.2;
    gamma = 1 / gamma;
    float3 lift = float3(1.05, 1.05, 1.1);
    float3 blend = float3(0.1, 0.1, 0.5);
    float weight = 0.5;

    float4 color = tex2D(k_color, l_texcoord);

    color.rgb = pow(color.rgb, gamma);
    color.rgb = saturate(overlay_mul(color.rgb, lift));
    float3 tint = saturate(overlay_blend(color.rgb, blend));
    color.rgb = lerp(color.rgb, tint, weight);

    o_color = color;
}
```

4. In Netbeans, press *F6* to run the application:

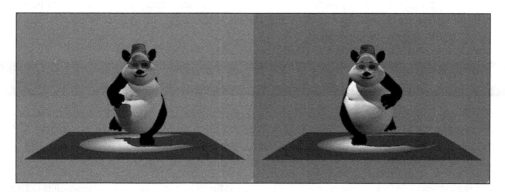

How it works...

Looking at the two screenshots (original color on the left, modified scene on the right) we can see that the color balance of the scene has changed dramatically due to our new filter. We shifted the color palette of the final image towards a cold and blue look, setting a nightly and full moon mood.

In this recipe, we are using only one render target that draws scene color into `colorTex`. This texture will be uploaded to the graphics card and used by our shader.

The shader found in `color.cg` is where all the color magic happens, so let's take a closer look!

Inside the `fshader()` function, which is the pixel shader applied to the final fullscreen quad, we first define a few parameters that will influence the color balance of our scene.

With the `gamma` variable, we change the gamma correction. The input color will be raised by the reciprocal of this value, resulting in a non-linear change in color intensity. Values greater than 1 will give low color intensities a boost, making the scene appear brighter, but also washed out as contrast decreases. With values below one, everything will appear dark with a lot of contrast and with lower intensities converging towards black.

The `lift` variable will be used with the `overlay_mul()` macro, multiplying the input color. With this, you can increase and decrease the intensities of color channels, emphasizing one channel while eliminating another one.

Using the blend variable, we define a color which is first blended with the source color using the `overlay_blend()` macro, which applies the overlay blending formula you may know from Photoshop or similar tools. This formula causes color channels with low intensities to be pushed harder towards the desired value than higher intensities, resulting in a balanced push towards the desired color. The result from this calculation is then linearly interpolated with the original color value, using `weight` to define how these colors are blended together.

In principle, what we do in our shader is similar to the steps we'd follow in an image manipulation program. First we change gamma correction and apply a channel multiplication filter. Then we create a new layer by blending the original image with a single color. Finally we alpha blend this layer onto our scene.

Adding a depth of field effect

An effect you can very commonly see in photography is objects that are very close to or very far away from the point of view. Therefore, appearing fuzzy and blurred while the middle portion of the image appears focused and sharp, emphasizing an object of interest in the scene. This focused part of the scene is referred to as 'depth of field'.

In this recipe you will learn how to mimic this cinematic effect in a post-processing filter. This will help you to emphasize the visual depth of a scene and focus a point of interest while blurring the background and foreground.

Getting ready

Set up the project structure found in *Setting up the game structure*, add a directory called `shaders` inside the project directory, make sure it is in the engine's search path and you're ready to go!

How to do it...

This recipe requires you to write some Python and Cg code as presented in the following steps:

1. Paste the following code into `Application.py`:

```python
from direct.showbase.ShowBase import ShowBase
from direct.actor.Actor import Actor
from panda3d.core import *
from direct.filter.FilterManager import *

class Application(ShowBase):
    def __init__(self):
        ShowBase.__init__(self)
        self.setupScene()
        self.setupLight()
        self.setupPostFx()

    def setupScene(self):
        self.panda = Actor("panda", {"walk": "panda-walk"})
        self.panda.reparentTo(render)
        self.panda.loop("walk")
```

```
smiley = loader.loadModel("smiley")
smiley.reparentTo(render)
smiley.setPos(5, -15, 10)

smiley = loader.loadModel("smiley")
smiley.reparentTo(render)
smiley.setPos(5, 0, 10)

smiley = loader.loadModel("smiley")
smiley.reparentTo(render)
smiley.setPos(5, 20, 10)

self.world = loader.loadModel("environment")
self.world.reparentTo(render)
self.world.setScale(0.5)
self.world.setPos(-8, 80, 0)

self.cam.setPos(0, -40, 6)
self.cam.node().getLens().setNearFar(1.0, 300.0)
```

2. Add this method to the `Application` class:

```
def setupLight(self):
    ambLight = AmbientLight("ambient")
    ambLight.setColor(Vec4(0.2, 0.1, 0.1, 1.0))
    ambNode = render.attachNewNode(ambLight)
    render.setLight(ambNode)

    dirLight = DirectionalLight("directional")
    dirLight.setColor(Vec4(0.1, 0.4, 0.1, 1.0))
    dirNode = render.attachNewNode(dirLight)
    dirNode.setHpr(60, 0, 90)
    render.setLight(dirNode)

    pntLight = PointLight("point")
    pntLight.setColor(Vec4(0.8, 0.8, 0.8, 1.0))
    pntNode = render.attachNewNode(pntLight)
    pntNode.setPos(0, 0, 15)
    self.panda.setLight(pntNode)

    sptLight = Spotlight("spot")
    sptLens = PerspectiveLens()
    sptLight.setLens(sptLens)
    sptLight.setColor(Vec4(1.0, 1.0, 1.0, 1.0))
    sptLight.setShadowCaster(True)
```

```
sptNode = render.attachNewNode(sptLight)
sptNode.setPos(-10, -10, 50)
sptNode.lookAt(self.panda)
render.setLight(sptNode)

render.setShaderAuto()
```

3. After the `setupLight()` method, add this last piece of code to `Application.py`:

```
def setupPostFx(self):
    self.filterMan = FilterManager(self.win, self.cam)

    colorTex = Texture()
    blurTex = Texture()
    depthTex = Texture()

    finalQuad = self.filterMan.renderSceneInto(colortex =
colorTex, depthtex = depthTex)
    blurQuad = self.filterMan.renderQuadInto(colortex =
blurTex, div = 4)
    blurQuad.setShader(loader.loadShader("blur.cg"))
    blurQuad.setShaderInput("color", colorTex)

    finalQuad.setShader(loader.loadShader("depth.cg"))
    finalQuad.setShaderInput("color", colorTex)
    finalQuad.setShaderInput("blur", blurTex)
    finalQuad.setShaderInput("depth", depthTex)
```

4. Add two new files called `blur.cg` and `depth.cg` to the `shaders` subdirectory.

5. Open `blur.cg` and add the following code:

```
//Cg

void vshader(float4 vtx_position : POSITION,
             out float4 l_position : POSITION,
             out float2 l_texcoord : TEXCOORD0,
             uniform float4 texpad_color,
             uniform float4x4 mat_modelproj)
{
    l_position = mul(mat_modelproj, vtx_position);
    l_texcoord = (vtx_position.xz * texpad_color.xy) + texpad_
color.xy;
}

void fshader(float2 l_texcoord : TEXCOORD0,
             uniform sampler2D k_color : TEXUNIT0,
```

```
                out float4 o_color : COLOR)
{
    float4 color = tex2D(k_color, l_texcoord);
    int samples = 16;
    float step = 0.001;

    for (float i = -(samples / 2) * step; i <= (samples / 2) *
step; i += step)
        color += tex2D(k_color, l_texcoord + float2(i, 0));
    color /= (samples + 1);

    samples /= 2;
    for (float i = -(samples / 2) * step; i <= (samples / 2) *
step; i += step)
        color += tex2D(k_color, l_texcoord + float2(0, i));
    color /= (samples + 1);

    o_color = color;
}
```

6. After pasting this piece of shader code to depth.cg you are done with coding for this sample:

```
//Cg

void vshader(float4 vtx_position : POSITION,
             out float4 l_position : POSITION,
             out float2 l_texcoord : TEXCOORD0,
             uniform float4 texpad_color,
             uniform float4x4 mat_modelproj)
{
    l_position = mul(mat_modelproj, vtx_position);
    l_texcoord = (vtx_position.xz * texpad_color.xy) + texpad_
color.xy;
}

float linearZ(uniform sampler2D tex, float2 uv)
{
    float near = 1.0;
    float far = 300.0;
    float z = tex2D(tex, uv);
    return (2.0 * near) / (far + near - z * (far - near));
}
```

```
void fshader(float2 l_texcoord : TEXCOORD0,
             uniform sampler2D k_color : TEXUNIT0,
             uniform sampler2D k_blur : TEXUNIT1,
             uniform sampler2D k_depth : TEXUNIT2,
             out float4 o_color : COLOR)
{
    float z_max = 0.3;
    float z_min = 0.16;
    float z = linearZ(k_depth, l_texcoord);

    float4 color = z > z_max ? tex2D(k_blur, l_texcoord) : z < z_
min ? tex2D(k_blur, l_texcoord) : tex2D(k_color, l_texcoord);
    o_color = color;
}
```

7. To run the sample, hit the *F6* key and watch how out-of-focus objects are being blurred:

How it works...

Before applying our post-processing effect, we need a scene which is created by the methods `setupScene()` and `setupLight()`. We also configure the near and far clipping planes of our camera using `setNearFar()` to define the depth boundaries of our scene.

Next, in `setupPostFx()`, we put together our render buffer setup. We're rendering scene color to `colorTex` and the depth buffer to `depthTex`. Additionally, we create an intermediate render step that produces a blurred and downsampled version of our color buffer.

Blurring the color buffer is implemented in the pixel shader of `blur.cg`. Here we first blur horizontally by taking the average of the color values to the left and the right of the current pixel. The same is done in vertical direction too, using only half as many samples as the horizontal blur. We're doing this to make the blur look more balanced, as using the same amount of samples tends to emphasize the vertical blur.

To create the final effect, the untouched scene color, the blurred scene, and the depth texture are passed to the depth of field shader found in `depth.cg`. First, notice the values `z_max` and `z_min`, which define the boundaries for the depth of field. Every pixel that has a scene depth below `z_min` or above `z_max` will appear blurred.

The depth values are converted to normalized, linear values produced by the `linearZ()` function to make it easier to define the blur boundaries. In our sample, everything that is below the first 16% of depth into the scene or further away than 30% of the maximum depth is blurred.

The line that chooses the color sample might look a bit cryptic, but does a really simple thing using nested ternary operators. First the depth value is checked against `z_max`. If it is greater, the current pixel will be sampled from the blurred texture. If not, there are two branches left—either z is smaller than `z_min`, which will also result in the blurred texture being used, or not—which means that we're in focus and the unaltered version of the pixel is drawn to the screen.

Building a deferred rendering pipeline

Although modern graphics cards are able to push millions of polygons per frame, their abilities in terms of lighting are quite limited when using the traditional, forward rendering approach, where all permutations of lights on scene objects have to be calculated to get the final scene lighting. Some engines circumvent this issue by limiting the number of lights that are allowed to affect the scene, by choosing the ones that are nearest.

But what if we wanted hundreds of lights in a scene? How would we realize that? In this recipe we will see how to solve this problem by building a deferred rendering pipeline that is limited by the number of pixels our hardware is able to push, but not the number of lights in our scene.

Getting ready

Create your project folders according to *Setting up the game structure*, add a directory called `shaders` and make sure it is in the engine's search path. If that is done, you're ready to go on.

How to do it...

Complete the following tasks to get your deferred rendering pipeline going:

1. Open `Application.py` and paste the following code below:

```
from direct.showbase.ShowBase import ShowBase
from direct.actor.Actor import Actor
from panda3d.core import *
from direct.filter.FilterManager import *
import random

loadPrcFileData('', 'show-buffers 1')

class Application(ShowBase):
    def __init__(self):
        ShowBase.__init__(self)
        self.setupScene()
        self.setupLight()
        self.setupCams()
        self.setupPostFx()

    def setupScene(self):
        self.scene = render.attachNewNode("scene")
        self.panda = Actor("panda", {"walk": "panda-walk"})
        self.panda.reparentTo(self.scene)
        self.panda.loop("walk")

        self.world = loader.loadModel("environment")
        self.world.reparentTo(self.scene)
        self.world.setScale(0.5)
        self.world.setPos(-8, 80, 0)

        self.scene.setShaderAuto()
```

2. Add the following method to the `Application` class:

```
    def setupCams(self):
        self.lightCam = self.makeCamera(self.win)
        self.lightCam.reparentTo(self.cam)

        sceneMask = BitMask32(1)
        lightMask = BitMask32(2)
        self.cam.node().setCameraMask(sceneMask)
        self.lightCam.node().setCameraMask(lightMask)
        self.lights.hide(sceneMask)
        self.ambient.hide(sceneMask)
        self.scene.hide(lightMask)
```

```
            self.cam.node().getDisplayRegion(0).setSort(1)
            self.lightCam.node().getDisplayRegion(0).setSort(2)
            self.win.setSort(3)

            self.lightCam.node().getDisplayRegion(0).
setClearColor(Vec4(0, 0, 0, 1))
            self.lightCam.node().getDisplayRegion(0).
setClearColorActive(1)

            self.cam.setPos(0, -40, 6)
```

3. Add another method to the class `Application`:

```
    def setupLight(self):
        self.lights = render.attachNewNode("lights")
        self.sphere = loader.loadModel("misc/sphere")

        for i in range(400):
            light = self.lights.attachNewNode("light")
            light.setPos(random.uniform(-15, 15), random.uniform(-
5, 50), random.uniform(0, 15))
            light.setColor(random.random(), random.random(),
random.random())
            light.setScale(5)
            self.sphere.instanceTo(light)

            vlight = self.scene.attachNewNode("vlight")
            vlight.setPos(light.getPos())
            vlight.setColor(light.getColor())
            vlight.setScale(0.1)
            self.sphere.instanceTo(vlight)

        cm = CardMaker("ambient")
        cm.setFrame(-100, 100, -100, 100)
        self.ambient = render.attachNewNode("ambient")
        self.ambient.attachNewNode(cm.generate())
        self.ambient.setColor(0.1, 0.1, 0.1, 1)
        self.ambient.reparentTo(self.cam)
        self.ambient.setPos(0, 5, 0)
```

4. The following `setupPostFx()` method is the last one you have to add to the `Application` class:

```
def setupPostFx(self):
        self.gbufMan = FilterManager(self.win, self.cam)
        self.lightMan = FilterManager(self.win, self.lightCam)
```

```
        albedo = Texture()
        depth = Texture()
        normal = Texture()
        final = Texture()

        self.gbufMan.renderSceneInto(colortex = albedo, depthtex =
depth, auxtex = normal, auxbits = AuxBitplaneAttrib.ABOAuxNormal)

        lightQuad = self.lightMan.renderSceneInto(colortex =
final)
        lightQuad.setShader(loader.loadShader("pass.cg"))
        lightQuad.setShaderInput("color", final)

        self.ambient.setShader(loader.loadShader("ambient.cg"))
        self.ambient.setShaderInput("albedo", albedo)

        self.ambient.setAttrib(ColorBlendAttrib.
make(ColorBlendAttrib.MAdd, ColorBlendAttrib.OOne,
ColorBlendAttrib.OOne))
        self.ambient.setAttrib(DepthWriteAttrib.
make(DepthWriteAttrib.MOff))

        self.lights.setShader(loader.loadShader("light.cg"))
        self.lights.setShaderInput("albedo", albedo)
        self.lights.setShaderInput("depth", depth)
        self.lights.setShaderInput("normal", normal)

        self.lights.setAttrib(ColorBlendAttrib.
make(ColorBlendAttrib.MAdd, ColorBlendAttrib.OOne,
ColorBlendAttrib.OOne))
        self.lights.setAttrib(CullFaceAttrib.make(CullFaceAttrib.
MCullCounterClockwise))
        self.lights.setAttrib(DepthWriteAttrib.
make(DepthWriteAttrib.MOff))
```

5. Go to the `shaders` subdirectory of the project and add 3 new files called `ambient.cg`, `light.cg`, and `pass.cg`.

6. Open `ambient.cg` in an editor and add the following code:

```
//Cg

void vshader(float4 vtx_position : POSITION,
             out float4 l_position : POSITION,
             out float4 l_screenpos : TEXCOORD0,
             uniform float4x4 mat_modelproj)
```

Chapter 5

```
    {
        l_position = mul(mat_modelproj, vtx_position);
        l_screenpos = l_position;
    }

    void fshader(float4 l_screenpos : TEXCOORD0,
                uniform sampler2D k_albedo : TEXUNIT0,
                uniform float4 texpad_albedo,
                uniform float4 attr_color,
                out float4 o_color : COLOR)
    {
        l_screenpos.xy /= l_screenpos.w;
        float2 texcoords = float2(l_screenpos.xy) * texpad_albedo.xy +
    texpad_albedo.xy;

        float4 albedo = tex2D(k_albedo, texcoords);
        o_color = albedo * attr_color;
    }
```

7. Add the following shader code to `light.cg`:

```
    //Cg

    void vshader(float4 vtx_position : POSITION,
                out float4 l_position : POSITION,
                out float4 l_screenpos : TEXCOORD0,
                uniform float4x4 mat_modelproj)
    {
        l_position = mul(mat_modelproj, vtx_position);
        l_screenpos = l_position;
    }

    void fshader(float4 l_screenpos : TEXCOORD0,
                uniform sampler2D k_albedo : TEXUNIT0,
                uniform sampler2D k_depth : TEXUNIT1,
                uniform sampler2D k_normal : TEXUNIT2,
                uniform float4 texpad_albedo,
                uniform float4 attr_color,
                uniform float4 vspos_model,
                uniform float4x4 vstrans_clip,
                uniform float4 row0_model_to_view,
                out float4 o_color : COLOR)
    {
```

```
        l_screenpos.xy /= l_screenpos.w;
        float2 texcoords = float2(l_screenpos.xy) * texpad_albedo.xy +
    texpad_albedo.xy;

        float4 albedo = tex2D(k_albedo, texcoords);
        float4 normal = tex2D(k_normal, texcoords);
        float depth = tex2D(k_depth, texcoords);

        float4 vspos_scene;
        vspos_scene.xy = l_screenpos.xy;
        vspos_scene.z = depth;
        vspos_scene.w = 1;
        vspos_scene = mul(vstrans_clip, vspos_scene);
        vspos_scene /= vspos_scene.w * 2;

        float3 vec = float3(vspos_model) - vspos_scene;
        float len = length(vec);
        float3 dir = vec / len;
        float atten = saturate(1.0 - (len / row0_model_to_view.x));
        float intensity = pow(atten, 2) * dot(dir, float3(normal));
        o_color = float4(albedo.xyz * attr_color.xyz * intensity, 1);
    }
```

8. Open and edit `pass.cg` so it contains this piece of code:

```
//Cg

void vshader(float4 vtx_position : POSITION,
             out float4 l_position : POSITION,
             out float2 l_texcoord : TEXCOORD0,
             uniform float4 texpad_color,
             uniform float4x4 mat_modelproj)
{
    l_position = mul(mat_modelproj, vtx_position);
    l_texcoord = (vtx_position.xz * texpad_color.xy) + texpad_
color.xy;
}

void fshader(float2 l_texcoord : TEXCOORD0,
             uniform sampler2D k_color : TEXUNIT0,
             out float4 o_color : COLOR0)
{
    o_color = tex2D(k_color, l_texcoord);
}
```

9. Press the *F6* key to launch the program you just created:

How it works...

The basic idea behind deferred rendering is very simple. The unlit scene, its normals, and the depth buffer are stored into textures in the first step of the technique. Then, the bounding volume of each light is rendered using a special shader that samples color, depth, and normal data at the current pixel and projects the screen position back into the scene to get the position relative to itself. Depending on this distance and the normal at that position, the pixel is lit or not.

This technique has the advantage that its performance only depends on how many pixels in the scene are actually lit. The downsides are that it consumes a lot of video memory and that it binds application performance to the graphics processor.

After this high level view on the topic, let's take a closer look at the parts this code sample is made of!

After filling our scene with the panda and the jungle background and instructing the engine to show the content of our buffers with the line `loadPrcFileData('', 'show-buffers 1')`, we go on to set up the lights and cameras.

In the `setupLight()` method, we create a new node that will be the parent for all the point lights in our scene, before the four hundred light volumes and the tiny dots that visualize the lights' center points are added to the scene. We also create an ambient light, which does not have a real light volume. In fact, it has an infinitely big one, but as this wouldn't be practical to implement, it is represented by a huge quad put in front of the camera.

Our camera setup is quite elaborate for this sample but unfortunately, it is necessary. We add a new camera and reparent it to the default camera so it always sees the same scene. Then we create a bit mask for each camera, which we use to hide the point and ambient lights from the default camera. The `lightCam` will in turn only record objects that act as light volumes.

In the following lines, we define the order in which the cameras will record the scene. This is very important, because the unlit scene has to be rendered before the lights are composited into the image. We also set the clear color of the `lightCam` to black, so unlit parts of the scene are rendered in a dark color.

This leaves us with the buffer and shader setup in the `setupPostFx()` method.

We are using two instances of `FilterManager`, each one attached to one of our cameras. The `gbufMan` instance is attached to the main camera to record scene color, normals, and depth, the so-called geometry buffer or short—G-buffer. With `lightMan`, we are recording the final image composition, which we will then render onto `lightQuad`, using a pass-through shader, to present the scene on the screen.

The lights will blend additively to make the scene appear brighter if more lights affect one spot and will not write to the depth buffer. After we're done with these render states, we can take a look at what's going on inside the light shaders.

The ambient light shader is really simple. It reconstructs the proper texture coordinates from the current screen coordinates to sample the albedo texture and multiply with the ambient quad's color.

Looking deeper into the inner workings of `light.cg`, the situation isn't so trivial anymore. First, we must find the current pixel position on the screen to determine the proper texture coordinates for the color, normal, and depth textures. Then, the view space position of the pixel is restored from clip space using the matrix `vstrans_clip` that is provided by Panda3D.

After the view space position of the current pixel is restored in `vspos_scene`, we can calculate the distance to the light that is currently rendered by subtracting it from `vspos_model`, which holds the view space position of the currently rendering model.

Using the distance from the current light's center and the direction to the pixel that is in question, we can calculate if that point actually is within the boundaries of the light volume. This is done by dividing `len` by `row0_model_to_view.x` and subtracting from one to compute the amount of distance-based attenuation. The latter of the variables stores the light volume's scale factor, which at the same time is its radius.

Finally, we determine the pixel's intensity using the famous **Lambertian** term (the dot product of the surface normal and the light direction) and the amount of attenuation. This is multiplied with the vertex color attribute holding the light's color and the albedo color sampled from the unlit scene buffer texture.

There's more...

This is a very basic deferred rendering setup that only supports ambient and point lights. Building on this sample, try adding directional lights, specular highlights, and shadows. A set up like this one opens many possibilities to create interesting effects!

6
2D Elements and User Interfaces

In this chapter, we will cover:

- ▸ Rendering text to the screen
- ▸ Rendering images to the 2D layer
- ▸ Playing a movie file
- ▸ Creating an interactive user interface
- ▸ Making the user interface data-driven using XML

Introduction

Apart from its 3D rendering capabilities, the Panda3D engine also has features for drawing two-dimensional graphics. This may be useful if you want to build a simple, side-scrolling platformer, but also when creating spectacular 3D action games. Score overlays, head-up displays, and movie clips all need the engine to draw "flat" to the screen, which is exactly what you will be learning over the course of this chapter.

Rendering text to the screen

This simple recipe will show you how to quickly put some text on the screen. This might be useful for debug output, but also for presenting the current score or hit points to the player.

Getting ready

If you haven't done it yet, set up your project according to the steps presented in the recipe *Setting up the game structure* before you proceed. You can find this recipe in *Chapter 1, Setting Up Panda3D and Configuring Development Tools*.

How to do it...

Let's put some text on the screen:

1. Open `Application.py` and add the following source code:

```python
from direct.showbase.ShowBase import ShowBase
from direct.gui.OnscreenText import OnscreenText
from panda3d.core import *

class Application(ShowBase):
    def __init__(self):
        ShowBase.__init__(self)
        font = loader.loadFont("cmr12.egg")
        props = TextProperties()
        props.setTextColor(1, 1, 0, 0.5)
        tp = TextPropertiesManager.getGlobalPtr()
        tp.setProperties("yellow", props)

        OnscreenText(text = "Panda3D Rocks!!",
                     frame = Vec4(1, 0, 0, 1),
                     bg = Vec4(1, 1, 0, 1),
                     pos = Vec2(-0.5, 0.5),
                     scale = 0.2,
                     font = font)

        wrapWidth = 6
        text = OnscreenText(text = "So long... \1yellow\1And
thanks for all the bamboo\2!!",
                            wordwrap = wrapWidth,
                            fg = Vec4(1, 1, 1, 1),
                            shadow = Vec4(0, 0, 0, 1),
                            scale = 0.07,
                            font = font)

        wrap = text.getScale()[0] * wrapWidth
        print "Word wrap after", wrap, "screen units"
```

2. Press *F6* and run the program:

How it works...

As you can see, outputting text is very easy using `OnscreenText()`. First, you import the proper package, which is `direct.gui.OnscreenText`. Then you load the font you wish to use, in this case the "cmr12" font that is included with Panda3D. If you wish to use a different font—no problem! Just use `loadFont()` to load any "Truetype" font you wish to use. Like other resources, such as models and textures, fonts need to be located in a directory that is configured to be a part of Panda3D's search path. See the description of the `model-path` configuration variable in the recipe *Understanding Panda3D's runtime configuration options* in *Chapter 1, Setting Up Panda3D and Configuring Development Tools*, for further information on adding directories to the search path.

`OnscreenText()` also allows you to set additional text properties, some of which are shown in the code you just added to your program, like `frame` for the red outline around the `Panda Rocks!!` text, `bg` for setting the background color, `fg` for setting the text color, `scale` for scaling the size of the text, `shadow` for defining a drop shadow below each font and `wordwrap` to set at which width to insert a line break. You may also use the `pos` parameter to position the text.

The `wordwrap` parameter sets the wrap width relative to the scale of the font. The last two lines of the sample code calculate the absolute wrap width in screen units and print it to the screen. In this case, this is $0.7 * 6$, so a line break is inserted after about a fifth of the screen width. If the `scale` parameter is omitted, the engine automatically chooses a scale factor to make the font fit onto the screen.

When you are positioning and scaling text or setting the word wrap width, you are working with a normalized coordinate system. The origin of this coordinate system is at the centre of the window, `(-1, 1)` is the top-left corner and `(1, -1)` are the coordinates of the bottom-right corner. This makes it easier to position elements independent from the screen resolution.

Text properties can also be set for sections of text. For getting this to work, you need to create a new instance of the TextProperties class, set the text properties you wish and register them with the global TextPropertiesManager. The custom text properties you create this way are then activated and deactivated using \1[name]\1 and \2. This works like a stack: A property name enclosed by \1 enables properties for any subsequent text. Putting \2 into a string pops and thus deactivates the text property you activated last. Watch how the text changes in the sample: The text color is set to yellow before the sentence And thanks for all the bamboo and deactivated again right before the two exclamation marks.

Rendering images to the 2D layer

In this easy-and-short recipe you will learn how to display images in the 2D layer of Panda3D. For example, if you want to build 2D games or display a HUD in a shooter, this recipe is the way to go!

Getting ready

Apart from using the project structure found in *Setting up the game structure* found in *Chapter 1, Setting Up Panda3D and Configuring Development Tools*, you will need two texture images that will be displayed. Also, add an additional directory called textures to the project folder structure.

> Putting the image files into the textures directory is optional (you could also put them into the source directory) but will help you to keep your code and resources organized. You may also use a different image file format for your textures. Panda3D also supports JPEG and DDS, for example.

How to do it...

Follow these steps to put some images into the 2D rendering layer:

1. Copy your texture image files to the textures directory and call them panda.png and test.png.

2. Add the following code to Application.py:

```
from direct.showbase.ShowBase import ShowBase
from direct.gui.OnscreenImage import OnscreenImage
from direct.actor.Actor import Actor
from panda3d.core import *
import random

class Application(ShowBase):
```

```
def __init__(self):
    ShowBase.__init__(self)

    self.panda = Actor("panda", {"walk": "panda-walk"})
    self.panda.reparentTo(render)
    self.panda.loop("walk")
    self.cam.setPos(0, -30, 5)

    files = ["panda.png", "test.png"]

    for i in range(30):
        OnscreenImage(random.sample(files, 1)[0],
                      scale = Vec3(0.15, 0, 0.15),
                      pos = Vec3(random.uniform(-1, 1), 0,
random.uniform(-1, 1)),
                      hpr = Vec3(0, 0, random.uniform(0,
360))))
```

3. Press *F6* to start the application:

How it works...

All it takes to display an image in the render2d layer of Panda3D is a call to
OnscreenImage(). This loads the texture, puts it on a quad and adds it to the render2d
scene graph, which is rendered using orthogonal projection after 3D drawing is done. The
function also returns the created node, so we can change its properties later on.

Playing a movie file

Whether it's showing your game studio's logo sequence at the start of the game, or it's telling an important part of your story using cutscenes—sometimes you need to play full motion video. That's why in this recipe you will learn how to load a video and replay it in the game window.

Getting ready

This sample uses the project structure created in *Setting up the game structure* found in *Chapter 1*. You also need to add a directory called `videos` to the project's source tree to keep your assets organized. Make sure that the `videos` directory is on Panda3D's content search path!

Of course, you need to provide a video file for playback. Panda3D uses the `FFmpeg` programming library for decoding video data, so it should be able to process any codec supported by `FFmpeg`. The sample code assumes you are using an AVI file.

How to do it...

To play a movie file, complete these tasks:

1. Copy your video file to the `videos` directory and rename it to `movie.avi`.

2. Open the `Application.py` file and add the following code:

```
from direct.showbase.ShowBase import ShowBase
from panda3d.core import *

loadPrcFileData("", "audio-library-name p3openal_audio")

class Application(ShowBase):
    def __init__(self):
        ShowBase.__init__(self)
        cm = CardMaker("plane")
        cm.setFrame(-1, 1, -1, 1)

        plane = render2d.attachNewNode(cm.generate())
        movie = loader.loadTexture("movie.avi")
        sound = loader.loadSfx("movie.avi")

        plane.setTexture(movie)
        plane.setTexScale(TextureStage.getDefault(), movie.
getTexScale())
```

```
movie.setLoop(0)
movie.synchronizeTo(sound)

sound.play()
```

3. Hit the *F6* key to run the application and watch the video play:

How it works...

First of all, we need to properly configure Panda3D to use OpenAL for audio output, using the `loadPrcFileData()` function. This is very important, because otherwise our code would not work!

To get the movie clip to play on the screen, we first use a `CardMaker` to create the quad the video will be put on as a dynamically updated texture image. We reparent plane to `render2d`, so it is rendered to Panda3D's 2D drawing layer.

Next, we load the video file into a texture object and set it as our target quad's texture image. Additionally, the texture matrix of plane is modified using `setTexScale()`. We have to do this because if the pixel width and height of our video is not a power of two, the movie texture Panda3D creates internally will be set to the nearest power-of-two measures. When we put video frames into this texture, it will cause a noticeable amount of stretching and/or squashing, distorting the video and making it appear rather odd.

Finally, we turn off looping the video over and over again and instruct the engine to synchronize the video to the audio data of the video. Note how we use the `loadSfx()` method to open the movie file a second time to retrieve the audio data!

The last line may appear a bit odd at first. Why would we want to start playing the sound if we want to see the video? The answer to this question can be found just one line above, where we ensure the audio to be synchronized with the video stream. This also causes movie playback to be bound to starting and stopping the sound.

Creating an interactive user interface

With very few exceptions, nearly every game features some kind of menu-based user interaction for selecting game modes, browsing servers, setting game, and graphics options, or chatting with other players. Most likely, the games you are going to create with Panda3D will also have such requirements and you will need to create buttons, text input fields, loading bars, or whatever controls suit your needs. To make things easier for you, the Panda3D engine comes with a set of user interface classes that make it very easy to place controls on the screen and make them react to the players' actions.

Getting ready

Go back to *Chapter 1* and follow the steps of the recipe *Setting up the game structure* if you haven't yet and you are set to go on with the following tasks.

How to do it...

Let's create a user interface:

1. Paste the following source code to `Application.py`:

```
from direct.showbase.ShowBase import ShowBase
from direct.gui.DirectGui import *
from direct.interval.IntervalGlobal import *
from panda3d.core import *

class Application(ShowBase):
    def __init__(self):
        ShowBase.__init__(self)
        self.nameEnt = DirectEntry(scale = 0.08, pos = Vec3(-0.4,
0, 0.15), width = 10)
        self.nameLbl = DirectLabel(text = "Hi, what's your name?",
                                    pos = Vec3(0, 0, 0.4),
                                    scale = 0.1,
                                    textMayChange = 1,
                                    frameColor = Vec4(0, 0, 0, 0))
        helloBtn = DirectButton(text = "Say Hello!",
                                scale = 0.1,
                                command = self.setName,
                                pos = Vec3(0, 0, -0.1))
```

```
                self.gender = [0]
                genderRdos = [DirectRadioButton(text = "Female",
                                                variable = self.gender,
                                                value = [0],
                                                scale = 0.05,
                                                pos = Vec3(-0.08, 0,
        0.05)),
                                DirectRadioButton(text = "Male",
                                                variable =self.gender,
                                                value = [1],
                                                scale = 0.05,
                                                pos = Vec3(0.16, 0,
        0.05))]
                for btn in genderRdos:
                    btn.setOthers(genderRdos)
```

2. Now add the methods for handling clicks on the **Say Hello!** button and the resulting dialog to the `Application` class:

```
        def setName(self):
            self.acceptDlg = YesNoDialog(text = "Are you sure?",
                                        command = self.acceptName)

        def acceptName(self, clickedYes):
            self.acceptDlg.cleanup()
            if clickedYes:
                self.loadName()
```

3. Next, it is time to add the code for creating and advancing a progress bar:

```
        def loadName(self):
            self.waitBar = DirectWaitBar(text = "Loading",
                                        range = 100,
                                        value = 0,
                                        pos = Vec3(0, 0, -0.3))
            inc = Func(self.loadStep)
            show = Func(self.setNameLabel)

            load = Sequence(Wait(1), inc, Wait(2), inc, Wait(1), inc,
        Wait(3), inc, show)
            load.start()

        def loadStep(self):
            self.waitBar["value"] += 25
```

4. Lastly, add the code for setting the label text to `Application.py`:

```
def setNameLabel(self):
    title = ""
    if self.gender[0]:
        title = "Mister"
    else:
        title = "Miss"

    self.nameLbl["text"] = "Hello " + title + " " + self.
nameEnt.get() + "!"
```

5. Press *F6* to start the program:

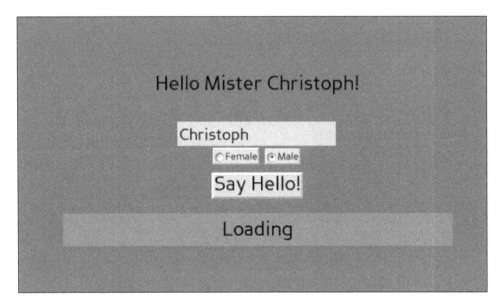

After importing the packages we need for this recipe—most notably, `direct.gui.`
`DirectGui` for the user interface functionality—we go on to add a text input field, a label,
a set of radio buttons and a button to confirm the name entry. We also use the pos, `scale`,
and `text` parameters to define the positions, scales, and the texts of the controls and hint
the label that its text will change by setting `textMayChange` to 1. Also note the `variable`
and `value` parameters used when setting up the radio buttons. The former defines the
variable that `value` will be stored into when the radio button is active. Don't forget to pass
data to `value` using a list! Further, we pass the method to call when being clicked by using
the `command` parameter of our confirmation button. To close step 1 of this sample, we iterate
over the radio buttons, informing each button about the other buttons in the radio group so
that only one option can be selected at a time.

In the next step, we add the `setName()` and `acceptName()` methods, which cause the application to display a confirmation popup after the user clicks the **Say Hello!** button. If the user clicks **Yes**, the program proceeds, otherwise the popup is hidden and nothing whatsoever happens.

We then proceed to step 3, where we add a progress bar to our user interface. The `range` parameter sets the maximum value for the progress bar, whereas `value` defines the initial progress shown after the control is added to the screen. We want to slow things down for this sample to see the progress bar in action. Therefore, we call `loadStep()` in a `Sequence` that waits a short moment between each step. This also allows us to see how we are able to update the progress bar's current `value`.

In the last method we add to the `Application` class, `setNameLabel()`, which is called last by the sequence that controls our progress bar. Here we finally modify the `text` attribute of the label control to display the name that is entered into the text input field.

There's more...

The GUI features of Panda3D go beyond what you have seen in this recipe so far, of course. The following section is meant to give you an idea about what else you can do with the engine's `DirectGui` library.

More controls

Besides the `DirectEntry`, `DirectLabel`, `DirectButton`, `DirectRadioButton`, `YesNoDialog`, and `DirectWaitBar` controls we used so far in this recipe, there are several more that might be useful for your purposes:

- ▶ `DirectCheckButton` is a button control that toggles between a checked and unchecked state every time it is clicked.
- ▶ `DirectDialog` is used for building popup dialogs like the confirmation used in the sample code. There are several pre-built default dialogs included in the `DirectGui` library like `YesNoDialog`, `OkDialog`, or `RetryCancelDialog`.
- ▶ `DirectFrame` acts as a container for controls. This allows us to group multiple controls and positions them relative to the frame.
- ▶ `DirectOptionMenu` works like a drop-down menu. When clicked, a menu opens and the control state is set to the selected item.
- ▶ `DirectScrolledList` is a container control similar to `DirectFrame`, with the difference that items are being placed in a scrollable list.
- ▶ `DirectSlider` is a control that allows the user to select an arbitrary value between two boundaries.
- ▶ `DirectScrollBar` allows you to build controls similar to `DirectScrolledList` by hand.
- ▶ `DirectScrolledFrame` works just like a `DirectFrame`, but it allows objects that are positioned outside of the container's boundaries to be reached using scroll bars.

More parameters

Apart from the parameters we used for setting up our sample GUI, there are some more common options that allow customizing Panda3D's user interface controls:

▶ `frameSize` makes it possible to set the measures of the control using a four-component vector that specifies the left, right, bottom, and top positions of its frame.

▶ `frameColor` sets the color of the user interface control element.

▶ `image` sets the texture that is rendered on the control.

▶ `geom` allows to set a `Geom` object that is rendered in place of the control.

▶ `suppressKeys` turns off global keyboard events when set to 1. This is useful for implementing a menu for the pause state of a game, as it makes sure that the game logic is not notified about any keys being pressed when interacting with the user interface.

▶ `suppressMouse` works like `suppressKeys`, but for the mouse.

Making the user interface data-driven using XML

A common practice in user interface programming is the division of design and program logic. In this recipe you will learn how to use one of the XML processing API that comes as a part of the standard libraries of the Python runtime used by Panda3D.

 Different versions of Panda3D might use different versions of Python. Don't assume these versions to be compatible as they might introduce changes to the standard library. You can check the version of the included Python runtime by issuing the command `ppython --version` on the console prompt.

Getting ready

Before proceeding, you will need to follow the recipe *Setting up the game structure* found in *Chapter 1* to have the proper project structure set and ready.

How to do it...

Complete the following tasks to create a data-driven user interface:

1. Add a new source file to the project and name it `GuiBuilder.py`.

2. Add the following code to `GuiBuilder.py`. `GuiHandler` is only a class stub. The following functions are not members of the `GuiHandler` class!

   ```
   from xml.etree.ElementTree import *
   from direct.gui.DirectGui import *
   ```

```python
from panda3d.core import *

class GuiHandler:
    def __init__(self):
        self.controls = {}

def GuiFromXml(fname, handler):
    elements = ElementTree()
    elements.parse(fname)

    handleButtons(elements, handler)
    handleLabels(elements, handler)
    handleEntries(elements, handler)
    handleRadioGroups(elements, handler)
```

3. Next, add the functions for finding all button, label, entry box, radio group, and radio button control descriptions contained in the XML structure to `GuiBuilder.py`:

```python
def handleButtons(elements, handler):
    buttons = elements.findall("button")
    for button in buttons:
        createButton(button, handler)

def handleLabels(elements, handler):
    labels = elements.findall("label")
    for label in labels:
        createLabel(label, handler)

def handleEntries(elements, handler):
    entries = elements.findall("entry")
    for entry in entries:
        createEntry(entry, handler)

def handleRadioGroups(elements, handler):
    rdoGroups = elements.findall("radiogroup")
    for group in rdoGroups:
        handleRadios(group, handler)

def handleRadios(elements, handler):
    radios = elements.findall("radio")
    created = []
    for radio in radios:
        created.append(createRadio(radio, handler))
    for btn in created:
        btn.setOthers(created)
```

4. Below the code you just added, paste the `getParams()` helper function. This function parses the parameters of an XML element and returns them in a dictionary:

```
def getParams(element):
    params = {}
    params["scale"] = float(element.findtext("scale", 1))
    params["text"] = element.findtext("text", "")
    params["mayChange"] = int(element.findtext("mayChange", 0))
    params["width"] = float(element.findtext("width", 1))
    params["value"] = [int(element.findtext("value", 0))]
    params["variable"] = element.findtext("variable", "")
    params["name"] = element.findtext("name", "")
    params["command"] = element.findtext("command", "")

    fcolorElem = element.find("frameColor")
    if fcolorElem != None:
        r = fcolorElem.get("r", 0)
        g = fcolorElem.get("g", 0)
        b = fcolorElem.get("b", 0)
        a = fcolorElem.get("a", 0)
        color = Vec4(float(r), float(g), float(b), float(a))
        params["frameColor"] = color
    else:
        color = Vec4(0, 0, 0, 0)
        params["frameColor"] = color

    posElem = element.find("pos")
    if posElem != None:
        x = posElem.get("x", 0)
        y = posElem.get("y", 0)
        z = posElem.get("z", 0)
        pos = Vec3(float(x), float(y), float(z))
        params["pos"] = pos
    else:
        pos = Vec3(0, 0, 0)
        params["pos"] = pos

    return params
```

5. The following code is the last you need to add to `GuiBuilder.py`. These functions create the actual user interface controls:

```
def createButton(element, handler):
    params = getParams(element)
    assert params["command"] != ""
    assert params["name"] != ""
```

```
            button = DirectButton(text = params["text"],
                                   scale = params["scale"],
                                   command = getattr(handler,
params["command"]),
                                   pos = params["pos"])
        handler.controls[params["name"]] = button

    def createLabel(element, handler):
        params = getParams(element)
        assert params["name"] != ""
        label = DirectLabel(text = params["text"],
                            pos = params["pos"],
                            scale = params["scale"],
                            textMayChange = params["mayChange"],
                            frameColor = params["frameColor"])
        handler.controls[params["name"]] = label

    def createEntry(element, handler):
        params = getParams(element)
        assert params["name"] != ""
        entry = DirectEntry(scale = params["scale"],
                            pos = params["pos"],
                            width = params["width"])
        handler.controls[params["name"]] = entry

    def createRadio(element, handler):
        params = getParams(element)
        assert params["variable"] != ""
        assert params["name"] != ""
        radio = DirectRadioButton(text = params["text"],
                                  variable = getattr(handler,
params["variable"]),
                                  value = params["value"],
                                  scale = params["scale"],
                                  pos = params["pos"])
        handler.controls[params["name"]] = radio
        return radio
```

6. Now open the `Application.py` file and implement the `Application` class like this:

```
from direct.showbase.ShowBase import ShowBase
from panda3d.core import *
from GuiBuilder import GuiHandler, GuiFromXml
```

```
class Application(ShowBase):
    def __init__(self):
        ShowBase.__init__(self)
        handler = MyHandler()
        GuiFromXml("gui.xml", handler)

class MyHandler(GuiHandler):
    def __init__(self):
        GuiHandler.__init__(self)
        self.gender = [0]

    def setName(self):
        title = ""
        if self.gender[0]:
            title = "Mister"
        else:
            title = "Miss"

        self.controls["nameLbl"]["text"] = "Hello " + title + " "
+ self.controls["nameEnt"].get() + "!"
```

7. Add a new file called gui.xml to the src directory.

8. Add this code to the gui.xml file:

```xml
<gui>
    <button>
        <name>helloBtn</name>
        <command>setName</command>
        <scale>0.1</scale>
        <text>Say Hello!</text>
        <pos x="0" y="0" z="-0.1"/>
    </button>
    <label>
        <name>nameLbl</name>
        <text>Hi, what's your name?</text>
        <pos x="0" y="0" z="0.4"/>
        <scale>0.1</scale>
        <mayChange>1</mayChange>
        <frameColor r="0" g="0" b="0" a="0"/>
    </label>
    <entry>
        <name>nameEnt</name>
        <scale>0.08</scale>
        <pos x="-0.4" y="0" z="0.15"/>
        <width>10</width>
```

```
            </entry>
            <radiogroup>
                <radio>
                    <name>femaleRdo</name>
                    <text>Female</text>
                    <variable>gender</variable>
                    <value>0</value>
                    <scale>0.05</scale>
                    <pos x="-0.08" y="0" z="0.05"/>
                </radio>
                <radio>
                    <name>maleRdo</name>
                    <text>Male</text>
                    <variable>gender</variable>
                    <value>1</value>
                    <scale>0.05</scale>
                    <pos x="0.16" y="0" z="0.05"/>
                </radio>
            </radiogroup>
        </gui>
```

9. Press *F6* to start the application:

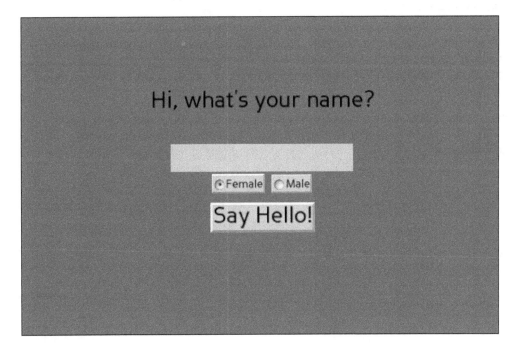

How it works...

In our newly added `GuiBuilder` library, we first add the `GuiHandler` class, which will be used as a base class for even handling. The central piece of this library is the `GuiFromXml()` function, that loads and parses the given XML file and calls the functions we added in step 3. Within these functions, we instruct the `ElementTree` object to look for the tags that represent user interface controls. If the appropriate tag is found, the according creation function is called, which first gets the parameters for the new control and then calls into Panda3D's `DirectGui` library to create the requested user interface element. The GUI controls are also added to the controls dictionary, so event-handling code is able to reference other user interface controls.

In `Application.py`, we then just add a new class that is derived from `GuiHandler`, containing a method that will set the label to the name given by the user. All the constructor of our `Application` class does then is create a new instance of `MyHandler` and call the `GuiFromXml()` function we created before to load the user interface data.

Finally, we add the XML data that defines our user interface. The tag names reflect the names of the controls and their properties. What's added now is the `<name>` tag that allows us to reference the control by name in the controls dictionary of the handler class.

There's more...

The code shown in this recipe is only a starting point for a data-driven user interface implementation and far from complete. For one, the `getParams()` function does not support all parameters yet. Also, besides not supporting all user interface controls found in the `DirectGui` library, the implemented elements do not even use all the parameters they could.

What's not complete is meant to be finished—feel free to complete and modify the `GuiBuilder` library to be able to elegantly divide the code and structure of your user interfaces!

7
Application Control

In this chapter, we will cover:

- ▸ Toggling window and fullscreen modes
- ▸ Controlling game state
- ▸ Decoupling modules using events
- ▸ Handling events more elegantly
- ▸ Managing recurring tasks

Introduction

So you wrote down your game idea into a nice design document? You convinced yourself and hopefully others, too, that it really would make a nice game once your vision has taken the form of an actual, completed, and polished product? Or maybe someone else inaugurated you into his or her game design ideas? Congratulations to you! This means you completed one very challenging step of the game production process!

Having a complete game design does not mean, however, that you are through with the challenges of creating a game. In fact, you are standing at the beginning of a very interesting journey towards the completion of your product.

Luckily, Panda3D provides you with a very impressive set of building blocks for implementing your game ideas at a level of abstraction that hides away many of the challenges, hassles, and annoyances of some lower-level programming APIs.

Unluckily for you, Panda3D cannot magically connect the single parts on its own to form the game you've imagined—ultimately it's your task to produce the application that implements the algorithms and rules that produce the entertaining behaviors described in your game design! That is where this book, and this chapter in particular, come in. This chapter will show you some tricks and techniques that put you in control of that application and enable you to connect the various modules that Panda3D provides.

Toggling window and fullscreen modes

Of course, game creators are always trying to immerse their customers into the colorful and fantastic worlds they are creating. This is why most games act quite selfish and take up the whole screen to present themselves in all their "awesome glory".

While this is true and understandable, some players just don't like this behavior. Maybe they are reading their email while the game is running. Maybe they want to be able to quickly minimize the game window in case their boss walks up behind them to check if they are busily working. Or maybe a developer just wants to switch from fullscreen to windowed mode to check the debug output window without having to tab through the window choices.

Whatever the reasons might be, PC games should be able to switch between windowed and fullscreen modes to accommodate the needs of players. So this recipe will show you how to achieve this with Panda3D.

Getting ready

Follow the steps of *Setting up the game structure* found in *Chapter 1*, *Setting Up Panda3D and Configuring Development Tools* before you go on with this recipe.

How to do it...

Let's create a sample program for switching between window and fullscreen modes:

1. Open `Application.py` and insert this code:

```
from direct.showbase.ShowBase import ShowBase
from direct.interval.IntervalGlobal import *
from direct.gui.OnscreenText import OnscreenText
from panda3d.core import *

class Application(ShowBase):
    def __init__(self):
        ShowBase.__init__(self)
        self.status = OnscreenText("Window Mode")
        toggle = Sequence(Wait(3),
                          Func(self.status.setText, "Switching to
Fullscreen Mode"),
                          Wait(2),
                          Func(self.toggleFullscreen, 1280, 800,
0, 0, 1),
                          Wait(3),
                          Func(self.status.setText, "Switching to
Window Mode"),
                          Wait(2),
```

```
                              Func(self.toggleFullscreen, 800, 600,
    50, 50, 0))
            toggle.start()

    def toggleFullscreen(self, width, height, posX, posY, full):
        winProps = WindowProperties()
        winProps.setOrigin(posX, posY)
        winProps.setSize(width, height)
        winProps.setFullscreen(full)
        self.win.requestProperties(winProps)

        if full:
            self.status.setText("Fullscreen Mode")
        else:
            self.status.setText("Window Mode");
```

2. Press *F6* to run the application:

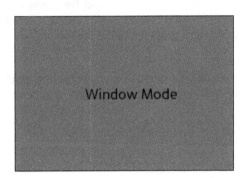

How it works...

While in our application class' constructor we set up a sequence that makes our program switch to fullscreen and back again to windowed mode. The interesting part in this code is the `toggleFullscreen()` method.

Here, the current properties of the game window are retrieved and modified. We pass the `posX` and `posY` parameters to `setOrigin()` to set the window's position. Then the window size is set using the values stored in `width` and `height`. For fullscreen mode, this describes the screen resolution that the application will switch to. Finally, we set the fullscreen flag of the window properties object and request our newly created screen mode from Panda3D's window handling system.

Panda3D handles errors quite transparently. If a given resolution is not supported, the engine will try to switch to the closest matching resolution. To check for errors manually we can also use the `getRejectedProperties()` of the window object after calling `requestProperties()`. This will retrieve a `WindowProperties` object containing the properties that could not be changed.

Controlling game state

No matter how simple your game might be, chances are that there will be multiple screens or modes the player will be able to interact with. Think of it for a moment—in most games there is a title screen, which is followed by a main menu, which lets you branch into various other sub-screens that let you set the game's difficulty or level of detail. Typically, you must navigate your way through many if not most of these screens and menus before you are finally ready to play the game itself.

All these varying screens and modes fall into the game development concept of **game states**. Each of these screens is seen as a state and might set the game to a different mode of operation. As the game transitions from one state to another, it is setting variables, loading content and finally, drawing different graphics to the screen or presenting new ways of interaction to the player.

This recipe will show you how to define and use a state machine that lets you easily define and cleanly switch back and forth through the differing states of a game.

Getting ready

As a prerequisite, please follow the instructions found in the recipe *Setting up the game structure* back in Chapter 1 before proceeding with the following tasks.

How to do it...

Let's get started with the practical part of this recipe:

1. Add a new Python source file called `AppState.py` to the project.

2. Insert the following code to `AppState.py`:

```python
from direct.fsm.FSM import FSM
from direct.gui.DirectGui import *
from panda3d.core import *

class AppState(FSM):
    def enterMenu(self):
        self.pandaBtn = DirectButton(text = "Panda",
                                     scale = 0.12,
                                     pos = Vec3(0, 0, 0.1),
```

```
                                           command = self.request,
                                           extraArgs = ["Panda"])
        self.smileyBtn = DirectButton(text = "Smiley",
                                           scale = 0.1,
                                           pos = Vec3(0, 0, -0.1),
                                           command = self.request,
                                           extraArgs = ["Smiley"])


    def exitMenu(self):
        self.pandaBtn.destroy()
        self.smileyBtn.destroy()
```

3. Below the code you just added, append the following two methods:

```
    def enterPanda(self):
        self.menuBtn = DirectButton(text = "Menu",
                                        scale = 0.1,
                                        pos = Vec3(0, 0, -0.8),
                                        command = self.request,
                                        extraArgs = ["Menu"])
        self.panda = loader.loadModel("panda")
        self.panda.reparentTo(render)
        base.cam.setPos(0, -40, 5)


    def exitPanda(self):
        self.menuBtn.destroy()
        self.panda.removeNode()
```

4. To finish the `AppState` class, add this code to it:

```
    def enterSmiley(self):
        self.menuBtn = DirectButton(text = "Menu",
                                        scale = 0.1,
                                        pos = Vec3(0, 0, -0.8),
                                        command = self.request,
                                        extraArgs = ["Menu"])
        self.smiley = loader.loadModel("smiley")
        self.smiley.reparentTo(render)
        base.cam.setPos(0, -20, 0)


    def exitSmiley(self):
        self.menuBtn.destroy()
        self.smiley.removeNode()
```

5. Open `Application.py` and paste the following piece of code:

```
from direct.showbase.ShowBase import ShowBase
from panda3d.core import *
from AppState import AppState

class Application(ShowBase):
    def __init__(self):
        ShowBase.__init__(self)
        state = AppState("Application")
        state.request("Menu")
```

6. That's it! Hit *F6* to run the code:

How it works...

For handling state in our code, Panda3D comes with the FSM (**finite state machine**) class, which we use as the base class for our `AppState` class. This class handles state switches for our sample application. This class is kept quite simple for the purpose of this recipe. A full game would feature a lot more states, of course.

The `AppState` class defines 3 states: `Menu`, `Panda`, and `Smiley`, all of which are implicitly defined by their respective `enter()` and `exit()` methods. These methods implement the actions that are performed if the state is entered, or when the state transitions to a different state.

Each state adds either some user interface controls or loads a model and then cleans up after itself, once another state is requested. Changing the state of our `AppState` object (and thus our application) is done using the `request()` method, passing the name of the state to switch to as the method parameter. This can be seen in the last line of `Application.py`, for example, where we set the initial `Menu` state.

Decoupling modules using events

Gameplay code can be a complex beast. In many cases, there are complex, many-to-many relationships between all sorts of different game entities. This can be good for the player, as he or she might enjoy the interesting emergent patterns of behavior created by this kind of game object interconnection.

For the programmer (that is you), who has to think about and write all the code that makes this happen, things look different, though. Having the game entity that creates an event which holds references to all the objects that will react to it could be problematic. This could lead to chaotic, messy code and a great deal of unnecessary coupling between otherwise independent and differing types of objects. The more complex the code, the more you need to create a more modular and maintainable design.

From a software engineering point of view, this situation cries out for a form of publish/subscribe design pattern that allows game entities (and other kinds of objects too, of course) to send and react to messages without knowing about the specific senders or receivers of the message.

Panda3D provides such a neat messaging subsystem, which we will take a look at in this recipe.

Getting ready

This recipe builds upon the project structure described in *Setting up the game structure* found in *Chapter 1*. Please follow these instructions before going on with the current recipe.

How to do it...

Follow the following instructions to learn how to use Panda3D's messaging system:

1. Edit `Application.py` so it contains the following code:

    ```
    from direct.showbase.ShowBase import ShowBase
    from direct.interval.IntervalGlobal import *
    from direct.showbase.DirectObject import DirectObject
    from panda3d.core import *
    ```

```
class Sender(DirectObject):
    def start(self):
        smiley = loader.loadModel("smiley")
        pause = Sequence(Wait(5), Func(messenger.send, "smiley-
done", [smiley]))
        pause.start()

class Receiver(DirectObject):
    def __init__(self):
        self.accept("smiley-done", self.showSmiley)

    def showSmiley(self, smiley):
        smiley.reparentTo(render)

class Application(ShowBase):
    def __init__(self):
        ShowBase.__init__(self)
        self.cam.setPos(0, -10, 0)
        rec = Receiver()
        snd = Sender()
        snd.start()
```

2. Press *F6* to start the program.

How it works...

In our little event sample, we create the classes `Sender` and `Receiver` that are communicating without ever knowing about each other's existence.

In the `start()` method of `Sender`, we load the smiley model and wait five seconds before sending the `"smiley-done"` message, passing the smiley model reference as a parameter to the `messenger.send()` method that adds the message to the global message queue of Panda3D.

By calling `accept()` in its constructor, each instance of `Receiver` subscribes to the `"smiley-done"` message. As soon as a `Sender` dispatches this message, the `showSmiley()` method will be called. This method reparents the smiley model to the scene root to make it visible.

Handling events more elegantly

Although Panda3D's event system is a great way for passing messages between objects, there are some things you should know before you are going to use it in your game. This recipe will show you an even more elegant way of integrating events into your code. You will learn how to use the introspection facilities of the Python language to create an annotation that marks a method as an event handler. Additionally, this article will discuss some problems you might encounter when using the messaging system of Panda3D.

Getting ready

Follow the tasks of _Setting up the game structure_ found in _Chapter 1_ prior to continuing with the current recipe.

How to do it...

The following are your tasks for this recipe:

1. Add a new file called `GameObject.py` to your project.

2. Insert the following source code into `GameObject.py`:

```python
from direct.showbase.DirectObject import DirectObject

def handle_event(event):
    def inner_event(func):
        func.event_name = event
        return func
    return inner_event

class GameObject(DirectObject):
    def __init__(self):
        for attrib in dir(self):
            method = getattr(self, attrib)
            if callable(method) and hasattr(method, 'event_name'):
                self.accept(method.event_name, method)

    def destroy(self):
        self.ignoreAll()
```

3. Open `Application.py` and add this following code to the file:

```python
from direct.showbase.ShowBase import ShowBase
from direct.interval.IntervalGlobal import *
from GameObject import GameObject
from GameObject import handle_event
from panda3d.core import *
```

```
class Sender(GameObject):
    def start(self):
        smiley = loader.loadModel("smiley")
        pause = Sequence(Wait(5), Func(messenger.send, "smiley-
done", [smiley]))
        pause.start()

class Receiver(GameObject):
    @handle_event("smiley-done")
    def showSmiley(self, smiley):
        smiley.reparentTo(render)
        messenger.send("smiley-shown")

class Application(ShowBase):
    def __init__(self):
        ShowBase.__init__(self)
        self.accept("smiley-shown", self.clean)
        self.cam.setPos(0, -10, 0)
        self.rec = Receiver()
        snd = Sender()
        snd.start()

    def clean(self):
        self.ignore("smiley-shown")
        self.rec.destroy()
```

4. Hit *F6* to run the program.

How it works...

This recipe introduces the `@handle_event()` decorator that allows you to mark methods to be event handlers for a given message. The decorator adds a new attribute called `event_name` to the method. The constructor of the `GameObject` class then iterates over all member methods, looking for this attribute and automatically calling `accept()` for the given event name and handler method. This can help a lot to keep code cleaner, especially in classes that listen for a lot of events. Instead of filling the constructor with calls to `accept()` to subscribe to messages, we can now simply mark a method to be an event handler, making its purpose clearer when reading the code.

One concept that this recipe is trying to teach you is that subscribing to a message has one slight side effect—it adds the object that registers for a kind of event to a list of listeners, thus increasing the object's reference count. This can result in surprising behavior and annoying bugs. Because of the entry in the list of subscribers, the reference count will never reach zero, keeping the object on reacting to events.

The effect of this can lead to the following situation: Let's suppose one of your game objects listens for an event called "explode", that displays a spectacular explosion on the screen and removes the object that was blown up from the scene graph. A few moments later, there occurs another "explode" event, but suddenly there's an explosion showing where it shouldn't. This is because the object from the first explosion still exists, eagerly listening for the order to explode.

To prevent this from happening, whenever an object that accepts messages isn't needed anymore, you should use `ignoreAll()` to stop listening for events. This will remove it from the subscriber list, allowing its reference count to reach zero so it can ultimately be deallocated.

There's more...

Panda3D's messaging system works within the boundary of a frame. This means that if you send a message in the first frame, all objects listening for that message will be reacting to it in the second frame.

This is usually sufficient for handling the needs of gameplay code, but should you somehow need to have an object react to a message immediately, or even multiple times within a frame, you will need to provide your own facilities or resort to Python libraries like `PubSub` or `PyDispatcher`.

Managing recurring tasks

Loops can be found in any video game running in real-time. Small incremental steps generally characterize gameplay simulation code. With each of these steps occurs a minimal frame-by-frame change of object transformations, creating the illusion of smooth movement.

Panda3D has its own way of handling code that needs to be called time and time again while the game is running. This recipe's topic is Panda3D's task system.

Getting ready

Please complete the tasks found in *Setting up the game structure* found in *Chapter 1* to get ready for this recipe.

How to do it...

Let's implement an application that uses the task system to execute a piece of code in every frame:

1. Open `Application.py` and insert the following code:

```python
from direct.showbase.ShowBase import ShowBase
from panda3d.core import *
import random

class Application(ShowBase):
    def __init__(self):
        ShowBase.__init__(self)
        self.smiley = loader.loadModel("smiley")
        self.smileyCount = 0
        self.cam.setPos(0, -100, 10)
        taskMgr.doMethodLater(0.1, self.addSmiley, "AddSmiley")
        taskMgr.add(self.updateSmileys, "UpdateSmileys", uponDeath
= self.removeSmileys)
        taskMgr.doMethodLater(60, taskMgr.remove, "RemoveUpdate",
extraArgs = ["UpdateSmileys"])

    def addSmiley(self, task):
        sm = render.attachNewNode("smiley-instance")
        sm.setPos(random.uniform(-20, 20), random.uniform(-30,
30), random.uniform(0, 30))
        sm.setPythonTag("velocity", 0)
        self.smiley.instanceTo(sm)
        self.smileyCount += 1

        if self.smileyCount == 100:
            return task.done

        return task.again

    def updateSmileys(self, task):
        for smiley in render.findAllMatches("smiley-instance"):
            vel = smiley.getPythonTag("velocity")
            z = smiley.getZ()
            if z <= 0:
                vel = random.uniform(0.1, 0.8)
            smiley.setZ(z + vel)
            vel -= 0.01
```

```
        smiley.setPythonTag("velocity", vel)
    return task.cont

def removeSmileys(self, task):
    for smiley in render.findAllMatches("smiley-instance"):
        smiley.removeNode()
```

2. Press F6 to run the application:

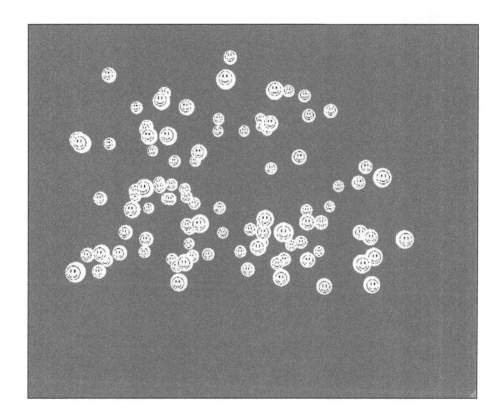

How it works...

To interface with Panda3D's task system, we are using the global `taskMgr` object. In total, we are adding three tasks to our application.

First we use `doMethodLater()` to add a task that calls the `addSmiley()` method after `0.1` seconds. As long as there are less than 100 smileys in the scene, the `addSmiley()` method will return `task.again`, which will put the task into the task queue again to be called after another tenth of a second has passed.

The second task we add is responsible for updating the positions of the smileys. This will be called every frame until the game is quit or the task is removed from the internal queue of `taskMgr`. For the latter case, we define that the `removeSmileys()` method should be called that removes all smileys from the scene.

Finally, we enqueue another method to be called later, which is the `remove()` method of `taskMgr`. This will stop the update task and also remove all smileys from the scene.

8
Collision Detection and Physics

In this chapter, we will cover:

- ▶ Using the built-in collision detection system
- ▶ Using the built-in physics system
- ▶ Using the ODE physics engine
- ▶ Using the PhysX physics engine
- ▶ Integrating the Bullet physics engine

Introduction

In a video game, the game world or level defines the boundaries within which the player is allowed to interact with the game environment. But how do we enforce these boundaries? How do we keep the player from running through walls?

This is where collision detection and response come into play.

Collision detection and response not only allow us to keep players from passing through the level boundaries, but also are the basis for many forms of interaction. For example, lots of actions in games are started when the player hits an invisible collision mesh, called a trigger, which initiates a scripted sequence as a response to the player entering its boundaries.

Simple collision detection and response form the basis for nearly all forms of interaction in video games. It's responsible for keeping the player within the level, for crates being pushable, for telling if and where a bullet hit the enemy.

What if we could add some extra magic to the mix to make our games even more believable, immersive, and entertaining? Let's think again about pushing crates around: What happens if the player pushes a stack of crates? Do they just move like they have been glued together, or will they start to tumble and eventually topple over?

This is where we add physics to the mix to make things more interesting, realistic, and dynamic.

In this chapter, we will take a look at the various collision detection and physics libraries that the Panda3D engine allows us to work with. Putting in some extra effort, we will also see that it is not very hard to integrate a physics engine that is not part of the Panda3D SDK.

Using the built-in collision detection system

Not all problems concerning world and player interaction need to be handled by a fully fledged physics API—sometimes a much more basic and lightweight system is just enough for our purposes. This is why in this recipe we dive into the collision handling system that is built into the Panda3D engine.

Getting ready

This recipe relies upon the project structure created in *Setting up the game structure* found in *Chapter 1, Setting Up Panda3D and Configuring Development Tools*.

How to do it...

Let's go through this recipe's tasks:

1. Open `Application.py` and add the include statements as well as the constructor of the `Application` class:

```
from direct.showbase.ShowBase import ShowBase
from panda3d.core import *
import random

class Application(ShowBase):
    def __init__(self):
        ShowBase.__init__(self)
        self.cam.setPos(0, -50, 10)
        self.setupCD()
        self.addSmiley()
        self.addFloor()
        taskMgr.add(self.updateSmiley, "UpdateSmiley")
```

2. Next, add the method that initializes the collision detection system:

```
def setupCD(self):
        base.cTrav = CollisionTraverser()
        base.cTrav.showCollisions(render)
        self.notifier = CollisionHandlerEvent()
        self.notifier.addInPattern("%fn-in-%in")
        self.accept("frowney-in-floor", self.onCollision)
```

3. Next, implement the method for adding the `frowney` model to the scene:

```
def addSmiley(self):
        self.frowney = loader.loadModel("frowney")
        self.frowney.reparentTo(render)
        self.frowney.setPos(0, 0, 10)
        self.frowney.setPythonTag("velocity", 0)

        col = self.frowney.attachNewNode(CollisionNode("frowney"))
        col.node().addSolid(CollisionSphere(0, 0, 0, 1.1))
        col.show()
        base.cTrav.addCollider(col, self.notifier)
```

4. The following methods will add a floor plane to the scene and handle the collision response:

```
def addFloor(self):
        floor = render.attachNewNode(CollisionNode("floor"))
        floor.node().addSolid(CollisionPlane(Plane(Vec3(0, 0, 1),
Point3(0, 0, 0))))
        floor.show()

def onCollision(self, entry):
        vel = random.uniform(0.01, 0.2)
        self.frowney.setPythonTag("velocity", vel)
```

5. Add this last piece of code. This will make the `frowney` model bounce up and down:

```
def updateSmiley(self, task):
        vel = self.frowney.getPythonTag("velocity")
        z = self.frowney.getZ()
        self.frowney.setZ(z + vel)
        vel -= 0.001
        self.frowney.setPythonTag("velocity", vel)
        return task.cont
```

6. Hit the *F6* key to launch the program:

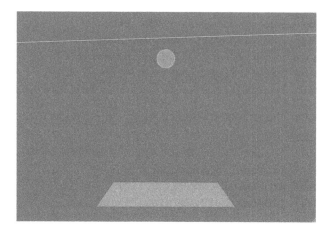

How it works...

We start off by adding some setup code that calls the other initialization routines. We also add the task that will update the smiley's position.

In the `setupCD()` method, we initialize the collision detection system. To be able to find out which scene objects collided and issue the appropriate responses, we create an instance of the `CollisionTraverser` class and assign it to `base.cTrav`. The variable name is important, because this way, Panda3D will automatically update the `CollisionTraverser` every frame. The engine checks if a `CollisionTraverser` was assigned to that variable and will automatically add the required tasks to Panda3D's update loop.

Additionally, we enable debug drawing, so collisions are being visualized at runtime. This will overlay a visualization of the collision meshes the collision detection system uses internally.

In the last lines of `setupCD()`, we instantiate a collision handler that sends a message using Panda3D's event system whenever a collision is detected. The method call `addInPattern("%fn-in-%in")` defines the pattern for the name of the event that is created when a collision is encountered the first time. `%fn` will be replaced by the name of the object that bumps into another object that goes by the name that will be inserted in the place of `%in`. Take a look at the event handler that is added below to get an idea of what these events will look like.

After the code for setting up the collision detection system is ready, we add the `addSmiley()` method, where we first load the model and then create a new collision node, which we attach to the model's node so it is moved around together with the model. We also add a sphere collision shape, defined by its local center coordinates and radius. This is the shape that defines the boundaries; the collision system will test against it to determine whether two objects have touched.

To complete this step, we register our new collision node with the collision traverser and configure it to use the collision handler that sends events as a collision response.

Next, we add an infinite floor plane and add the event handling method for reacting on collision notifications. Although the debug visualization shows us a limited rectangular area, this plane actually has an unlimited width and height. In our case, this means that at any given x- and y-coordinate, objects will register a collision when any point on their bounding volume reaches a z-coordinate of 0. It's also important to note that the floor is not registered as a collider here. This is contrary to what we did for the `frowney` model and guarantees that the model will act as the collider, and the floor will be treated as the collide when a contact between the two is encountered.

While the `onCollision()` method makes the smiley model go up again, the code in `updateSmiley()` constantly drags it downwards. Setting the velocity tag on the `frowney` model to a positive or negative value, respectively, does this in these two methods. We can think of that as forces being applied. Whenever we encounter a collision with the ground plane, we add a one-shot bounce to our model. But what goes up must come down, eventually. Therefore, we continuously add a gravity force by decreasing the model's velocity every frame.

There's more...

This sample only touched a few of the features of Panda3D's collision system. The following sections are meant as an overview to give you an impression of what else is possible. For more details, take a look into Panda3D's API reference.

Collision Shapes

In the sample code, we used `CollisionPlane` and `CollisionSphere`, but there are several more shapes available:

- `CollisionBox`: A simple rectangular shape. Crates, boxes, and walls are example usages for this kind of collision shape.

- `CollisionTube`: A cylinder with rounded ends. This type of collision mesh is often used as a bounding volume for first and third person game characters.

- `CollisionInvSphere`: This shape can be thought of as a bubble that contains objects, like a fish bowl. Everything that is outside the bubble is reported to be colliding. A `CollisionInvSphere` may be used to delimit the boundaries of a game world, for example.

- `CollisionPolygon`: This collision shape is formed from a set of vertices, and allows for the creating of freeform collision meshes. This kind of shape is the most complex to test for collisions, but also the most accurate one. Whenever polygon-level collision detection is important, when doing hit detection in a shooter for example, this collision mesh comes in handy.

- ▶ CollisionRay: This is a line that, starting from one point, extends to infinity in a given direction. Rays are usually shot into a scene to determine whether one or more objects intersect with them. This can be used for various tasks like finding out if a bullet shot in the given direction hit a target, or simple AI tasks like finding out whether a bot is approaching a wall.

- ▶ CollisionLine: Like CollisionRay, but stretches to infinity in both directions.

- ▶ CollisionSegment: This is a special form of ray that is limited by two end points.

- ▶ CollisionParabola: Another special type of ray that is bent. The flying curves of ballistic objects are commonly described as parabolas. Naturally, we would use this kind of ray to find collisions for bullets, for example.

Collision Handlers

Just like it is the case with collision shapes for this recipe, we only used CollisionHandlerEvent for our sample program, even though there are several more collision handler classes available:

- ▶ CollisionHandlerPusher: This collision handler automatically keeps the collider out of intersecting vertical geometry, like walls.

- ▶ CollisionHandlerFloor: Like CollisionHandlerPusher, but works in the horizontal plane.

- ▶ CollisionHandlerQueue: A very simple handler. All it does is add any intersecting objects to a list.

- ▶ PhysicsCollisionHandler: This collision handler should be used in connection with Panda3D's built-in physics engine. Whenever a collision is found by this collision handler, the appropriate response is calculated by the simple physics engine that is built into the engine.

Using the built-in physics system

Panda3D has a built-in physics system that treats its entities as simple particles with masses to which forces may be applied. This physics system is a great amount simpler than a fully featured rigid body one. But it still is enough for cheaply, quickly, and easily creating some nice and simple physics effects.

Getting ready

To be prepared for this recipe, please first follow the steps found in *Setting up the game structure* found in *Chapter 1*. Also, the collision detection system of Panda3D will be used, so reading up on it in *Using the built-in collision detection system* might be a good idea!

How to do it...

The following steps are required to work with Panda3D's built-in physics system:

1. Edit `Application.py` and add the required `import` statements as well as the constructor of the `Application` class:

```
from direct.showbase.ShowBase import ShowBase
from panda3d.core import *
from panda3d.physics import *


class Application(ShowBase):
    def __init__(self):
        ShowBase.__init__(self)
        self.cam.setPos(0, -50, 10)
        self.setupCD()
        self.setupPhysics()
        self.addSmiley()
        self.addFloor()
```

2. Next, add the methods for initializing the collision detection and physics systems to the `Application` class:

```
    def setupCD(self):
        base.cTrav = CollisionTraverser()
        base.cTrav.showCollisions(render)
        self.notifier = CollisionHandlerEvent()
        self.notifier.addInPattern("%fn-in-%in")
        self.notifier.addOutPattern("%fn-out-%in")
        self.accept("smiley-in-floor", self.onCollisionStart)
        self.accept("smiley-out-floor", self.onCollisionEnd)


    def setupPhysics(self):
        base.enableParticles()
        gravNode = ForceNode("gravity")
        render.attachNewNode(gravNode)
        gravityForce = LinearVectorForce(0, 0, -9.81)
        gravNode.addForce(gravityForce)
        base.physicsMgr.addLinearForce(gravityForce)
```

3. Next, implement the method for adding a model and physics actor to the scene:

```
    def addSmiley(self):
        actor = ActorNode("physics")
        actor.getPhysicsObject().setMass(10)
        self.phys = render.attachNewNode(actor)
        base.physicsMgr.attachPhysicalNode(actor)
```

```
self.smiley = loader.loadModel("smiley")
self.smiley.reparentTo(self.phys)
self.phys.setPos(0, 0, 10)

thrustNode = ForceNode("thrust")
self.phys.attachNewNode(thrustNode)
self.thrustForce = LinearVectorForce(0, 0, 400)
self.thrustForce.setMassDependent(1)
thrustNode.addForce(self.thrustForce)

col = self.smiley.attachNewNode(CollisionNode("smiley"))
col.node().addSolid(CollisionSphere(0, 0, 0, 1.1))
col.show()
base.cTrav.addCollider(col, self.notifier)
```

4. Add this last piece of source code that adds the floor plane to the scene to `Application.py`:

```
def addFloor(self):
    floor = render.attachNewNode(CollisionNode("floor"))
    floor.node().addSolid(CollisionPlane(Plane(Vec3(0, 0, 1),
Point3(0, 0, 0))))
    floor.show()

def onCollisionStart(self, entry):
    base.physicsMgr.addLinearForce(self.thrustForce)

def onCollisionEnd(self, entry):
    base.physicsMgr.removeLinearForce(self.thrustForce)
```

5. Start the program by pressing *F6*:

How it works...

After adding the mandatory libraries and initialization code, we proceed to the code that sets up the collision detection system. Here we register event handlers for when the smiley starts or stops colliding with the floor. The calls involved in `setupCD()` are very similar to the ones used in *Using the built-in collision detection system*. Instead of moving the smiley model in our own update task, we use the built-in physics system to calculate new object positions based on the forces applied to them.

In `setupPhysics()`, we call `base.enableParticles()` to fire up the physics system. We also attach a new `ForceNode` to the scene graph, so all physics objects will be affected by the gravity force. We also register the force with `base.physicsMgr`, which is automatically defined when the physics engine is initialized and ready.

In the first couple of lines in `addSmiley()`, we create a new `ActorNode`, give it a mass, attach it to the scene graph and register it with the physics manager class. The graphical representation, which is the smiley model in this case, is then added to the physics node as a child so it will be moved automatically as the physics system updates.

We also add a `ForceNode` to the physics actor. This acts as a thruster that applies a force that pushes the smiley upwards whenever it intersects the floor. As opposed to the gravity force, the thruster force is set to be mass dependant. This means that no matter how heavy we set the smiley to be, it will always be accelerated at the same rate by the gravity force. The thruster force, on the other hand, would need to be more powerful if we increased the mass of the smiley.

The last step when adding a smiley is adding its collision node and shape, which leads us to the last methods added in this recipe, where we add the floor plane and define that the thruster should be enabled when the collision starts, and disabled when the objects' contact phase ends.

Using the ODE physics engine

The **Open Dynamics Engine (ODE)** in short, is a very powerful and feature-rich implementation of a rigid body physics system. It has been successfully integrated into various commercial simulation and game projects like World of Goo and Nail'd, for example. Panda3D comes with this proven piece of physics technology included out of the box. This leaves it to us to enable and use ODE in our code, so let's get started!

Getting ready

To get set for this recipe, please follow *Setting up the game structure* first. You can find this recipe in *Chapter 1*.

How to do it...

The ODE physics engine is used like the following in a Panda3D application:

1. Open `Application.py` and add this code:

```python
from direct.showbase.ShowBase import ShowBase
from panda3d.core import *
from panda3d.ode import *
import random

class Application(ShowBase):
    def __init__(self):
        ShowBase.__init__(self)
        self.smiley = loader.loadModel("smiley")
        self.smileyCount = 0
        self.cam.setPos(0, -100, 10)

        self.setupODE()
        self.addGround()

        taskMgr.doMethodLater(0.01, self.addSmiley, "AddSmiley")
        taskMgr.add(self.updateODE, "UpdateODE")
```

2. Append the following code to the file:

```python
    def setupODE(self):
        self.odeWorld = OdeWorld()
        self.odeWorld.setGravity(0, 0, -9.81)
        self.odeWorld.initSurfaceTable(1)
        self.odeWorld.setSurfaceEntry(0, 0, 200, 0.7, 0.2, 0.9,
0.00001, 0.0, 0.002)

        self.space = OdeSimpleSpace()
        self.space.setAutoCollideWorld(self.odeWorld)
        self.contacts = OdeJointGroup()
        self.space.setAutoCollideJointGroup(self.contacts)

    def addGround(self):
        cm = CardMaker("ground")
        cm.setFrame(-500, 500, -500, 500)
        ground = render.attachNewNode(cm.generate())
        ground.setColor(0.2, 0.4, 0.8)
        ground.lookAt(0, 0, -1)
        groundGeom = OdePlaneGeom(self.space, Vec4(0, 0, 1, 0))
```

3. Next, add these methods:

```
def addSmiley(self, task):
    sm = render.attachNewNode("smiley-instance")
    sm.setPos(random.uniform(-20, 20), random.uniform(-30,
30), random.uniform(10, 30))
    self.smiley.instanceTo(sm)

    body = OdeBody(self.odeWorld)
    mass = OdeMass()
    mass.setSphereTotal(10, 1)
    body.setMass(mass)
    body.setPosition(sm.getPos())
    geom = OdeSphereGeom(self.space, 1)
    geom.setBody(body)

    sm.setPythonTag("body", body)
    self.smileyCount += 1

    if self.smileyCount == 1000:
        return task.done

    return task.again

def updateODE(self, task):
    self.space.autoCollide()
    self.odeWorld.quickStep(globalClock.getDt())

    for smiley in render.findAllMatches("smiley-instance"):
        body = smiley.getPythonTag("body")
        smiley.setPosQuat(body.getPosition(), Quat(body.
getQuaternion()))

    self.contacts.empty()
    return task.cont
```

4.   Press *F6* to launch the program and see the smileys roll, tumble, and bounce:

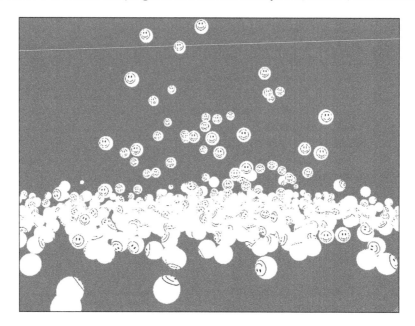

How it works...

For ODE to work, we need to do the following things.

We create a new `OdeWorld`, set its gravity, and add a default surface description. The surface description defines the properties of two surfaces that collide. The first two parameters of `setSurfaceEntry()` are indices in the surface table, with index zero being the default surface. The next parameter is the friction coefficient, which sets how slippery or sticky the surfaces react to each other. The higher this value is set, the higher the friction will be. The fourth parameter describes the bounciness on a scale between 0 and 1, while the fifth parameter sets the minimum velocity that is required for an object to bounce at all. The next two parameters define the values for error reduction and constraint force mixing, which influence to which extent objects are allowed to penetrate each other and how much force will be applied to push objects out of each other. This is followed by the `slip` parameter that is used to set a force-dependent slip value, which is useful for simulating car tires, for example. The last parameter sets a damping coefficient, which helps to keep the simulation more stable.

Next, we create an `OdeSimpleSpace`, which represents a space within which ODE tests for collisions. We configure ODE to automatically detect and resolve collisions. This requires a joint group, because whenever two objects intersect in ODE, a temporary joint is created between them that pushes the objects off each other.

In the `addGround()` method, we create a static ground plane, both in our visible scene as well as in ODE's simulation world.

Whenever a new smiley is added, we create a new `OdeBody`, set its mass and position and assign it to a new `OdeSphereGeom`. We then assign the ODE physics body to a tag of the smiley `NodePath`. This part of the code also shows a very important principle of ODE—the `OdeBody` is used for physics calculations, whereas the geometry is used for collision detection.

The `updateOde()` method is run every frame as a task. It first runs collision detection, then steps the physics simulation, and updates the positions of the objects in the scene graph. Before the method returns, we must not forget to clear the list of contact groups to keep the automatic collision response working properly.

Using the PhysX physics engine

PhysX is a proprietary physics programming library made by the graphics card specialist nVidia that simulates the behavior of rigid bodies. One of the library's major features is its ability to leverage the computing abilities of a graphics card to accelerate the calculation of the internal physics formulas used for the simulation. If a suitable graphics adapter cannot be found, the physics engine falls back to the system's CPU so that nobody's left behind.

This recipe will give you some insight into the wrapper that the Panda3D developers have created around this physics API.

Getting ready

This recipe builds upon the framework created in *Setting up the game structure* found in *Chapter 1*.

Additionally, you need to have the PhysX SDK installed on your system. For more information on licensing and how to download, see this website: `http://developer.nvidia.com/object/physx_downloads.html`.

How to do it...

These are the tasks required to create a program that uses PhysX:

1. Copy the file `NxCharacter.dll` from `C:\Program Files (x86)\NVIDIA Corporation\NVIDIA PhysX SDK\v2.8.4_win\Bin\win32` to `C:\Panda3D-1.7.0\bin`.

2. Open `Application.py` and add the required imports and the constructor:
    ```
    from direct.showbase.ShowBase import ShowBase
    from panda3d.core import *
    from panda3d.physx import *
    import random
    ```

```
class Application(ShowBase):
    def __init__(self):
        ShowBase.__init__(self)
        self.box = loader.loadModel("misc/rgbCube")
        self.boxCount = 0
        self.cam.setPos(0, -100, 10)

        self.setupPhysX()
        self.addGround()

        taskMgr.doMethodLater(0.01, self.addBox, "AddBox")
        taskMgr.add(self.updatePhysX, "UpdatePhysX")
```

3. Append the methods for initializing PhysX and adding a ground plane:

```
    def setupPhysX(self):
        scene = PhysxSceneDesc()
        scene.setGravity(Vec3(0, 0, -9.81))
        self.physxScene = PhysxManager.getGlobalPtr().
createScene(scene)

        mat = self.physxScene.getMaterial(0)
        mat.setRestitution(0.7)
        mat.setStaticFriction(0.5)
        mat.setDynamicFriction(0.8)

    def addGround(self):
        cm = CardMaker("ground")
        cm.setFrame(-500, 500, -500, 500)
        ground = render.attachNewNode(cm.generate())
        ground.setColor(0.2, 0.2, 0.2)
        ground.lookAt(0, 0, -1)

        shape = PhysxPlaneShapeDesc()
        shape.setPlane(Vec3(0, 0, 1), 0)
        actor = PhysxActorDesc()
        actor.addShape(shape)
        self.physxScene.createActor(actor)
```

4. Add the methods for adding boxes and updating the physics simulation:

```
    def addBox(self, task):
        bx = render.attachNewNode("box-instance")
        self.box.instanceTo(bx)
```

```
        shape = PhysxBoxShapeDesc()
        shape.setDimensions(Vec3(0.5, 0.5, 0.5))
        body = PhysxBodyDesc()
        body.setMass(10)
        actor = PhysxActorDesc()
        actor.setBody(body)
        actor.addShape(shape)
        actor.setGlobalPos(Point3(random.uniform(-20, 20), random.
uniform(-30, 30), random.uniform(10, 30)))
        physxActor = self.physxScene.createActor(actor)
        physxActor.attachNodePath(bx)

        self.boxCount += 1

        if self.boxCount == 1000:
            return task.done

        return task.again

    def updatePhysX(self, task):
        self.physxScene.simulate(globalClock.getDt())
        self.physxScene.fetchResults()
        return task.cont
```

5. Press *F6* to run the sample:

How it works...

First, we make sure to place `NxCharacter.dll` in the right location, or else we won't be able to use the API. The exact path of the source directory might vary slightly, depending on which version of the PhysX SDK is installed.

After adding the boilerplate code for loading modules and setting up the `Application` class, we can proceed to the `setupPhysX()` method, where we create a new PhysX scene with earth-like gravitation. We also modify the material stored at index zero—the default material—to be a bit more bouncy and also have more friction.

We then add a ground plane by creating a shape description, adding it to an actor description, and creating the new physics actor using the `createActor()` method.

In the `addSmiley()` method, we connect a shape, used for collision detection, and body, which is used for physics calculations, to form a new actor. We also attach the created smiley `NodePath` to the newly created actor, so its transformation is automatically updated as PhysX advances the simulation.

Finally, we add the code for the task that keeps on updating the simulation. This method first performs a simulation step and afterwards instructs the PhysX API to collect and apply the results of the calculations it performed.

Integrating the Bullet physics engine

As a sample for integrating a third party library that is not built into Panda3D into a game, this recipe dives into the C++ side of Panda3D to create a scene that is driven by the excellent and free Bullet physics engine.

Getting ready

This recipe builds on the project setup described in *Creating a scene using C++* found in *Chapter 2*. Follow the steps of this recipe before proceeding!

You also need a copy of the Bullet source code. The latest version can be retrieved from this website: `http://code.google.com/p/bullet/downloads/list`.

How to do it...

Integrating the Bullet physics engine into a Panda3D program involves these tasks:

1. In the top-level solution directory, create a directory named `Lib`.
2. Unpack the Bullet source code into the `Lib` directory so that the top-level directory, containing the file `AUTHORS` and the directory `msvc`, of Bullet is `Lib\bullet-2.77`.

3. Navigate to the `msvc\2008` subdirectory of the Bullet source tree and open the file `BULLET_PHYSICS.sln`.

4. Switch the build configuration to **Release** and build the solution.

5. Quit Visual Studio.

6. Edit the `PandaSettings.vsprops` file and replace its content with the following configuration data:

```xml
<?xml version="1.0" encoding="Windows-1252"?>
<VisualStudioPropertySheet
   ProjectType="Visual C++"
   Version="8.00"
   Name="PandaSettings"
   >
   <Tool
     Name="VCCLCompilerTool"
     AdditionalIncludeDirectories="&quot;..\Lib\bullet-2.77\src&quot;;&quot;C:\Panda3D-1.7.0\python\include&quot;;&quot;C:\Panda3D-1.7.0\include&quot;"
   />
   <Tool
     Name="VCLinkerTool"
     AdditionalDependencies="BulletDynamics.lib BulletCollision.lib LinearMath.lib libp3framework.lib libpanda.lib libpandafx.lib libpandaexpress.lib libp3dtool.lib libp3dtoolconfig.lib libp3pystub.lib libp3direct.lib"
     AdditionalLibraryDirectories="&quot;..\Lib\bullet-2.77\msvc\2008\lib\Release&quot;;&quot;C:\Panda3D-1.7.0\python\libs&quot;;&quot;C:\Panda3D-1.7.0\lib&quot;"
   />
</VisualStudioPropertySheet>
```

7. Open your solution again.

8. Edit `main.cpp` and add the `main` function:

```cpp
#include "Application.h"

PandaFramework framework;

int main(int argc, char* argv[])
{
  Application app(argc, argv);
  app.run();
  return 0;
}
```

9. Add a new file called `Application.h` and add the declaration of the `Application` and `BulletTask` classes:

```cpp
#pragma once

#include <pandaFramework.h>
#include <pandaSystem.h>
#include <asyncTask.h>
#include <btBulletDynamicsCommon.h>

class Application
{
public:
  Application(int argc, char* argv[]);
  ~Application();
  void run();

private:
  void init();
  void setupBullet();
  void addGround();
  void updateBullet();

private:
  NodePath render;
  NodePath cam;
  NodePath smiley;
  WindowFramework* win;
  PandaFramework framework;

  btBroadphaseInterface*  broadphase;
  btCollisionDispatcher*  dispatcher;
  btConstraintSolver*  solver;
  btDefaultCollisionConfiguration* collisionConfiguration;
  btDynamicsWorld* btWorld;
};

class BulletTask
{
public:
  static AsyncTask::DoneStatus updateBullet(GenericAsyncTask*
task, void* data);
};
```

10. Create another new file called `SmileyMotionState.h`. Insert the following code for declaring the `SmileyMotionState` class:

```
#pragma once

#include <pandaFramework.h>
#include <pandaSystem.h>
#include <btBulletDynamicsCommon.h>


class SmileyMotionState : public btMotionState
{
public:
  SmileyMotionState(const btTransform& start, const NodePath& sm);
  virtual ~SmileyMotionState() {}
  virtual void getWorldTransform(btTransform& trans) const;
  virtual void setWorldTransform(const btTransform& trans);

protected:
  btTransform transform;
  NodePath smiley;
};
```

11. Add a new header file called `SmileyTask.h` and add another class declaration:

```
#pragma once

#include <pandaFramework.h>
#include <pandaSystem.h>
#include <asyncTask.h>
#include <randomizer.h>
#include <btBulletDynamicsCommon.h>

class SmileyTask
{
public:
  SmileyTask(NodePath& rndr, NodePath& sm, btDynamicsWorld*
world);
  static AsyncTask::DoneStatus addSmiley(GenericAsyncTask* task,
void* data);

  NodePath render;
  NodePath smiley;
  btDynamicsWorld* btWorld;
  int smileyCount;
};
```

12. Add a new code file to the solution. Call it `SmileyTask.cpp` and populate it with the following code:

```cpp
#include "SmileyTask.h"
#include "SmileyMotionState.h"

SmileyTask::SmileyTask(NodePath& rndr, NodePath& sm,
btDynamicsWorld* world)
{
  smileyCount = 0;
  smiley = sm;
  render = rndr;
  btWorld = world;
}

AsyncTask::DoneStatus SmileyTask::addSmiley(GenericAsyncTask*
task, void* data)
{
  SmileyTask* add = reinterpret_cast<SmileyTask*>(data);
  NodePath render = add->render;
  NodePath smiley = add->smiley;
  btDynamicsWorld* btWorld = add->btWorld;

  NodePath sm = render.attach_new_node("smiley-instance");
  Randomizer rnd;
  smiley.instance_to(sm);

  btCollisionShape* shape = new btSphereShape(btScalar(1));

  btTransform trans;
  trans.setIdentity();
  trans.setOrigin(btVector3(rnd.random_real(40) - 20, rnd.random_
real(20) + 10, rnd.random_real(60) - 30));

  btScalar mass(10);
  btVector3 inertia(0, 0, 0);
  shape->calculateLocalInertia(mass, inertia);

  SmileyMotionState* ms = new SmileyMotionState(trans, sm);
  btRigidBody::btRigidBodyConstructionInfo info(mass, ms, shape,
inertia);
  info.m_restitution = btScalar(0.5f);
  info.m_friction = btScalar(0.7f);
  btRigidBody* body = new btRigidBody(info);
```

```
btWorld->addRigidBody(body);

add->smileyCount++;
if (add->smileyCount == 100)
  return AsyncTask::DS_done;

return AsyncTask::DS_again;
}
```

13. Create another file called `SmileyMotionState.cpp` and fill it with this following snippet:

```
#include "SmileyMotionState.h"

SmileyMotionState::SmileyMotionState(const btTransform& start,
const NodePath& sm)
{
  transform = start;
  smiley = sm;
}

void SmileyMotionState::getWorldTransform(btTransform& trans)
const
{
  trans = transform;
}

void SmileyMotionState::setWorldTransform(const btTransform&
trans)
{
  transform = trans;
  btQuaternion rot = trans.getRotation();
  LQuaternionf prot(rot.w(), -rot.x(), -rot.z(), -rot.y());
  smiley.set_hpr(prot.get_hpr());
  btVector3 pos = trans.getOrigin();
  smiley.set_pos(pos.x(), pos.z(), pos.y());
}
```

14. Add one last file called `Application.cpp` and add the code below:

```
#include <cardMaker.h>
#include "Application.h"
#include "SmileyTask.h"

Application::Application(int argc, char* argv[])
{
```

```
    framework.open_framework(argc, argv);
    win = framework.open_window();
    cam = win->get_camera_group();
    render = win->get_render();
}

Application::~Application()
{
}

void Application::run()
{
    init();
    framework.main_loop();
    framework.close_framework();
}

void Application::init()
{
    setupBullet();
    PT(AsyncTaskManager) taskMgr = AsyncTaskManager::get_global_
ptr();

    smiley = win->load_model(framework.get_models(), "frowney");
    SmileyTask* add = new SmileyTask(render, smiley, btWorld);
    PT(GenericAsyncTask) addSmiley = new GenericAsyncTask("AddSmiley
", &SmileyTask::addSmiley, add);
    addSmiley->set_delay(0.01);
    taskMgr->add(addSmiley);

    PT(GenericAsyncTask) bt = new GenericAsyncTask("UpdateBullet",
&BulletTask::updateBullet, btWorld);
    taskMgr->add(bt);

    addGround();
    cam.set_pos(0, -100, 10);
}

void Application::setupBullet()
{
    collisionConfiguration = new btDefaultCollisionConfiguration();
    dispatcher = new btCollisionDispatcher(collisionConfiguration);
    broadphase = new btDbvtBroadphase();
```

```
  btSequentialImpulseConstraintSolver* sol = new
btSequentialImpulseConstraintSolver;
  solver = sol;


  btWorld = new btDiscreteDynamicsWorld(dispatcher, broadphase,
solver, collisionConfiguration);
  btWorld->setGravity(btVector3(0, -9.81f, 0));
}

void Application::addGround()
{
  CardMaker cm("ground");
  cm.set_frame(-500, 500, -500, 500);
  NodePath ground = render.attach_new_node(cm.generate());
  ground.look_at(0, 0, -1);
  ground.set_color(0.2f, 0.6f, 0.2f);

  btCollisionShape* shape = new btBoxShape(btVector3(btScalar(500)
, btScalar(0.5f), btScalar(500)));

  btTransform trans;
  trans.setIdentity();
  trans.setOrigin(btVector3(0, -0.5f, 0));

  btDefaultMotionState* ms = new btDefaultMotionState(trans);
  btScalar mass(0);
  btVector3 inertia(0, 0, 0);
  btRigidBody::btRigidBodyConstructionInfo info(mass, ms, shape,
inertia);
  info.m_restitution = btScalar(0.5f);
  info.m_friction = btScalar(0.7f);
  btRigidBody* body = new btRigidBody(info);

  btWorld->addRigidBody(body);
}

AsyncTask::DoneStatus BulletTask::updateBullet(GenericAsyncTask*
task, void* data)
{
  btScalar dt(ClockObject::get_global_clock()->get_dt());
  btDynamicsWorld* btWorld = reinterpret_cast<btDynamicsWorld*>(da
ta);
  btWorld->stepSimulation(dt);
  return AsyncTask::DS_cont;
}
```

15. Press *Ctrl* + *F5* to compile and run the program:

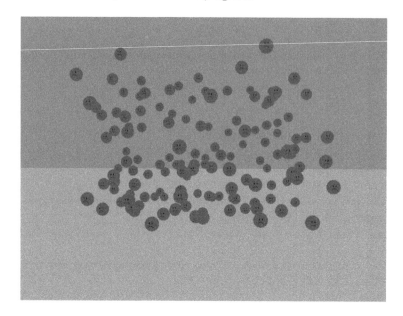

How it works...

First, we need to set up our environment: We unpack Bullet to the right location and compile it. We also modify the property file to add the search paths for Bullet's libraries and header files.

After we completely rewrite main.cpp, we go on to define the interfaces of the classes for our little sample program. The Application class, just like in the Python code samples, keeps everything together and controls the application behavior. BulletTask only contains the static method that is used to perform simulation steps. A SmileyMotionState is created for every new smiley created throughout the program's runtime. Motion state objects are a convenient way for Bullet to keep object transformations up-to-date as they provide a per-object callback mechanism that allows Bullet to inject new and updated data. Lastly, we define the interface of SmileyTask, which is responsible for creating new smileys.

The next thing we add is the implementation of SmileyTask. In the static member function, we first retrieve the necessary objects from the context data we pass into the function using the data parameter.

Additionally, we can observe how Bullet's interface for adding a new object to the simulation works. We need to combine a shape, mass, inertia, and motion state into a btRigidBodyConstructionInfo object that we can also use to set the object's material parameters for bounciness and friction. This info is then used to construct the new object, which is then added to our physics world.

In the implementation of `SmileyMotionState`, nothing too obscure is happening. The getter and setter methods return and set transformation data and where necessary convert between the data types of Bullet and Panda3D.

Bullet uses a different coordinate system than Panda3D. In Bullet's representation of the scene, the y-axis points up, while in Panda3D, the z-axis points up. Since they are different, in the sample code, the z- and y-axes are flipped to accommodate this situation.

The code in `Application.cpp` is responsible for opening the application window and initializing the Panda3D framework. It also sets up Bullet's `btDiscreteDynamicsWorld` and sets up the scene.

9
Networking

In this chapter, we will cover:

- ▸ Downloading a file from a server
- ▸ Using assets hosted on a server
- ▸ Sending high scores to a server
- ▸ Establishing a network connection
- ▸ Sending and receiving custom datagrams
- ▸ Synchronizing object state between server and client

Introduction

Thanks to the adoption of networking features, today's video games provide a great deal of additional value. While you are reading this, millions of gamers across the globe are playing their favorite games against each other or cooperatively, submitting scores to online leaderboards or retrieving the latest package of downloadable bonus content. Without a doubt, games providing networking features are opening the doors for players to compete, communicate, and connect.

Panda3D, being the engine behind Disney Interactive's Pirates of the Caribbean Online, comes with a set of built-in features for developing features that make use of network connections. In this chapter you will learn how to access remote content and how to implement a very simple online leaderboard. You will also be introduced to the basics of writing a custom network protocol and replicating the state of an object across hosts.

Downloading a file from a server

It is a very common property of today's games—even those that are strictly single player—to connect to a server at some point in time to retrieve data such as the latest headlines from the game's official website, leaderboards, patches or the latest bonus content package. By the end of this recipe you will be able to do so as well.

Hosting files on a web server is very simple to set up and reasonably priced these days. Additionally, this makes it easy to use Panda3D's built in networking features. The engine comes with a class called `HTTPClient` that hides the complexities of communicating with a web server.

In this sample you will learn how to connect to a server, download some data and display it on the screen.

Getting ready

This recipe will use the framework presented in *Setting up the game structure* found in *Chapter 1, Setting Up Panda3D and Configuring Development Tools*. Please set up your project prior to going on with the following tasks.

How to do it...

Complete these tasks to make Panda3D download files from a server:

1. Open `Application.py` and fill in the following code:

```
from direct.showbase.ShowBase import ShowBase
from panda3d.core import *
from direct.gui.OnscreenImage import OnscreenImage

class Application(ShowBase):
    def __init__(self):
        ShowBase.__init__(self)
        self.http = HTTPClient.getGlobalPtr()
        self.channel = self.http.makeChannel(False)
        self.channel.beginGetDocument(DocumentSpec("http://www.
panda3d.org/images/panda-logo-2.png"))
        self.channel.downloadToFile(Filename("panda.png"))
        taskMgr.add(self.downloadData, "downloadData")

    def downloadData(self, task):
        if self.channel.run():
            return task.cont

        if not self.channel.isDownloadComplete():
            print "Unable to download file."
            return task.done
```

```
else:
    OnscreenImage("panda.png", scale = Vec3(0.2, 0, 0.2))
    return task.done
```

2. Press *F6* to launch the program. After a short moment you should be able to see the following result:

How it works...

Now that our little program is able to download an image file to disk and display it on the screen, let's take a look at the steps that are necessary to achieve this goal.

First, we retrieve a reference to the global singleton instance of HTTPClient that Panda3D creates for us automatically. We could also create a new instance here, which wouldn't alter anything about this program's behavior apart from a minimally increased memory footprint.

We then go on to create a new HTTPChannel object by calling the makeChannel() method on our HTTPClient. This channel object represents the communication line to the server over which we will retrieve the image file. We also pass False as an argument, which makes the channel non-persistent. This means that immediately after the requested file has finished downloading, the connection will be closed. This fits our use case pretty well as we want to retrieve only one single file from the server. If we wanted to download a series of files, we would use a persistent connection. This is more efficient as the connection is kept open and reused instead of opening a new one for each request.

The next two calls, beginGetDocument() and downloadToFile(), are used to set which file to request from the server and where to store it. We try to retrieve a file hosted on the website of Panda3D, but we could easily replace it with a URL that points to a different resource, hosted on another server. Note, however, how we need to hand the URL to a new DocumentSpec object, which is responsible for handling whether the file can be retrieved from the local cache or needs to be downloaded.

By using downloadToFile(), we configure our HTTPChannel to download the requested data into a local file. Alternatively, we could also use downloadToRam() to store the data in a Ramfile object that represents a virtual file that uses the system's RAM for storage instead of the hard disk.

The call to `beginGetDocument()` is non-blocking. This means that instead of waiting for the complete download to finish within the execution of this method, it places a request for the desired file. Then the call returns and the program continues execution from that point onward. To actually download data after requesting it, we need to periodically update our channel using the `run()` method that is called periodically inside the `downloadData` task. This task will keep on updating the channel as long as there is data incoming before checking if the download has finished. As soon as the file is retrieved to the local hard drive, a new `OnscreenImage` is created to display the downloaded image.

Using assets hosted on a server

Panda3D features a very advanced virtual file system that makes it possible to transparently handle and load file data from various sources, such as directories in the local file system or archive files that contain resources themselves (See *Chapter 12, Packaging and Distribution* for more info on multifile archives and packages). Every time you call `loader.loadModel()`, the engine tries to find and load the requested model from one of the sources that have been added to the file system structure before.

However, files do not have to be stored on the local system to be used by Panda3D. The virtual file system also allows mounting directories hosted on web servers. Files that reside on the remote system are downloaded transparently as needed whenever they are requested by your application, without having to write any extra code apart from the call that adds the resources on the server to Panda3D's file system.

This can be very practical for games that feature constantly evolving worlds or for hosting in-game advertisements. This also allows you to build a very lean version of your game that only contains some basic assets—keeping the initial download size small. Additional game content will then be streamed in on-demand as the player progresses through the game.

Getting ready

Before going on, set up a new project as shown in *Setting up the game structure* as found in *Chapter 1*.

How to do it...

Let's see how we can use some remotely hosted assets:

1. Edit `Application.py` to exactly resemble the following lines of code:

```
from direct.showbase.ShowBase import ShowBase
from panda3d.core import *
from direct.gui.OnscreenImage import OnscreenImage
```

```
class Application(ShowBase):
    def __init__(self):
        ShowBase.__init__(self)
        vfs = VirtualFileSystem.getGlobalPtr()
        vfs.mount(VirtualFileMountHTTP("http://www.panda3d.org/
images/"), "/http", VirtualFileSystem.MFReadOnly)
        getModelPath().appendDirectory("/http")
        OnscreenImage("panda-logo-2.png", scale = Vec3(0.2, 0,
0.2))
```

2. Press *F6* to run the sample. You should be able to see the same output as in *Downloading a file from a server*.

How it works...

This little program is a great sample for how Panda3D wraps an advanced feature into an easy to use API. All we need to do is get the pointer to the global `VirtualFileSystem` object and `mount()` our new source. We're passing the `MFReadOnly` flag, as we only need to read from, but never write to, our remotely hosted data.

The server directory is added to the virtual file system at the mount point `/http`. This means that all files and directories found in the server's directory will be visible as children of the `http` directory. The `http` directory in turn is a subdirectory of the virtual file system's root directory.

To make things even easier, `getModelPath().appendDirectory("/http")` adds the `http` directory to the model path so we do not need to provide full file paths when loading assets, given that there are no name clashes, of course.

Finally, the last line of our program's code shows a remote file being referenced. There is no visible difference to loading a local file. The internals of the engine are taking care of downloading the file from the server and adding its contents to the scene.

Sending high scores to a server

In this recipe we are going to take a look at the very basics of implementing a feature that allows us to submit scores to a server that processes and stores the data we are sending. Additionally, we will be able to view the list of submitted scores using a web browser.

The server side of this project will be implemented using the Twisted framework (`http://twistedmatrix.com`). The libraries contained in Twisted make it very easy to implement servers and clients for all kinds of common and custom network protocols. For our purpose, we are going to implement a little custom web server that will accept POST requests for submitting data and will serve the static scoreboard page.

It is important to note that there are several other Python frameworks like Twisted available. Tornado (`http://www.tornadoweb.org`) and Diesel (`http://dieselweb.org`) are just two examples of network programming frameworks similar to Twisted. All of them have their upsides and downsides, but in the end Twisted was chosen here out of pure preference as well as for its ease of use. Not to mention that it is implemented in Python, which makes it a good fit among all the other Python code in this recipe and this book.

Getting ready

Before we can begin working on the following steps, we need to install the Twisted framework first using a collection of Python scripts called "setuptools". This is a set of command line tools that handle installing and managing additional third-party libraries from the Python Package Index hosted on `http://pypi.python.org/pypi`. This is a great source for Python programming libraries and frameworks, definitely worth some time to browse and explore!

To get set for the following tasks, first follow these steps:

1. Open your browser and go to `http://pypi.python.org/pypi/setuptools`.

2. Scroll down the page until you find the following table of download links:

File	Type	Py Version	Uploaded on	Size	# downloads
setuptools-0.6c11-1.src.rpm (md5) built for redhat 4.3	RPM	any	2009-10-20	263KB	9477
setuptools-0.6c11-py2.3.egg (md5)	Python Egg	2.3	2009-10-20	1MB	6531
setuptools-0.6c11-py2.4.egg (md5)	Python Egg	2.4	2009-10-20	329KB	119632
setuptools-0.6c11-py2.5.egg (md5)	Python Egg	2.5	2009-10-20	325KB	205436
setuptools-0.6c11-py2.6.egg (md5)	Python Egg	2.6	2009-10-20	325KB	292394
setuptools-0.6c11-py2.7.egg (md5)	Python Egg	2.7	2010-07-08	324KB	43110
setuptools-0.6c11.tar.gz (md5)	Source		2009-10-20	250KB	108036
setuptools-0.6c11.win32-py2.3.exe (md5)	MS Windows installer	2.3	2009-10-20	218KB	3608
setuptools-0.6c11.win32-py2.4.exe (md5)	MS Windows installer	2.4	2009-10-20	222KB	3764
setuptools-0.6c11.win32-py2.5.exe (md5)	MS Windows installer	2.5	2009-10-20	222KB	24971
setuptools-0.6c11.win32-py2.6.exe (md5)	MS Windows installer	2.6	2009-10-20	222KB	75119
setuptools-0.6c11.win32-py2.7.exe (md5)	MS Windows installer	2.7	2010-07-08	222KB	13316

3. Download the file `setuptools-0.6c11.win32-py2.6.exe`. The exact filename and version may vary slightly because of newer releases but it is important to watch for the string `win32-py2.6` in the filename to match the version of Python used in Panda3D.

4. After the file has finished downloading, launch the executable. This will start an installer program. Click **Next** until you see the following screen:

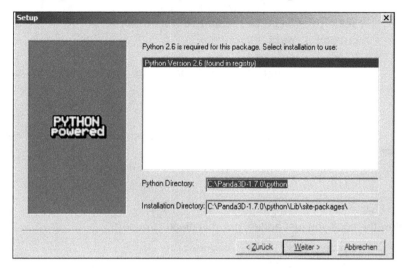

5. Choose the Python installation that comes with Panda3D, if you happen to have multiple versions of Python installed on your system. Double check the **Python Directory** field – this has to match your Panda3D installation directory!

6. After the installer has finished, add the directory `C:\Panda3D-1.7.0\python\Scripts` to the system search path.

7. Open a command prompt and enter the command `easy_install Twisted`. This will download and set up all components needed for using the Twisted framework.

Now that the dependencies are installed and ready, it is time to finish the preparation steps by creating two projects. For the first one, follow *Setting up the game structure* found in *Chapter 1* and name the project **PostScore**. This will be our client application.

When creating the second project, follow the same recipe again, but only up to step 3, naming the project **ScoreServer**. This is where we will implement the server side of this sample.

How to do it...

This recipe consists of the following tasks:

1. Open the `main.py` file that's part of the **ScoreServer** project and replace its content with the following code:

```
from twisted.web.server import Site
from twisted.web.resource import Resource
from twisted.internet import reactor
import sqlite3
```

```
class ScorePage(Resource):
    def __init__(self):
        Resource.__init__(self)
        self.db = sqlite3.connect("scores.db")
        cursor = self.db.cursor()
        args = ("scores",)
        cursor.execute("select name from sqlite_master where
name=?", args)

        if len(cursor.fetchall()) == 0:
            cursor.execute("create table scores (player text,
score integer)")
            self.db.commit()

        cursor.close()
```

2. Below the code you just added, put this piece of code:

```
def render_POST(self, request):
    cursor = self.db.cursor()

    args = (request.args["player"][0],)
    cursor.execute("select * from scores where player=?",
args)

    if len(cursor.fetchall()) > 0:
        args = (request.args["score"][0], request.
args["player"][0])
        cursor.execute("update scores set score=? where
player=?", args)
    else:
        args = (request.args["player"][0], request.
args["score"][0])
        cursor.execute("insert into scores values (?,?)",
args)

    self.db.commit()
    cursor.close()
    return "OK"
```

3. Then, add the following method:

```
def render_GET(self, request):
    cursor = self.db.cursor()
    cursor.execute("select * from scores order by score desc")
    data = cursor.fetchall()
    cursor.close()
```

```
        result = str("\n".join(["%s %s" % (p, s) for p, s in
    data]))
        request.setHeader("Content-Type", "text/plain;
    charset=utf-8")
        return result
```

4. Now we need to add the following main function that will start up our server:

```
if __name__ == "__main__":
    root = Resource()
    root.putChild("score", ScorePage())
    factory = Site(root)
    reactor.listenTCP(80, factory)
    reactor.run()
```

5. For implementing the client, open the file Application.py and fill in the code below:

```
from direct.showbase.ShowBase import ShowBase
from panda3d.core import *

class Application(ShowBase):
    def __init__(self):
        ShowBase.__init__(self)
        self.http = HTTPClient.getGlobalPtr()
        self.channel = self.http.makeChannel(False)
        self.channel.beginPostForm(DocumentSpec("http://localhost/
    score"), "player=Foo&score=1337")
        self.ram = Ramfile()
        self.channel.downloadToRam(self.ram)
        taskMgr.add(self.updateChannel, "updateChannel")

    def updateChannel(self, task):
        if self.channel.run():
            return task.cont
        elif self.channel.isDownloadComplete():
            print self.ram.getData()
            return task.done
        else:
            print "Error posting score."
```

6. To start the server, right-click the **ScoreServer** node in the project tree and click on **Run**, as shown in the following screenshot:

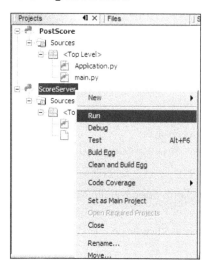

7. Repeat the last step to run the **PostScore** project.

8. To view the list of scores, open a browser and go to `http://localhost/score`.

9. To stop the server, find the entry in NetBean's status bar (at the bottom right of the window, as shown in the screenshot) that reads **ScoreServer** and **Running** and click the little **x** button next to it.

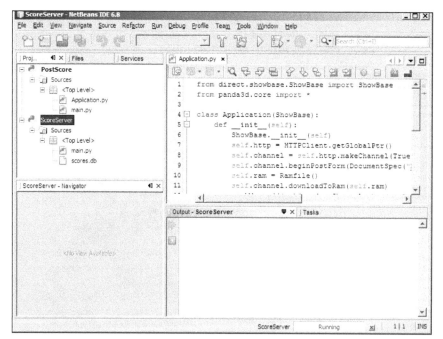

How it works...

First, let's take a look at how our server works. For this we need to understand the programming model of the Twisted framework: At the core of our application we find the `reactor` object that is responsible for opening ports and polling them in its internal event loop. In our case, port 80 (the standard for a HTTP server) is opened to listen for TCP connections, which leads us directly to the next layer.

When opening the server port, we pass a new object of the class `Site` that is responsible for processing the data that is received and sent over our newly opened port as HTTP requests. This means that with these steps, we have already created a web server. The only problem is that as our web server currently is, it would not provide any interesting data.

To add resources that can be queried and retrieved, we first add an empty Resource at the site's root folder. We do not want our server to host anything there. The only thing a client will receive if they request at the document root of our server is an error code, specifically 503. This error means that it is forbidden to access the requested resource. Instead, we add a new child to our virtual directory tree called `score`. This causes our service to be reachable via the URL `http://localhost/score`.

To be able to accept new scores being submitted by players and present the score list, we add our custom `ScorePage` subclass of `Resource` to the aforementioned virtual server directory.

In the constructor of `ScorePage`, we connect to an `SQLite` database, check if a table called `scores` exists, and create it if necessary. `SQLite` is a very lightweight SQL database implementation that stores its data in a specially formatted local file. It is mainly intended for small, single user applications, which means that for a serious attempt at implementing a server that stores scores, we should think about using a database system that is aimed at bigger scale use cases.

Querying the database requires us to use a cursor object. After executing the query, the cursor holds the results, which we then can retrieve using the `fetchall()` method. If we made changes to the database's layout or data, we need to `commit()` these changes, or they will be dropped. Also, after we are done with our queries, we should not forget to `close()` the cursor to free any resources or handles we might still be holding.

This leaves the `render_POST()` and `render_GET()` methods to be discussed on the server side of our project. The `render_POST()` method is called whenever a client sends data to our server. We then check if a player with the given name has already submitted a score that we need to update or if we need to create a new record in our database. After the data is processed and stored in the database, we're done receiving the request and return the string `"OK"` to the client to signal that no error occurred.

An `HTTP GET` request asks the server to return the data it hosts at a given address. The `render_GET()` method builds this data on the fly as new requests for retrieving the resource located at the score directory of the server are received by the server. Our code queries the database to return all submitted scores, ordered by score in descending order. We build a plain text list of strings, where each line contains a player name and a score, hence the `text/plain` MIME type is set in the header of the reply that will be sent back to the client. Of course, we could also return a string that contains HTML and omit setting the MIME type so the client (that is most likely going to be a web browser) will interpret it as a web page.

Before going on to discussing the client side, we should stop and think about an important issue that we have not addressed so far in the server code: security. First, our little server does not perform any sanity checks on the data submitted to it. In a production system, make sure to define which ranges and data types are allowed and add checking routines to prevent possible attacks based on submitting malicious data.

The second point we did not address is client authentication and authorization. So far, any program that is able to send a `POST` request could possibly submit data to our server. Surely, we would only want our game to be able to submit data to prevent cheaters from submitting arbitrarily crafted scores, so some mechanisms for verifying clients and encrypting the submitted data will have to be put into place.

Finally, we can take a look at the client, where we use the `HTTPClient` to send our request and retrieve the server's reply, which has already been discussed in the recipe *Downloading a file from a server* found earlier in this chapter. Instead of requesting a document, we use the `beginPostForm()` method to send data to the server. What's particularly interesting about this call is the second parameter it accepts, which is the data to send.

The data is sent using a key-value form. Each of these key-value pairs takes the following form `key=value`. We can send multiples of these pairs in one request, as shown in the sample code, using the ampersand (&) sign as a delimiter between each key-value pair.

Establishing a network connection

While the recipes preceding this one have shown off some neat networking features of the Panda3D engine using standard communication protocols, none of them have touched upon the topic of implementing the lower-level custom network protocols needed for synchronizing game objects across players connected to a game server. Starting with this recipe though, we change that situation. The rest of this chapter will be dedicated to how to open a connection and exchange custom crafted data between hosts.

Why games might require special network handling, such that you need to know about lower-level custom networking protocols?

The problems game developers have to solve when developing online multiplayer games are plenty. First of all, each game is a unique case on its own: First, there are different types of games, like shooters, racing games, or online role-playing games. Every game out of any category offers a different set of game modes, gameplay, game mechanics, objects, and ways of interaction. Apart from offering non-standardized experiences, each online game has a different set of requirements for its multiplayer functionality: An MMO has to be able to let thousands of players share the same world at the same time, while a fast-paced shooter has to minimize the communication lag between hosts to allow precise and accurate player movement and hit detection.

These are just a few simple samples, but ultimately it's up to us game developers to find solutions for all of these problems. This means that we need to be in control over how, when and which data is sent to meet our games' requirements.

This recipe marks the beginning of a three-part series. First we will shed some light on the components that are involved in getting Panda3D to talk over a network and how to establish a connection. Second, we will implement a tiny custom protocol for learning how to build and send custom datagrams across a network. Finally, in the third part of the series, we will implement a basic sample for synchronizing the state of a game object as a start for implementing a custom network protocol for a game.

Getting ready

We will build this sample on the foundation created in *Setting up the game structure* found in *Chapter 1*. Take a step back to read that recipe before continuing if you're unsure.

Unlike the other recipes in this chapter, we will be building this sample from our basic project setup without using any additional libraries or frameworks.

How to do it...

Let's implement a basic client and server and open a connection between them:

1. Add the required `import` statements and the `NetCommon` class to `Application.py`:

```python
from direct.showbase.ShowBase import ShowBase
from panda3d.core import *

class NetCommon:
    def __init__(self, protocol):
        self.manager = ConnectionManager()
        self.reader = QueuedConnectionReader(self.manager, 0)
        self.writer = ConnectionWriter(self.manager, 0)
        self.protocol = protocol
```

```
                    taskMgr.add(self.updateReader, "updateReader")

        def updateReader(self, task):
            if self.reader.dataAvailable():
                data = NetDatagram()
                self.reader.getData(data)
                reply = self.protocol.process(data)

                if reply != None:
                    self.writer.send(reply, data.getConnection())

            return task.cont
```

2. Below `NetCommon`, implement the `Server` class:

```
    class Server(NetCommon):
        def __init__(self, protocol, port):
            NetCommon.__init__(self, protocol)
            self.listener = QueuedConnectionListener(self.manager, 0)
            socket = self.manager.openTCPServerRendezvous(port, 100)
            self.listener.addConnection(socket)
            self.connections = []

            taskMgr.add(self.updateListener, "updateListener")

        def updateListener(self, task):
            if self.listener.newConnectionAvailable():
                connection = PointerToConnection()
                if self.listener.getNewConnection(connection):
                    connection = connection.p()
                    self.connections.append(connection)
                    self.reader.addConnection(connection)
                    print "Server: New connection established."

            return task.cont
```

3. Now it's time to add the implementation of the `Client` and `Protocol` classes:

```
    class Client(NetCommon):
        def __init__(self, protocol):
            NetCommon.__init__(self, protocol)

        def connect(self, host, port, timeout):
            self.connection = self.manager.openTCPClientConnection(hos
    t, port, timeout)
```

```
        if self.connection:
            self.reader.addConnection(self.connection)
            print "Client: Connected to server."

    def send(self, datagram):
        if self.connection:
            self.writer.send(datagram, self.connection)

class Protocol:
    def process(self, data):
        return None
```

4. To finish coding for this recipe, it's time to modify the `Application` class to look like this:

```
class Application(ShowBase):
    def __init__(self):
        ShowBase.__init__(self)
        server = Server(Protocol(), 9999)
        client = Client(Protocol())
        client.connect("localhost", 9999, 3000)
```

5. Start the program. If everything went right you will be able to see the following lines in the **Output** area of NetBeans:

Client: Connected to server.

Server: New connection established.

How it works...

To avoid duplication of code, we begin this recipe by adding the `NetCommon` class to `Application.py`. In the constructor we can already see some of the main components needed for implementing custom network functionality in Panda3D.

The `ConnectionManager` class handles opening ports, initiating connections to remote hosts and encapsulates all the low level IO operations involved when communicating over a network. Additionally, we need to create `QueuedConnectionReader` and a `ConnectionWriter`, responsible for reading and writing data respectively. `QueuedConnectionReader` is a subclass of `ConnectionReader` that buffers all incoming datagrams so they can be processed one after another in the `updateReader()` task. This task periodically polls the reader object for newly available data. If anything has been received, it is handed to the `process()` method of a `Protocol` object, which decides how to react to the received data and which reply to send.

Currently, we only have a `Protocol` class that doesn't do anything. This will change in the following recipes, where we will use different protocol implementations to define the behaviors of client and server.

The NetCommon class already contains a good part of what's necessary for sending and receiving data over a network, but to create a server we still need to derive a new class and add some additional features. We need a QueuedConnectionListener to listen for new connections on the network port that is opened using the call to openTCPServerRendezvous(). The first parameter defines the port number our server will listen on for connections. The second parameter sets the maximum amount of simultaneous connection attempts. If the number of requests exceeds this value, new connection attempts are simply ignored.

Similar to the QueuedConnectionReader class, QueuedConnectionListener buffers requests for new connections and needs to be polled in a task where new connections are put into a list and registered to the QueuedConnectionReader owned by the class so incoming data is received and processed.

All we need to add to the Client class, on the other hand, are the connect() and send() methods. The former opens a new connection to a server. For this we need to specify the target host and port as well as the maximum time to wait for a reply before considering the connection to be terminated. The latter method is just a wrapper for sending a datagram.

In the constructor of Application we finally create a new Server and Client object and connect them using the internal loopback connection. Both client and server are using our stub protocol that does nothing yet. If you want this to change, go on to the next recipe!

Sending and receiving custom datagrams

After having built the groundwork for opening network connections, it's time to implement our first self-defined network protocol. To achieve this goal, we are going to implement new classes derived from Protocol that will piece together custom datagrams. We will then send these datagrams back and forth between our client and server to have them a nice little chat.

Getting ready

This recipe directly continues where the last one left off. So if you didn't read that part yet, take one step back and start from the beginning to create the prerequisites for this recipe and better understand what will be shown here.

How to do it...

Follow these steps to implement your own network protocol:

1. Open Application.py and add the following import statements to the top of the file:

```
from direct.distributed.PyDatagram import PyDatagram
from direct.distributed.PyDatagramIterator import
PyDatagramIterator
```

2. Add the following two methods to the `Protocol` class:

```
def printMessage(self, title, msg):
    print "%s %s" % (title, msg)

def buildReply(self, msgid, data):
    reply = PyDatagram()
    reply.addUint8(msgid)
    reply.addString(data)
    return reply
```

3. Directly below the code of the `Protocol` class, add this:

```
class ServerProtocol(Protocol):
    def process(self, data):
        it = PyDatagramIterator(data)
        msgid = it.getUint8()

        if msgid == 0:
            return self.handleHello(it)
        elif msgid == 1:
            return self.handleQuestion(it)
        elif msgid == 2:
            return self.handleBye(it)

    def handleHello(self, it):
        self.printMessage("Server received:", it.getString())
        return self.buildReply(0, "Hello, too!")

    def handleQuestion(self, it):
        self.printMessage("Server received:", it.getString())
        return self.buildReply(1, "I'm fine. How are you?")

    def handleBye(self, it):
        self.printMessage("Server received:", it.getString())
        return self.buildReply(2, "Bye!")
```

4. Now add the `ClientProtocol` class below `ServerProtocol`:

```
class ClientProtocol(Protocol):
    def process(self, data):
        it = PyDatagramIterator(data)
        msgid = it.getUint8()

        if msgid == 0:
            return self.handleHello(it)
```

```
            elif msgid == 1:
                return self.handleQuestion(it)
            elif msgid == 2:
                return self.handleBye(it)

        def handleHello(self, it):
            self.printMessage("Client received:", it.getString())
            return self.buildReply(1, "How are you?")

        def handleQuestion(self, it):
            self.printMessage("Client received:", it.getString())
            return self.buildReply(2, "I'm fine too. Gotta run! Bye!")

        def handleBye(self, it):
            self.printMessage("Client received:", it.getString())
            return None
```

5. Modify the `Application` class to resemble the code below:

```
class Application(ShowBase):
    def __init__(self):
        ShowBase.__init__(self)
        server = Server(ServerProtocol(), 9999)
        client = Client(ClientProtocol())
        client.connect("localhost", 9999, 3000)

        data = PyDatagram()
        data.addUint8(0)
        data.addString("Hello!")
        client.send(data)
```

6. Start the program and watch the **Output** area. You should be able to observe the following output:

Client: Connected to server.

Server: New connection established.

Server received: Hello!

Client received: Hello, too!

Server received: How are you?

Client received: I'm fine. How are you?

Server received: I'm fine too. Gotta run! Bye!

Client received: Bye!

How it works...

As we can see in this sample, sending and receiving data over a network connection is really easy, thanks to the API provided by Panda3D. To send data, we need to create a new `PyDatagram` and add data fields using methods like `addString()` and `addUint8()` before passing it to a `ConnectionWriter` instance for sending. We are not limited to sending strings and 8 bit unsigned integers, though. `PyDatagram` features a whole lot of these `add*()` methods for floating point numbers and integers of various bit widths, for example.

To retrieve data that has been received over a network connection we have to pass it to a `PyDatagramIterator`. With the help of this class we are able to unpack the data fields from the datagram. Of course, this works quick and easy, but there's a catch to it that is very important to keep in mind: When retrieving data from a datagram using a `PyDatagramIterator`, the fields need to be accessed in exactly the same order as they were added to the `PyDatagram` before sending!

Using this knowledge, we were able to build a simple communication protocol that sends a numerical message id and a string. The receiver displays the string it got on the console and sends a reply containing a new message id and string based on the numerical id it received.

Synchronizing object state between server and client

Now that we know how to send custom data across a network connection, we can proceed to address one of the hardest issues of programming online games: game object synchronization.

There are two main challenges to this that we need to take on: The number one issue for networked multiplayer games is the communication lag between clients and the server. In many cases this is out of the hands of the developer, but we will find a way to smooth this out so that it is at least less noticeable on the client side.

The second problem is closely related to the lag issue: We just can't send a complete update of all active game objects' states every frame. This means state updates are sent to the client at a much lower rate than the game makes updates to its local state. Again, the trick is about smoothing things out to hide the issue from the player.

Getting ready

This recipe is the last part of a three-part series. Before proceeding, you should have followed and understood the recipes *Establishing a network connection* and *Sending and receiving custom datagrams* also found in this chapter. The following tasks will build upon the code created in the first part of the series.

How to do it...

Complete the tasks below to achieve the goal of this recipe and synchronize object state between two network hosts:

1. Append the following import statements to the ones already present in `Application.py`:

```
from direct.distributed.PyDatagram import PyDatagram
from direct.distributed.PyDatagramIterator import
PyDatagramIterator
import random
```

2. Add the class `ServerSmiley` to your code:

```
class ServerSmiley:
    def __init__(self):
        self.pos = Vec3(0, 0, 30)
        self.vel = 0

    def update(self):
        z = self.pos.getZ()
        if z <= 0:
            self.vel = random.uniform(0.1, 0.8)
        self.pos.setZ(z + self.vel)
        self.vel -= 0.01
```

3. Modify the constructor of the `Server` class to match the following code:

```
    def __init__(self, protocol, port):
        NetCommon.__init__(self, protocol)
        self.listener = QueuedConnectionListener(self.manager, 0)
        socket = self.manager.openTCPServerRendezvous(port, 100)
        self.listener.addConnection(socket)
        self.connections = []

        self.smiley = ServerSmiley()
        self.frowney = loader.loadModel("frowney")
        self.frowney.reparentTo(render)

        taskMgr.add(self.updateListener, "updateListener")
        taskMgr.add(self.updateSmiley, "updateSmiley")
        taskMgr.doMethodLater(0.5, self.syncSmiley, "syncSmiley")
```

4. Add these methods to the `Server` class:

```
    def updateSmiley(self, task):
        self.smiley.update()
        self.frowney.setPos(self.smiley.pos)
        return task.cont
```

```
        def syncSmiley(self, task):
            sync = PyDatagram()
            sync.addFloat32(self.smiley.vel)
            sync.addFloat32(self.smiley.pos.getZ())
            self.broadcast(sync)
            return task.again

        def broadcast(self, datagram):
            for conn in self.connections:
                self.writer.send(datagram, conn)
```

5. Add the class `ClientProtocol` to your code:

```
class ClientProtocol(Protocol):
    def __init__(self, smiley):
        self.smiley = smiley

    def process(self, data):
        it = PyDatagramIterator(data)
        vel = it.getFloat32()
        z = it.getFloat32()
        diff = z - self.smiley.getZ()
        self.smiley.setPythonTag("velocity", vel + diff * 0.03)
        return None
```

6. Modify the `Application` class so it resembles the code that follows below:

```
class Application(ShowBase):
    def __init__(self):
        ShowBase.__init__(self)
        server = Server(Protocol(), 9999)

        self.smiley = loader.loadModel("smiley")
        self.smiley.setPythonTag("velocity", 0)
        self.smiley.reparentTo(render)
        self.smiley.setPos(0, 0, 30)
        self.cam.setPos(0, -100, 10)

        client = Client(ClientProtocol(self.smiley))
        client.connect("localhost", 9999, 3000)

        taskMgr.add(self.updateSmiley, "updateSmiley")

    def updateSmiley(self, task):
        vel = self.smiley.getPythonTag("velocity")
        z = self.smiley.getZ()
```

```
if z <= 0:
    vel = random.uniform(0.1, 0.8)
self.smiley.setZ(z + vel)
vel -= 0.01
self.smiley.setPythonTag("velocity", vel)
return task.cont
```

7. Start the program. You should now see a smiley and a frowney bounce up and down very close to each other:

How it works...

In our little demo program, the server simulates the bouncy behavior of a ball and sends information about the ball's position and velocity to all connected clients. Because the server has control over the ball and its data will always be considered to be correct by the client, we say that the server has the authority over the ball.

While the simulation is running at full speed, the `syncSmiley()` function is only called once every 0.5 seconds to simulate lag and the limited server and bandwidth resources. If we just took the data coming from the server and replaced the current position and velocity values with the ones sent by the server, we would get some interesting but useless results. The client is, and will always be, behind the server state—this is a fact we cannot change. Updated data will arrive with a bit of delay every time and as soon as the client processes it, it is already out of date. This generates some uncertainty about the ball's actual position on the client side. This situation is visualized using the blue ball to show the position on the server, while the white and yellow ball shows the position on the client side. What we want is little to no distance between those two balls.

The first step we are taking to even out network and server lag is to duplicate the simulation on the client side. This keeps the game running smoothly on the player's computer and prevents objects from jumping from one point to the other because of the delayed arrival of updates.

But now there's another problem: Our client side simulation makes a call to a random number generator that does not deliver the same values as the one on the server, causing the local simulation to make the ball jump differently than the one simulated by the server. Why are we doing this? How are we going to fix it?

The reason for adding this additional amount of uncertainty to the client side is to show that the client always has to assume that its data is not precise or just plainly and simply wrong. Sure, it is a rather drastic sample, but this is what happens in real world applications more often than any developer would wish for. Possible causes for this, other than lag, can be physics engines that operate in a nondeterministic way or different floating point rounding errors.

To solve this issue, we built a clever little piece of code into the `process()` method of our `ClientProtocol` class. When the client receives an update from the server, it does not directly set the client ball's position and velocity (which should be avoided anyway, as it only results in jerky behavior of client side objects). Instead we add a small fraction of the vector that points from the client ball's position to the location of the ball on the server to the client's velocity value. This has the result of the ball on the client side slowly converging towards the correct position without giving the impression of objects jumping or being teleported between two points.

10
Debugging and Performance

In this chapter, we will cover:

- ▶ Debugging Python code
- ▶ Debugging C++ code
- ▶ Using the PStats tool for finding performance bottlenecks
- ▶ Improving performance by flattening scenes
- ▶ Implementing performance critical code in C++

Introduction

As game programmers, our job is to translate the rules, ways of interaction, and ideas defined either by us or the game designers and producers in our development team into program code. We act as the interface between the language of the designers and the language of the computer.

Most of the time we're doing fine when expressing game rules as clever algorithms, but from time to time things go wrong and bugs and errors are introduced to the game. While violations of programming language rules are detected and pointed out to us programmers by compilers and interpreters, errors caused by misinterpretations of the design specifications or by faulty algorithms are the ones that are putting us into all sorts of trouble.

Many of these programming mistakes cause wrong and unintended behavior that is immediately visible to players, who will at best be disappointed by a buggy and broken game. This means that we need to find and fix these errors to keep up quality and produce excellent games. To achieve this goal, we must realize two things: One, programming errors do happen—there's nothing to be ashamed of about that. What we should be ashamed of is being unable to find out what the problem is and how to fix it. Secondly, locating software bugs in big codebases can be a daunting, cumbersome, and even a near impossible task without the support of proper tools.

This is the reason why this chapter will introduce common programs and workflows involved in searching and fixing erroneous program code. Running a program in a debugger and stepping through the code line by line while inspecting its behavior is a part of the basics any programmer has to know!

While our first goal when developing program code should always be to write correct and working implementations of algorithms, there also are functional requirements we need to fulfill. In the case of game development, this mostly means one thing: Maintaining program performance to keep the game updating smoothly, at an interactive rate of thirty times per second or more.

This would be a much easier task if there were not game entity behaviors to be executed, collisions to be found and resolved, animations to be updated, and geometry to be rendered in every frame. A lot of things are going on when one single frame of a game is rendered, and whenever we hit a performance problem, we need to find the root of the problem and find a solution to the problem.

Of course this is not done by trial and error, but by measuring and observing the various components of our game code and the engine. For this purpose, we are going to use the profiling tool included with the Panda3D engine to learn about the possibilities and features it provides for locating performance problems.

Complex scenes containing lots of models are the cause of many performance problems. This is why this chapter will introduce the measures Panda3D provides for simplifying scenes to decrease the load on the scene management and the rendering stages of the engine.

Finally, we will take a look at how to add modules written in C++ to the engine, which can be useful for implementing very complex algorithms that perform poorly when written and run in Python.

Debugging Python code

As already stated in the introduction to this chapter, knowing the debugger of the language you are developing in and how to put it to use is part of the bread-and-butter business of a programmer, just like writing the code in the first place. In case of Python, this means knowing how to use the pdb debugger, which will be introduced throughout the course of this recipe.

The pdb debugger operates as an interactive prompt, accepting simple text commands that trigger actions like advancing program execution, or setting break points that stop program execution at a given line. In the following tasks, you will be walked through an example debug session, teaching you all the commands needed for analyzing code and hunting down those nasty bugs!

However, note that pdb is not the only debugger available for Python. There are plenty of alternatives available like pydbgr, pudb, or Winpdb that might provide more features or a user interface that's easier to use. Though the big plus point for pdb, on the other hand, is that it comes included with the Python runtime, that's part of the Panda3D engine.

Getting ready

The program you are going to debug is the one developed in the recipe *Managing recurring tasks*, found in *Chapter 7, Application Control*. Please prepare the code and before proceeding, make the following changes to the source code:

1. Delete the `removeSmileys()` method.

2. Find and delete the following line in the constructor:

    ```
    taskMgr.doMethodLater(60, taskMgr.remove, "RemoveUpdate",
    extraArgs = ["UpdateSmileys"])
    ```

3. Remove the `uponDeath` parameter from the call that adds the `updateSmileys()` method to the task manager.

Finally, check if Panda3D's `bin` directory can be found in the system search path. You can do this by opening a command prompt and issuing the command `ppython`. This should start an interactive Python session.

How to do it...

Let's take a look at the Python debugger:

1. Open a new command prompt window and navigate to the `src` subdirectory of your project directory.

2. Use the following command to start debugging the program:

    ```
    > ppython -m pdb main.py
    ```

3. In the newly opened command prompt, we first want to get an overview of the available commands:

    ```
    (Pdb) help
    ```

4. Place a temporary breakpoint at the first line of the `addSmiley()` method:

    ```
    (Pdb) tbreak Application.py:15
    ```

5. Create another breakpoint at the `updateSmileys()` method and set a condition for triggering the breakpoint:

   (Pdb) break Application.py:27

   (Pdb) condition 2 self.smileyCount > 50

6. List all active breakpoints:

   (Pdb) break

7. The program is in a halted state. Continue execution by entering the following command:

   (Pdb) continue

8. After a short moment of running, the application is stopped at the first breakpoint. Gather some context about where the execution flow was stopped. List an excerpt of the source code surrounding the breakpoint:

   (Pdb) list

9. Inspect the arguments that were passed to the method:

   (Pdb) args

10. Execute the `addSmiley()` method until the point from which it is going to return:

    (Pdb) return

11. Print the value of the `smileyCount` variable:

    (Pdb) p self.smileyCount

12. Continue execution until the next breakpoint is triggered:

    (Pdb) c

13. Display a stack trace:

    (Pdb) where

14. Execute the current and next line of code:

    (Pdb) next

    (Pdb) n

15. Check the type of the local variable `vel`:

    (Pdb) whatis vel

16. Change the value of the `smileyCount` variable and continue execution:

    (Pdb) !self.smileyCount = 55

    (Pdb) c

17. Clear the breakpoint in `updateSmileys()` and let the program continue execution:

    (Pdb) clear 2

    (Pdb) continue

How it works...

The pdb debugger is actually implemented as a Python module, which we load from the library search path using the `-m pdb` parameters we pass to the Python runtime. This starts up the debugger's command shell, loads our `main.py` file, and pauses program execution.

We then go on to add breakpoints to our code. A breakpoint marks a line of code so the debugger halts the program when it is reached while the program is executed. While a standard breakpoint, created with the `break` command, causes program execution to be stopped whenever it is hit, we add some special cases of breakpoints: A temporary and a conditional breakpoint.

Temporary breakpoints are deleted after being hit once. This is useful if you're only interested in the first iteration of a loop, for example. If you want to narrow down the cause of a bug in more detail, or want to skip loop iterations, conditional breakpoints allow the contents of variables to be examined and evaluated. Only if the expression provided evaluates to true, the program gets stopped.

Beneath breakpoints, another set of commands is dedicated to controlling how to run the program. Using `next`, `return`, and `continue`, we are able to execute step by step, to the point where the current function is about to return, or until the next breakpoint is hit.

Additionally to these commands, there's `step`, which we didn't use in this recipe. This command steps the program line by line just like `next`, with the exception that instead of stepping over function calls, it jumps into the body of the function being executed. This makes it possible to observe what's going on inside a function instead of just seeing the result or return value of the current call.

The last group of commonly used commands is used for gathering information about where in the code we currently are (`list`), how we got there (`where`), and the types as well as the values of variables and function parameters (`whatis`, `p`, `args`). These are the essentials for observing program state and finding problems with our code!

One additional great thing about this debugger is the possibility to execute Python code directly within the debug session. Lines beginning with an exclamation mark are directly passed to the Python runtime to be interpreted, which makes it possible to halt execution using a breakpoint, change the value of a variable or the state of an object before proceeding the execution. This can be quite useful for quickly trying fixes or finding program states that cause erroneous behavior.

Debugging C++ code

Although this book is very Python-centric, we should not forget that the core of Panda3D is written in C++. Additionally, it is possible to extend the engine with our own native libraries. Not only that, but we're even able to drop Python and write our games in pure C++.

Even if we intend to write our games completely in Python, there might be this one occasion coming up in the future where we wished we had read the recipe about using the C++ debugger of Visual Studio 2008. The following recipe will prepare us for this situation, even if it is unlikely to occur.

Getting ready

In this recipe, you are going to debug the C++ code you created in *Creating a scene using C++* found in *Chapter 2, Creating and Building Scenes*. For this to work, you need to add the property sheet containing your project settings to the **Debug** configuration just as you did for the **Release** configuration.

To be able to debug the code of the Panda3D engine on top of your own source code, you will need a debug build of the engine. If you want to use the release runtime from the installer package and just want to debug your own code, you need to apply the following workaround to be able to produce a debug build of your program:

1. Search for the string `python26_d.lib`.
2. Replace any occurrence of it with `python26.lib`.

How to do it...

The Visual Studio 2008 C++ debugger is a powerful tool. Let's see what can be done with it:

1. Load the project in Visual Studio 2008 and open the file `main.cpp`.
2. Place a new breakpoint in the line shown in the following screenshot by left-clicking the grey area to the left of the source code editor:

```cpp
int main(int argc, char* argv[])
{
    framework.open_framework(argc, argv);
    WindowFramework* win = framework.open_window();
    NodePath camera = win->get_camera_group();

    NodePath teapot = win->load_model(framework.get_models(), "teapot");
    teapot.reparent_to(win->get_render());
    teapot.set_pos(-5, 0, 0);
```

3. Right-click the breakpoint and select **Condition...**:

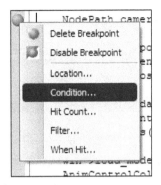

4. In the **Breakpoint Condition** window, tick the **Condition** checkbox and enter the string **win != 0** into the textbox and confirm your input by clicking **OK**:

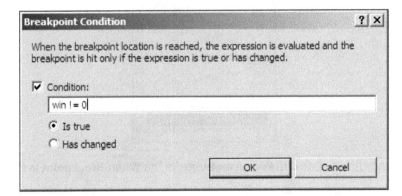

5. Right-click the breakpoint and select **Hit Count...**:

6. In the **Breakpoint Hit Count** window, choose the settings shown in the following screenshot and click **OK**:

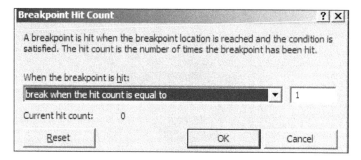

7. Right-click the breakpoint again and select **When Hit...**:

8. Tick the checkbox next to **Print a message:** in the **When Breakpoint Is Hit** window:

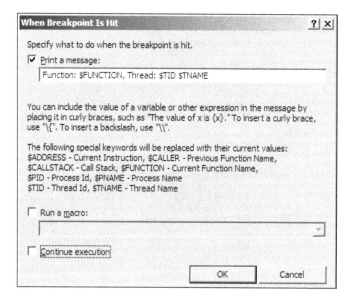

9. Start the debug session by clicking the toolbar button shown in the following screenshot, or by pressing *F5*:

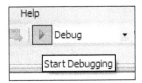

10. Wait until the breakpoint is hit. If the program is halted at a breakpoint it is marked with a little arrow:

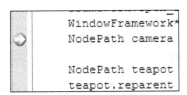

11. Use the toolbar buttons shown next to continue and halt the program, to stop debugging, restart the program, and to step through the code line by line. Click your way through the buttons and watch the results. Your actions may cause the program to stop, which will also cause the debugging session to end. In that case, just start the program again.

12. While stepping through the code, observe the areas at the bottom of the screen. **Autos** shows recently accessed or changed variables:

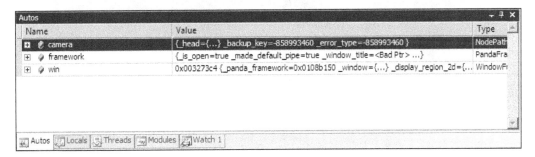

13. **Locals** lets you observe all variables in the current local scope:

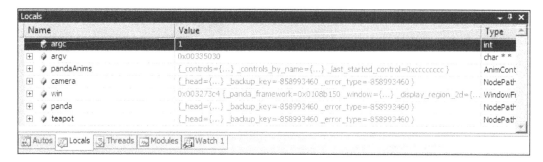

14. The **Call Stack** area shows which function calls led to the current point of execution:

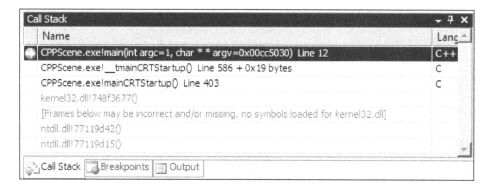

15. **Breakpoints** lists all active breakpoints as well as the conditions that need to be fulfilled to trigger them:

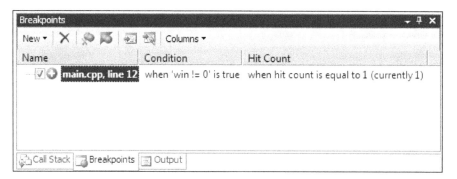

16. The **Output** area shows the debug text and console output of the program:

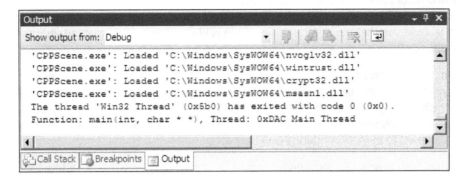

```
Output                                                          ▼ ₽ ✕
Show output from:  Debug                          ▼ | 🗐 | 🗐 🗐 | 🗐 🗐
    'CPPScene.exe':  Loaded  'C:\Windows\SysWOW64\nvoglv32.dll'      ▲
    'CPPScene.exe':  Loaded  'C:\Windows\SysWOW64\wintrust.dll'
    'CPPScene.exe':  Loaded  'C:\Windows\SysWOW64\crypt32.dll'
    'CPPScene.exe':  Loaded  'C:\Windows\SysWOW64\msasn1.dll'
    The thread 'Win32 Thread' (0x5b0) has exited with code 0 (0x0).
    Function: main(int, char * *), Thread: 0xDAC Main Thread
                                                                    ▼
◄                                                                  ►
  🔎Call Stack  🗐Breakpoints  🗐 Output
```

How it works...

Compared to the textmode debugger for Python, presented in the recipe found right before this one, the workflow doesn't differ too much. Basically, it's only the interface that differs drastically.

What we do with the tool is absolutely the same though. We set a breakpoint, define conditions that need to be fulfilled for triggering it, and create an action that prints a diagnostic message to the output window. While we are stepping through the code, we are watching variables as they change in the **Autos** and **Locals** windows. The **Call Stack** window shows us how we got to where we currently are in the program flow, the **Breakpoints** window is there to manage the breakpoints that are possibly scattered throughout the code of our game or library, and the **Output** window prints diagnostics and log messages.

Using the PStats tool for finding performance bottlenecks

From a plain technological point of view, most video games fall into the category of so-called "soft real time multi-agent simulations". This means that in games, we are simulating, by stepping frame by frame, a collection of multiple interacting game entities or agents within soft real time boundaries. Or even simpler: We are moving models and actors around in our game world while trying to maintain a frame rate high enough to create the illusion of smooth movement.

In practice this imposes limits to our games' usage of computing resources, because dropping frame rates and stuttering gameplay need to be avoided at all cost. Additionally, we want our games to be able to run on a wealth of hardware configurations, even ones that do not feature top of the line hardware.

The reasons for a game to perform poorly are manifold: Inefficient algorithms, too many models and actors per scene, too much geometry to draw per model or actor, too many changes of render states, too many transforms—the list of possible causes goes on and on. The fact is, however, that the program as a whole is almost never slow. Instead, in most cases, performance problems are caused by single bottlenecks within the program.

We could just try to find performance problems by randomly crossing off items from our imaginary list of possible causes but in this case, the odds for actually finding anything are not very high. The right way to go about performance problems in our code is to observe, measure, and finally locate the points in our code that make the game exceed the maximum time it is allowed to take for rendering one frame.

Luckily, Panda3D is able to collect detailed profiling data. Together with the PStats tool, which will be introduced in the following tasks, we are able to display and observe this data to quickly find out where precious CPU cycles are wasted in our programs.

Getting ready

We are going to profile the sample program created in the recipe *Managing recurring tasks*, found in *Chapter 7*. Please prepare this sample before proceeding to be able to follow the tasks as closely as possible.

How to do it...

These are some of the common tasks where you will be using PStats in your projects:

1. Open `Application.py` and add the following line to the constructor of the `Application` class:

   ```
   PStatClient.connect()
   ```

2. Navigate to `C:\Panda3D-1.7.0\bin` and launch `pstats.exe`. Your firewall might show a popup window asking if you want to allow PStats to listen on a network port. If so, allow the port to be opened.

3. Launch the application. The following window will pop up:

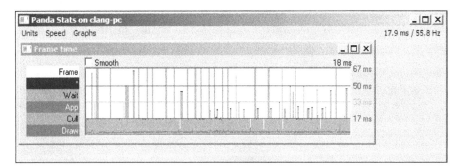

4. Click **Graphs | Frame components | App components | Show code components | UpdateSmileys**. An additional child window will be created:

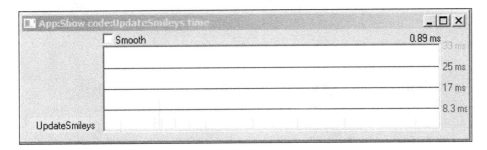

5. Click **Graphs | Nodes** to view the following graph:

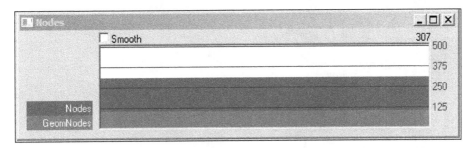

6. Clicking **Graphs | System memory** will bring up the following display:

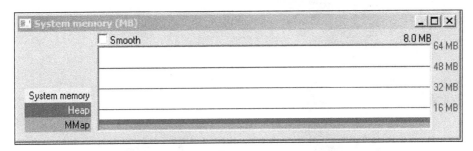

7. Click **Graphs | Vertices**. This will show the following child window:

8. By clicking **Graphs | State changes**, the application will present the following graph:

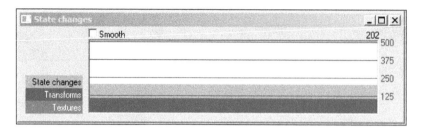

9. Finally, click **Graphs | Piano Roll** to view the following profiling data representation:

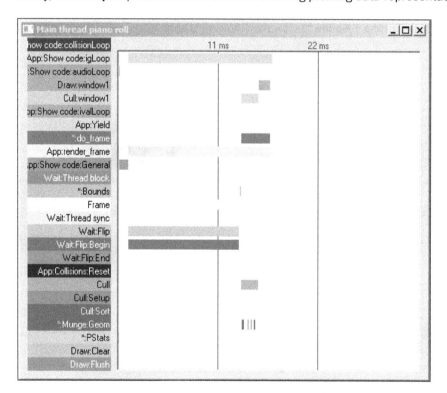

How it works...

PStats is a network server program that once started, listens for incoming connections from a Panda3D runtime. At application startup time, in the constructor of the Application class, we instruct the engine to connect to the PStats instance running on the local machine. We could also run PStats on an additional machine and pass a string containing its host name or IP address to `PStatClient.connect()`—a great feature if we intend to run the game in full screen mode.

As soon as a connection is established, PStats shows its window and displays the **Frame time** graph to give a very general performance overview. The tool allows us to get exact timing data on individual tasks, the number of nodes in the scene, memory usage statistics, the number of vertices that are drawn, how many state changes there have been in a frame, and a detailed list of which component takes which amount of time to execute, among others.

There is no fixed way of using this tool. The goal should be to observe and interpret the readings. Watch for sudden anomalies and keep an eye on how the readings change over time. Big spikes in the graphs or constantly growing values should make you suspicious.

Improving performance by flattening scenes

While the scene graph and renderer of the Panda3D engine generally do a good job managing and drawing scene data, they are easily overloaded with data. Too many different models consisting of lots of geometry nodes while all being transformed to various positions will quickly push the scene graph to its limits, while the renderer has to wait for the graphics card because all these models in the scene need to be sent one by one to the graphics card for drawing to the screen.

The easiest step to decreased scene complexity, for sure, is to remove objects from the scene graph. This works, but it removes details from our game and may make it look empty and cheap.

Fortunately, there's an alternative solution we can try before starting to cut models from our scenes. Panda3D provides an API for simplifying scenes by precalculating transformations as well as combining scene nodes and their geometry to please the graphics card by sending this data in one big batch.

Getting ready

Setup a new game project structure as described in *Chapter 1, Setting Up Panda3D and Configuring Development Tools* before going on with the following tasks.

How to do it...

For optimizing a scene, you will need to follow these steps:

1. Edit `Application.py` and fill in the following code:

```
from direct.showbase.ShowBase import ShowBase
from panda3d.core import *
import random

class Application(ShowBase):
    def __init__(self):
        ShowBase.__init__(self)
```

```
        self.cam.setPos(0, -100, 10)
        self.setFrameRateMeter(True)

        envRoot = render.attachNewNode("envRoot")
        for i in range(100):
            self.addEnvironment(envRoot)
        envRoot.flattenStrong()

        combiner = RigidBodyCombiner("cmb")
        self.smRoot = render.attachNewNode(combiner)
        for i in range(200):
            self.addSmiley(self.smRoot)
        combiner.collect()
            taskMgr.add(self.updateSmileys, "UpdateSmileys")
```

2. Below the code you just added, append the following:

```
    def addSmiley(self, parent):
        sm = loader.loadModel("smiley")
        sm.reparentTo(parent)
        sm.setPos(random.uniform(-20, 20), random.uniform(-30,
30), random.uniform(0, 30))
        sm.setPythonTag("velocity", 0)

    def updateSmileys(self, task):
        for smiley in self.smRoot.findAllMatches("smiley.egg"):
            vel = smiley.getPythonTag("velocity")
            z = smiley.getZ()
            if z <= 0:
                vel = random.uniform(0.1, 0.8)
            smiley.setZ(z + vel)
            vel -= 0.01
            smiley.setPythonTag("velocity", vel)
        return task.cont

    def addEnvironment(self, parent):
        env = loader.loadModel("environment")
        env.reparentTo(parent)
        env.setScale(0.01, 0.01, 0.01)
        env.setPos(render, random.uniform(-20, 20), random.
uniform(-30, 30), random.uniform(0, 30))
```

How it works...

The important parts about this code sample are the `flattenStrong()` method and the `RigidBodyCombiner` class.

Actually, `flattenStrong()` is part of a group of methods of the `NodePath` class used for simplifying the subtree of child nodes under the scene node the method is being called on. Using `flattenLight()`, the vertices of child nodes are multiplied by their nodes' transformation matrices. This has the effect that these nodes do not need to be transformed to their positions anymore, sparing the CPU a set of matrix multiplications per frame. The `flattenMedium()` method does a `flattenLight()` pass and additionally makes the scene tree hierarchy simpler by removing and combining obsolete nodes and their children. We can try to use this method to increase performance of static scenes with a very deep and nested node hierarchy. By calling `flattenStrong()` on a node in the scene graph, the complete scene node subtree under the affected node is flattened and combined to one single node, making it possible to send the node geometry in one big batch, which can greatly decrease the time needed for rendering the scene. The price for this gain though, is that this is a destructive action because after using this method, the hierarchy of child nodes connected to the modified node is destroyed.

We are using a similar optimization technique for the subtree containing the smileys. But while the nodes we applied `flattenStrong()` to were static, our smileys are moved every frame, which is why we are using the `RigidBodyContainer` class in this case. Although used in a slightly different way than the flattening methods, the concept behind `RigidBodyContainer` and its effect on how the scene is rendered is very similar. Before being sent to the renderer, the child nodes of the combiner node are joined into one, causing only one batch of geometry to be sent to the graphics device.

These optimization methods are no magic bullet, however. In some cases they are able to greatly improve performance, while in others it can even become worse than before. Therefore it is very important for us to keep on experimenting with the various degrees of flattening while profiling our game to observe the results!

Implementing performance critical code in C++

While in direct comparison, compiled C++ code performs better than the same code ported to Python, it would be wrong to generally state that the use of the Python interpreter in Panda3D is detrimental to the performance of your game. This would be wrong and utter nonsense, as Python just acts as a simpler interface to the engine's core libraries. Most of a game's code that uses the Python interface of Panda3D consists of calls to the engine's APIs, which are implemented in C++ and simply forwarded by the Python runtime.

While this architecture generally delivers quite acceptable performance, there might be an occasion or two where, after thoroughly profiling and optimizing your Python code, you still might not have reached the performance goals you set for that piece of code. Only if you are sure about there not being any gains possible to achieve anymore should you start thinking about writing a C++ implementation of your code.

This recipe will show you the steps necessary for adding a new C++ class to the Panda3D engine and making it available to be instantiated from Python code. You will add the new module containing the newly created class to Panda3D's API and build it with the rest of the engine's source code. This approach might seem bloated and overly complex, but while it is possible to build custom libraries for Panda3D outside the engine's source tree, it is a lot harder and cumbersome to set up. Furthermore, the documentation on adding C++ classes to the engine is really very sparse. Following the example of the rest of the source code of Panda3D does at least provide you with lots of sample material you can compare your custom efforts to. Finally and very importantly, this way the code is already prepared to be integrated into the official source code in case you wish to contribute the code to the community. Panda3D is an open source project and available for free, so giving back is just fair!

Getting ready

Prior to going on with this recipe you should have read and understood the recipe about building Panda3D from source code found in *Chapter 1*.

How to do it...

To complete this recipe, work your way through these tasks:

1. In `panda\src`, create a new directory called `bounce`.
2. Copy the files `config_skel.cxx`, `config_skel.h`, `skel_composite.cxx`, `skel_composite1.cxx`, `Sources.pp`, `typedSkel.cxx`, `typedSkel.h`, and `typedSkel.I` from `panda\src\skel` to `panda\src\bounce`.
3. In `panda\src\bounce`, rename `config_skel.cxx` to `config_bounce.cxx`, `config_skel.h` to `config_bounce.h`, `skel_composite.cxx` to `bounce_composite.cxx`, `skel_composite1.cxx` to `bounce_composite1.cxx` as well as `typedSkel.cxx`, `typedSkel.h`, and `typedSkel.I` to `bounce.cxx`, `bounce.h` and `bounce.I`, respectively.
4. Open `Sources.pp` in a text editor and replace its content with the following lines:

```
#define OTHER_LIBS interrogatedb:c dconfig:c dtoolconfig:m \
                   dtoolutil:c dtoolbase:c dtool:m prc:c

#define USE_PACKAGES
#define BUILDING_DLL BUILDING_PANDABOUNCE
```

```
#begin lib_target
  #define TARGET bounce
  #define LOCAL_LIBS \
    putil

  #define COMBINED_SOURCES $[TARGET]_composite1.cxx

  #define SOURCES \
    config_bounce.h \
    bounce.I bounce.h

  #define INCLUDED_SOURCES \
    config_bounce.cxx \
    bounce.cxx

  #define INSTALL_HEADERS \
    bounce.I bounce.h

  #define IGATESCAN all

#end lib_target
```

5. Edit `bounce_composite.cxx` so it contains the following line:

```
#include "bounce_composite1.cxx"
```

6. Change `bounce_composite1.cxx` so it contains the following two lines:

```
#include "config_bounce.cxx"
#include "bounce.cxx"
```

7. Open `bounce.h` and change its content to reflect the following code:

```
#ifndef BOUNCE_H
#define BOUNCE_H

#include "pandabase.h"
#include "typedObject.h"
#include "randomizer.h"

class EXPCL_PANDABOUNCE Bounce : public TypedObject {
PUBLISHED:
  INLINE Bounce();
  INLINE ~Bounce();
  INLINE float get_z();
  INLINE void set_z(float z);
  void update();
```

```
  private:
    float _velocity;
    float _z;
    Randomizer _rand;

  public:
    static TypeHandle get_class_type() {
      return _type_handle;
    }
    static void init_type() {
      TypedObject::init_type();
      register_type(_type_handle, "Bounce",
                    TypedObject::get_class_type());
    }
    virtual TypeHandle get_type() const {
      return get_class_type();
    }
    virtual TypeHandle force_init_type() {init_type(); return get_
class_type();}

  private:
    static TypeHandle _type_handle;
};

#include "bounce.I"
#endif
```

8. After you are done with bounce.cxx it should look like the following:

```
#include "bounce.h"

TypeHandle Bounce::_type_handle;

void Bounce::
update() {
  if (_z <= bounce_floor_level)
    _velocity = _rand.random_real(0.7f) + 0.1f;

  _z = _z + _velocity;
  _velocity -= 0.01f;
}
```

9. Now open `bounce.I` and change the code to the following:

```
INLINE Bounce::
Bounce() {
  _z = 0;
  _velocity = 0;
}

INLINE Bounce::
~Bounce() {
}

INLINE float Bounce::
get_z() {
  return _z;
}

INLINE void Bounce::
set_z(float z) {
  _z = z;
}
```

10. Make sure `config_bounce.h` contains the following lines of code:

```
#ifndef CONFIG_BOUNCE_H
#define CONFIG_BOUNCE_H

#include "pandabase.h"
#include "notifyCategoryProxy.h"
#include "configVariableDouble.h"

NotifyCategoryDecl(bounce, EXPCL_PANDABOUNCE, EXPTP_PANDABOUNCE);

extern ConfigVariableDouble bounce_floor_level;
extern EXPCL_PANDABOUNCE void init_libbounce();

#endif
```

11. Edit `config_bounce.cxx`. The file's content should look as follows:

```
#include "config_bounce.h"
#include "bounce.h"
#include "dconfig.h"

Configure(config_bounce);
NotifyCategoryDef(bounce, "");
```

```
ConfigureFn(config_bounce) {
  init_libbounce();
}

ConfigVariableDouble bounce_floor_level
("bounce-floor-level", 0);

void
init_libbounce() {
  static bool initialized = false;
  if (initialized) {
    return;
  }
  initialized = true;

  Bounce::init_type();
}
```

12. Open the file `panda\src\pandabase\pandasymbols.h`. Look for the following block of code and add the highlighted code:

```
#ifdef BUILDING_PANDASKEL
  #define EXPCL_PANDASKEL __declspec(dllexport)
  #define EXPTP_PANDASKEL
#else
  #define EXPCL_PANDASKEL __declspec(dllimport)
  #define EXPTP_PANDASKEL extern
#endif

#ifdef BUILDING_PANDABOUNCE
  #define EXPCL_PANDABOUNCE __declspec(dllexport)
  #define EXPTP_PANDABOUNCE
#else
  #define EXPCL_PANDABOUNCE __declspec(dllimport)
  #define EXPTP_PANDABOUNCE extern
#endif
```

13. Still in `pandasymbols.h`, look out for the following code and add the marked lines:

```
#define EXPCL_PANDASKEL
#define EXPTP_PANDASKEL

#define EXPCL_PANDABOUNCE
#define EXPTP_PANDABOUNCE
```

14. Search for the following block of code in `makepanda\makepanda.py`:

```
if (not RUNTIME):
  OPTS=['BUILDING:PANDASKEL', 'ADVAPI']

  TargetAdd('libpandaskel_module.obj', input='libskel.in')
  TargetAdd('libpandaskel_module.obj', opts=OPTS)
  TargetAdd('libpandaskel_module.obj', opts=['IMOD:pandaskel',
'ILIB:libpandaskel'])

  TargetAdd('libpandaskel.dll', input='skel_composite.obj')
  TargetAdd('libpandaskel.dll', input='libskel_igate.obj')
  TargetAdd('libpandaskel.dll', input='libpandaskel_module.obj')
  TargetAdd('libpandaskel.dll', input=COMMON_PANDA_LIBS)
  TargetAdd('libpandaskel.dll', opts=OPTS)
```

15. Directly below the aforementioned block of code add the following:

```
if (not RUNTIME):
  OPTS=['DIR:panda/src/bounce', 'BUILDING:PANDABOUNCE', 'ADVAPI']
    TargetAdd('bounce_composite.obj', opts=OPTS, input='bounce_
composite.cxx')
    IGATEFILES=GetDirectoryContents("panda/src/bounce", ["*.h", "*_
composite.cxx"])
    TargetAdd('libbounce.in', opts=OPTS, input=IGATEFILES)
    TargetAdd('libbounce.in', opts=['IMOD:pandabounce', 'ILIB:
libbounce', 'SRCDIR:panda/src/bounce'])
    TargetAdd('libbounce_igate.obj', input='libbounce.in',
opts=["DEPENDENCYONLY"])

    TargetAdd('libpandabounce_module.obj', input='libbounce.in')
    TargetAdd('libpandabounce_module.obj', opts=OPTS)
    TargetAdd('libpandabounce_module.obj', opts=['IMOD:pandabounce',
'ILIB:libpandabounce'])

    TargetAdd('libpandabounce.dll', input='bounce_composite.obj')
    TargetAdd('libpandabounce.dll', input='libbounce_igate.obj')
    TargetAdd('libpandabounce.dll', input='libpandabounce_module.
obj')
    TargetAdd('libpandabounce.dll', input=COMMON_PANDA_LIBS)
    TargetAdd('libpandabounce.dll', opts=OPTS)
```

16. Add the highlighted line to `direct\src\ffi\panda3d.py`:

```
panda3d_modules = {
    "core"        :("libpandaexpress", "libpanda"),
    "dtoolconfig" : "libp3dtoolconfig",
    "physics"     : "libpandaphysics",
```

```
        "fx"          : "libpandafx",
        "direct"      : "libp3direct",
        "egg"         : "libpandaegg",
        "ode"         : "libpandaode",
        "vision"      : "libp3vision",
        "physx"       : "libpandaphysx",
        "ai"          : "libpandaai",
        "bounce"      : "libpandabounce",
    }
```

17. Compile the Panda3D source code using the makepanda tool.

18. Add your custom built version of Panda3D to NetBeans. Follow steps 13 to 17 of the recipe *Downloading and configuring NetBeans to work with Panda3D* found in *Chapter 1*. Instead of the ppython.exe file in the Panda3D installation directory, choose the one found in the built\python subdirectory of the Panda3D source code. Type **CustomPython** into the **Platform Name** field of the **Python Platform Manager** window.

19. Create a new project as described in *Setting up the game structure*. Be sure to choose **CustomPython** in step 3.

20. Open Application.py and replace its content with the following:

```python
from direct.showbase.ShowBase import ShowBase
from panda3d.core import *
from panda3d.bounce import *
import random

class Application(ShowBase):
    def __init__(self):
        ShowBase.__init__(self)
        self.smiley = loader.loadModel("smiley")
        self.smileyCount = 0
        self.cam.setPos(0, -100, 10)
        taskMgr.doMethodLater(0.1, self.addSmiley, "AddSmiley")
        taskMgr.add(self.updateSmileys, "UpdateSmileys", uponDeath
= self.removeSmileys)
        taskMgr.doMethodLater(60, taskMgr.remove, "RemoveUpdate",
extraArgs = ["UpdateSmileys"])

    def addSmiley(self, task):
        sm = render.attachNewNode("smiley-instance")
        sm.setPos(random.uniform(-20, 20), random.uniform(-30,
30), random.uniform(0, 30))
        bounce = Bounce()
        bounce.setZ(sm.getZ())
```

```
        sm.setPythonTag("bounce", bounce)
        self.smiley.instanceTo(sm)
        self.smileyCount += 1

        if self.smileyCount == 300:
            return task.done

        return task.again

    def updateSmileys(self, task):
        for smiley in render.findAllMatches("smiley-instance"):
            bounce = smiley.getPythonTag("bounce")
            bounce.update()
            smiley.setZ(bounce.getZ())
        return task.cont

    def removeSmileys(self, task):
        for smiley in render.findAllMatches("smiley-instance"):
            smiley.removeNode()
        return task.done
```

21. Press *F6* to launch the program.

How it works...

After copying and renaming the files of the skeleton module provided with the rest of the Panda3D source code, our first real task is preparing the files needed by the build system.

In `Sources.pp`, we need to list the source and header files that make up our project, as well as the libraries our code depends on and needs to be linked against. Additionally, we set the name of the build target to `bounce`, which will be the name of the library being built from our code. This file also defines which header files will be distributed with the build, and is needed for automatically generating the Python bindings for our class.

Using `#include` on C++ source files instead of just using it on headers may seem a bit odd, but this is how the build system works. Panda3D is built using a compilation technique that is very specific to C++ projects called "unity build". In this kind of setup, instead of compiling individual source files to object files and linking them, the preprocessor is used to generate one big file containing all of the source code. This big, unified source file is then compiled as one, which can reduce build times of big C++ projects.

Next, we define the interface of our class. Because we want our new class to be exposed to the Python runtime, we need to derive from `TypedObject` and add the `init_type()` and `get_type()` member functions that will be called by the engine to register and initialize our class with Python's type system. In `init_type()` we have to call the `init_type()` function of the base class and fill in the type name we are going to use in Python. So if we wanted to derive a new class called `Tumble` from `Bounce`, the derived class' `init_type()` function would have to look like this:

```
static void init_type() {
  Bounce::init_type();
  register_type(_type_handle, "Tumble", Bounce::get_class_type());
}
```

Besides the type system management code, we mark the member functions we want to be exposed to Python as `PUBLISHED`. To the C++ compiler, these are just public member functions, but the tools invoked by Panda3D's build system will pick it up for automatically generating Python bindings for the class.

We then go on to implementing the Bounce class and adding functions for configuring and initializing the library. In the files `config_bounce.h` and `config_bounce.cxx`, we register a new category for log messages using the `NotifyCategoryDecl` and `NotifyCategoryDef` macros. In addition, we add a new configuration variable, so we are able to change the behavior of our class library using the engine's configuration file. `ConfigVariableDouble` for floating point values is not the only possible type for configuration variables. There are also the types `ConfigVariableBool`, `ConfigVariableInt` and `ConfigVariableString`.

Before building, we need to add a few preprocessor symbols. The `EXPCL_PANDABOUNCE` and `EXPTP_PANDABOUNCE` symbols are defined differently, depending on whether they are used for building the engine code or they are included in client code. This avoids having to keep around two versions of the file for these two use cases.

After adding the directory that contains our source to the `makepanda` script and adding our library to the list of submodules of `panda3d`, we can go on to build the source code. When this rather lengthy process has finished, all we have to do is register our customized runtime version to the IDE, setup our project and use our Bounce class just like any other type found in the Panda3D API.

11
Input Handling

In this chapter, we will cover:

- ▶ Handling keyboard and mouse input
- ▶ Implementing an abstraction layer for supporting multiple input methods
- ▶ Handling input from an Xbox 360 controller
- ▶ Recording and simulating user input
- ▶ Reading audio data from a microphone
- ▶ Reading video data from a webcam
- ▶ Reading input data from a network

Introduction

The one important feature that sets video games apart from other media like movies or books is the player's ability to interact and be a part of the experience. Just think about it for a moment: A piece of literature defines itself by what it tells and which images it creates in the reader's imagination. Movies are trying to engage and entertain by showing, not telling. The video game medium, while of course being able to tell stories and visualize the action in spectacular ways, requires its audience to take an active part and take control of what's happening on the screen. This is a fundamental difference to the other forms of entertainment media, where the audience is put into the role of a passive consumer. Reading user input and providing immediate on-screen responses, representing the state of the game and prompting the player for more input, this feedback loop operates at the core of every video game.

Input data can originate from various sources and take many different forms. Be it binary data from keyboard and mouse buttons, the absolute two-dimensional screen position of a mouse pointer, or the normalized distance and direction an analog stick is being tilted. Apart from the classic and widely used standard input methods, designers also have found uses for more complex devices, like microphones and cameras, to immerse players even further.

Panda3D provides nice wrappers around most of the details of handling all of these different devices. This chapter will discuss and show how to use these abstraction layers and how to process the provided data to create measures of interaction.

Handling keyboard and mouse input

With the exception of karaoke and guitar games like Rock Band or Guitar Hero, it is generally a pretty bad idea to require a specialized controller or other input device for a video game. So, unless you have the marketing budget for advertising your new and special controller, you should always opt to use the most common and most widely available devices.

On consoles you would therefore aim for the standard gamepad, while the most widespread input measure for PC games is a combination of keyboard and mouse. Because Panda3D is targeted towards PC game production, in this example, you will learn how to handle input data received from the latter input method.

Getting ready

This recipe will of course be using our standard application skeleton that we created in the first chapter. Additionally, we will reuse the FollowCam class from the recipe *Making the camera smoothly follow an object* in *Chapter 2, Creating and Building Scenes*. Be sure to implement that class and place the source file called FollowCam.py inside the src subdirectory of the project.

How to do it...

Implement keyboard and mouse input by following these steps:

1. Import the required libraries and implement the constructor of the Application class as well as the resetMouse() method:

```
from direct.showbase.ShowBase import ShowBase
from direct.actor.Actor import Actor
from panda3d.core import *
from FollowCam import FollowCam

class Application(ShowBase):
    def __init__(self):
        ShowBase.__init__(self)
        self.world = loader.loadModel("environment")
        self.world.reparentTo(render)
        self.world.setScale(0.5)
        self.world.setPos(-8, 80, 0)
```

```
        self.panda = Actor("panda", {"walk": "panda-walk"})
        self.panda.reparentTo(render)

        self.followCam = FollowCam(self.cam, self.panda)

        base.disableMouse()
        props = WindowProperties.getDefault()
        props.setCursorHidden(True)
        base.win.requestProperties(props)

        self.resetMouse()

        # don't use -repeat because of slight delay after keydown
        self.pandaWalk = False
        self.pandaReverse = False
        self.pandaLeft = False
        self.pandaRight = False

        self.accept("escape", exit)
        self.accept("w", self.beginWalk)
        self.accept("w-up", self.endWalk)
        self.accept("s", self.beginReverse)
        self.accept("s-up", self.endReverse)
        self.accept("a", self.beginTurnLeft)
        self.accept("a-up", self.endTurnLeft)
        self.accept("d", self.beginTurnRight)
        self.accept("d-up", self.endTurnRight)

        taskMgr.add(self.updatePanda, "update panda")

    def resetMouse(self):
        cx = base.win.getProperties().getXSize() / 2
        cy = base.win.getProperties().getYSize() / 2
        base.win.movePointer(0, cx, cy)
```

2. Add these keyboard event handling methods to the `Application` class:

```
    def beginWalk(self):
        self.panda.setPlayRate(1.0, "walk")
        self.panda.loop("walk")
        self.pandaWalk = True

    def endWalk(self):
        self.panda.stop()
        self.pandaWalk = False
```

```
        def beginReverse(self):
            self.panda.setPlayRate(-1.0, "walk")
            self.panda.loop("walk")
            self.pandaReverse = True

        def endReverse(self):
            self.panda.stop()
            self.pandaReverse = False

        def beginTurnLeft(self):
            self.pandaLeft = True

        def endTurnLeft(self):
            self.pandaLeft = False

        def beginTurnRight(self):
            self.pandaRight = True

        def endTurnRight(self):
            self.pandaRight = False
```

3. Extend the `Application` class further by adding this method:

```
        def updatePanda(self, task):
            if base.mouseWatcherNode.hasMouse():
                self.panda.setH(self.panda, -base.mouseWatcherNode.
getMouseX() * 10)

            self.resetMouse()

            if self.pandaWalk:
                self.panda.setY(self.panda, -0.2)
            elif self.pandaReverse:
                self.panda.setY(self.panda, 0.2)

            if self.pandaLeft:
                self.panda.setH(self.panda, 0.8)
            elif self.pandaRight:
                self.panda.setH(self.panda, -0.8)

            return task.cont
```

4. Start the program. Use the *W* and *S* keys to walk forward and backward. Press *A*, *D*, or use the mouse to turn left and right. Press the *Escape* key to quit.

How it works...

After loading and positioning all the scene objects and setting up the `FollowCam` class to follow the panda, we encounter the line `base.disableMouse()`. The method name is somewhat misleading, as it does not literally do what it says. After calling `base.disableMouse()` the engine will still receive mouse input but the default mouse-based camera controls will be disabled.

We then hide the mouse cursor by setting the appropriate flag in `WindowProperties` and use the `resetMouse()` method to reset the mouse pointer to the center of the window. This is important for detecting mouse movement later on in the code.

Next, we initialize a set of Boolean flags. These will be used to inform the updating task which action to perform and in which direction to move the panda. These flags are modified by the event handling methods we register for keyboard presses in the following lines.

After the line that adds the task for updating the panda's position, we can find the keyboard event handling methods. Here we set the movement flags `pandaWalk`, `pandaReverse`, `pandaLeft`, and `PandaRight` and activate the appropriate animations depending on the key being pressed. We need the Boolean flags to make the panda move as long as the key is in a pressed state, where the flag is set to `True`. As soon as an `"-up"` event occurs, the flag is set back to `False` and the panda stops moving.

We explicitly do not use the `"-repeat"` events here for a reason: The engine starts to send this type of event a short moment after the key was initially pressed. In our case this would cause the panda to twitch, pause, and then move on normally, which is not what we intend to achieve.

Finally, we implement the `updatePanda()` method. At runtime, this code is called at every frame and is responsible for moving the panda around, based on which of the movement flags are set. It is also the place where we finally handle mouse movement: First we check if the mouse is within our window. The position of the mouse pointer in Panda3D is relative to the center of the window. We use this fact to check how far the mouse pointer was moved from the window center since the last frame to change the heading of the panda model. Of course, we need to reset the mouse pointer to the center of the window again to keep this technique working and prevent it from leaving the window.

There's more...

As we can see, Panda3D automatically creates various events for when a key is pressed down or released again. This reduces accepting keyboard events to simply adding the correct event handlers for these events.

Character and number keys create events named after the symbol on the key. The events for character keys are always in lower case. Special and control keys have their own, but not hard to guess, event names: `"enter"`, `"lshift"`, `"ralt"`, `"f1"`, `"f2"`, `"page_down"`, and so on. The same applies for mouse buttons, which are named consecutively, starting with `"mouse1"` and `"mouse2"` for the left and right mouse buttons.

For handling keys being held down or being released after having been pressed, the event names are modified with a set of post- and prefixes. In our sample, we can see the `"-up"` modifier that is used when the player takes a finger off a key. Apart from that, there are also the `"time-"` and `"-repeat"` variants of each event. The former passes the time when the event occurred to the event handler, while the latter is sent continuously if a key is held down over a period of time. These modifiers can also be mixed: `"time-enter"`, `"time-f1-repeat"`, `"a-up"`, and `"time-lshift-up"` are all valid samples of event names to accept.

Implementing an abstraction layer for supporting multiple input methods

In this recipe we are going to rework the code produced in *Handling keyboard and mouse input*. We are going to add an abstraction layer to the input handling sections of our code to hide away the specifics of the input device being used. This means that the gameplay code that controls animation and movement of the panda will not be handling any specific keys being pressed. Instead, there will be just a set of unified events for the actions the panda should be able to perform.

The reason for adding such a layer can already be found in the title of this recipe. We want to generalize our gameplay code to be able to support more input devices than just the classic keyboard and mouse combination. Further down in this chapter we will use this approach to add gamepad support to our demo, for example. We could also use the approach of this recipe as a starting point for implementing artificial intelligence for a game—why not let the AI controlled bots use a virtual gamepad, keyboard, or mouse to send the same commands as a human player would do?

Not only will this approach open new possibilities like the ones just stated, it will also make the character and gameplay handling code a bit shorter and easier to comprehend.

Getting ready

Although this recipe can be finished on its own, it is recommended to follow and understand the first recipe in this chapter before proceeding. This will help you to better understand the benefits of adding an abstraction layer to your input handling code. Also note that the following code will be discussed further based on the recipe *Handling keyboard and mouse input* dealing with keyboard and mouse input.

How to do it...

To finish this recipe, complete the tasks below:

1. Add a new file called `InputHandler.py` and insert the following code:

```python
from direct.showbase.DirectObject import DirectObject
from panda3d.core import *

class InputHandler(DirectObject):
    def __init__(self):
        DirectObject.__init__(self)

        self.walk = False
        self.reverse = False
        self.left = False
        self.right = False

        taskMgr.add(self.updateInput, "update input")

    def beginWalk(self):
        messenger.send("walk-start")
        self.walk = True

    def endWalk(self):
        messenger.send("walk-stop")
        self.walk = False

    def beginReverse(self):
        messenger.send("reverse-start")
        self.reverse = True

    def endReverse(self):
        messenger.send("reverse-stop")
        self.reverse = False

    def beginTurnLeft(self):
        self.left = True

    def endTurnLeft(self):
        self.left = False

    def beginTurnRight(self):
        self.right = True

    def endTurnRight(self):
        self.right = False
```

```
        def dispatchMessages(self):
            if self.walk:
                messenger.send("walk", [-0.1])
            elif self.reverse:
                messenger.send("reverse", [0.1])

            if self.left:
                messenger.send("turn", [0.8])
            elif self.right:
                messenger.send("turn", [-0.8])


        def updateInput(self, task):
            return task.cont
```

2. Add another new file and name it `KeyboardMouseHandler.py`. Open it and implement the following class:

```
from InputHandler import InputHandler
from panda3d.core import *


class KeyboardMouseHandler(InputHandler):
    def __init__(self):
        InputHandler.__init__(self)

        base.disableMouse()
        props = WindowProperties()
        props.setCursorHidden(True)
        base.win.requestProperties(props)

        self.accept("escape", exit)
        self.accept("w", self.beginWalk)
        self.accept("w-up", self.endWalk)
        self.accept("s", self.beginReverse)
        self.accept("s-up", self.endReverse)
        self.accept("a", self.beginTurnLeft)
        self.accept("a-up", self.endTurnLeft)
        self.accept("d", self.beginTurnRight)
        self.accept("d-up", self.endTurnRight)

        taskMgr.add(self.updateInput, "update input")

    def resetMouse(self):
        cx = base.win.getProperties().getXSize() / 2
        cy = base.win.getProperties().getYSize() / 2
        base.win.movePointer(0, cx, cy)
```

```
        def updateInput(self, task):
            if base.mouseWatcherNode.hasMouse():
                messenger.send("turn", [-base.mouseWatcherNode.
getMouseX() * 10])

            self.resetMouse()
            self.dispatchMessages()

            return task.cont
```

3. Open `Application.py` and replace its contents with the following source code:

```
from direct.showbase.ShowBase import ShowBase
from direct.actor.Actor import Actor
from panda3d.core import *
from FollowCam import FollowCam
from KeyboardMouseHandler import KeyboardMouseHandler

class Application(ShowBase):
    def __init__(self):
        ShowBase.__init__(self)
        self.world = loader.loadModel("environment")
        self.world.reparentTo(render)
        self.world.setScale(0.5)
        self.world.setPos(-8, 80, 0)

        self.panda = Actor("panda", {"walk": "panda-walk"})
        self.panda.reparentTo(render)

        self.followCam = FollowCam(self.cam, self.panda)

        self.keyInput = KeyboardMouseHandler()
        self.accept("walk-start", self.beginWalk)
        self.accept("walk-stop", self.endWalk)
        self.accept("reverse-start", self.beginReverse)
        self.accept("reverse-stop", self.endReverse)
        self.accept("walk", self.walk)
        self.accept("reverse", self.reverse)
        self.accept("turn", self.turn)

    def beginWalk(self):
        self.panda.setPlayRate(1.0, "walk")
        self.panda.loop("walk")
```

```
def endWalk(self):
    self.panda.stop()

def beginReverse(self):
    self.panda.setPlayRate(-1.0, "walk")
    self.panda.loop("walk")

def endReverse(self):
    self.panda.stop()

def walk(self, rate):
    self.panda.setY(self.panda, rate)

def reverse(self, rate):
    self.panda.setY(self.panda, rate)
```

4. Launch the program. If nothing about the input response has changed, you did just fine!

How it works...

In this recipe we moved the event handling methods, the movement flags, and the updating task to the `InputHandler` class. In this class, we implement the general parts of the input system. It acts as an abstraction layer between the game code and the input handling code, translating input device events to generalized, device-agnostic events.

The `KeyboardMouseHandler` class shows us one of the benefits of this architecture, as it only contains device specific code. Instead of having to deal with one big piece of code as before, we have now moved this part of the implementation in a separate, concise, and easy to understand class. This way writing implementations for new devices only requires wiring events to the appropriate handling functions and providing an implementation of `updateInput()` that at least calls `dispatchMessages()`.

With this change, we now are able to add support for new input devices without having to touch gameplay code. In fact, the gameplay logic has become completely independent from how input is generated. Here we added a handler for keyboard and mouse, but we might as well add support for joysticks and gamepads, as can be seen in the recipe *Handling input from an Xbox 360 controller* found in this chapter.

Finally, we can take a look at our cleaned up implementation of the `Application` class. First we need to create an instance of our `KeyboardMouseHandler` class (or any other device-specific derived implementation of the `InputHandler` class). We then just need to register and implement a few event handlers for the device-independent messages and that's it!

Handling input from an Xbox 360 controller

Having been sold together with millions of Xbox 360 game consoles, the Xbox 360 controller is one of the most widespread and well-known types of input devices for gamers. But it is not only console gamers who are able to use this kind of controller as it can easily be plugged into a Windows PC too. Apart from the device being recognized by the operating system, many PC games are officially supporting the Xbox 360 controller as a possible input device.

In case you want to create a game with support for this gamepad, this recipe is for you. But also if you intend to support any other type of joystick or game controller you will find interesting resources ahead because the API you are going to use is not bound to any device in particular. Nonetheless, this recipe will show you how to read data from the Xbox 360 controller's analog sticks and buttons, and will provide you with a minimal class that maps the raw button and axis indices to more meaningfully named variables.

Getting ready

This recipe builds upon the code and knowledge presented in the recipe *Implementing an abstraction layer for supporting multiple input methods*. Before going on, you are required to follow and understand that recipe!

Additionally, as Panda3D does not have built-in support for analog input devices like joysticks and gamepads, you need to add the `pygame` programming library to your installation of the Panda3D engine:

1. Start your web browser and go to `www.pygame.org/download.shtml`.

2. Scroll down the page until you find the following list of download links:

Windows

Get the version of pygame for your version of python. You may need to uninstall old versions of pygame first.
NOTE: if you had pygame 1.7.1 installed already, please uninstall it first. Either using the uninstall feature - or remove the files: c:\python25\lib\site-packages\pygame . We changed the type of installer, and there will be issues if you don't uninstall pygame 1.7.1 first (and all old versions).

- pygame-1.9.1release.win32-py2.4.exe 3MB
- pygame-1.9.1release.win32-py2.5.exe 3MB
- pygame-1.9.1.win32-py2.5.msi 3MB (**python2.5.4 is the best python on windows** at the moment)
- pygame-1.9.1.win32-py2.6.msi 3MB
- pygame-1.9.1.win32-py3.1.msi 3MB
- (optional) Numeric for windows python2.5 (note: Numeric is old, best to use numpy) http://rene.f0o.com/~rene/stuff/Numeric-24.2.win32-py2.5.exe
- windows 64bit users note: use the 32bit python with this 32bit pygame.

---

3. Download the file `pygame-1.9.1.win32-py2.6.msi`. The version number might not match. In that case watch out for the `-py2.6` postfix in the filename.

4. Launch the installer and click **Next** until you reach the following step of the install wizard:

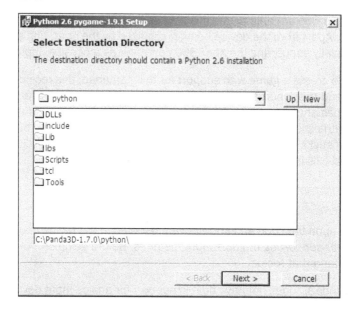

5. Make sure the directory actually is the `python` subdirectory of your Panda3D installation. The screenshot shows the default installation path.

6. Finish the installation and you are ready to go.

How to do it...

Let's write some code for handling gamepad input:

1. Add a new source file called `XboxControllerHandler.py` and insert the following code:

```python
from panda3d.core import *
import pygame
import math

class XboxControllerState:
    A = 0
    B = 1
    X = 2
    Y = 3
    LB = 4
    RB = 5
```

```
            BACK = 6
            START = 7
            LS = 8
            RS = 9

            def __init__(self, joy):
                self.joy = joy
                self.leftStick = Vec2()
                self.rightStick = Vec2()
                self.dpad = Vec2()
                self.triggers = 0.0
                self.buttons = [False] * self.joy.get_numbuttons()

            def update(self):
                self.leftStick.setX(self.joy.get_axis(0))
                self.leftStick.setY(self.joy.get_axis(1))
                self.rightStick.setX(self.joy.get_axis(4))
                self.rightStick.setY(self.joy.get_axis(3))
                self.triggers = self.joy.get_axis(2)

                for i in range(self.joy.get_numbuttons()):
                    self.buttons[i] = self.joy.get_button(i)
```

2. Add the `XboxControllerHandler` class below the code of `XboxControllerState`:

```
class XboxControllerHandler(InputHandler):
    def __init__(self):
        InputHandler.__init__(self)

        self.wasWalking = False
        self.wasReversing = False
        self.controller = None

        pygame.init()
        pygame.joystick.init()

        for i in range(pygame.joystick.get_count()):
            joy = pygame.joystick.Joystick(i)
            name = joy.get_name()

            if "Xbox 360" in name or "XBOX 360" in name:
                joy.init()
                self.controller = joy
                self.state = XboxControllerState(joy)

        taskMgr.add(self.updateInput, "update input")
```

```
def updateInput(self, task):
    pygame.event.pump()

    if self.controller:
        self.state.update()

    x = self.state.rightStick.getX()
    y = self.state.leftStick.getY()

    if y < -0.5 and not self.wasWalking:
        self.wasWalking = True
        self.beginWalk()
    elif not y < -0.5 and self.wasWalking:
        self.wasWalking = False
        self.endWalk()
    elif y > 0.5 and not self.wasReversing:
        self.wasReversing = True
        self.beginReverse()
    elif not y > 0.5 and self.wasReversing:
        self.wasReversing = False
        self.endReverse()

    if math.fabs(x) > 0.2:
        messenger.send("turn", [-x])

    self.dispatchMessages()
    return task.cont
```

3. Open `Application.py` and add the highlighted line to the constructor of the `Application` class:

```
self.keyInput = KeyboardMouseHandler()
self.xboxInput = XboxControllerHandler()
```

4. Start the application and control the panda using the left analog stick for moving forward and backward and the right stick for turning left and right.

How it works...

In the constructor of the `XboxControllerHandler` class we can see the `pygame` library and its joystick module being initialized before we iterate over all connected devices to see if we can find an Xbox 360 controller. If this routine is successful, a new instance of `XboxControllerState` is created.

This class is a container for storing the state of an Xbox 360 controller and provides easier access to the controller data than using numeric indices. The class' `leftStick` and `rightStick` variables store the state of the two analog sticks, while `dpad` and `triggers` store the states of the cross-shaped directional pad and the analog triggers on the back of the controller. Data about the various buttons on the controller being up or down can be accessed using the `buttons` list. To make accessing these buttons easier, the `A`, `B`, `X`, and other class variables, found right under the class declaration, can be used to address buttons by name rather than by a numeric index.

This leaves the `updateInput()` method of the `XboxControllerHandler` class open for discussion. Here, we keep the internal message loop of `pygame` running by calling `pygame.event.pump()`. Handling the input for walking forwards and backwards requires special care as we are degrading the left analog stick to a binary control scheme. We do not care how far the stick was pushed forward. Instead, we just set a flag based on whether the stick has been moved forward or backward.

Because we are not receiving any events for when an analog stick has become active, we need to take care of detecting this case ourselves. Therefore we need to store and check if we were not walking or reversing before any of the `-start` events are triggered. The same applies for the `-stop` events, where we need to determine if we were in a walking or reversing state, respectively.

The data read from the analog sticks on the Xbox 360 controller does not just simply go back to zero if they are centered. Instead, we receive a lot of noise from the controller. This is the reason why the `turn` event is starting to be triggered after the controller was moved more than 20% of the way towards one direction, or else the panda would be twitching uncontrollably and never stand still. We apply this low-cut filter in the code using the conditional expression `if math.fabs(x) > 0.2`.

Recording and simulating user input

In this recipe you will learn how to record the stream of user inputs and replay it at a later point. This can be useful in several areas of game development, such as playtesting and AI.

While testing a game, you could capture all of the playtesters' actions, for example. If a bug is encountered, the data file containing the input that led to a crash or unintended behavior can then be attached to the bug report so that a programmer is able to easily reproduce the steps that led to the problem and fix it.

Apart from being able to save input streams for reproducing bugs, this data could also be used to automate playtesting. You have to realize that testing a game means playing the same section of it over and over again, just to make sure everything works properly. To relieve your testers from this repetitive kind of work, using a technique similar to the one shown here could enable them to record a stream of interactions once for every test case. This way, as long as there are no fundamental changes to the level or the gameplay, testers would just need to hit "play" and wait for unexpected things to happen.

Prerecorded input could also be used as a starting point for computer controlled opponents. You could, for example, record the input of several hundred players and let the AI toggle between these command streams or just parts of them. This will of course not work for every game and might not be convincing enough, but a fake AI is still better than no AI if you didn't implement that part of your game yet.

Getting ready

We will use the recipe *Implementing an abstraction layer for supporting multiple input methods* found in this chapter as the base for this sample (*Handling input from an Xbox 360 controller* works too). If you haven't read and implemented it yet, take a step back and complete that recipe first!

How to do it...

The following steps are necessary for recording and simulating user input:

1. Create a new source file. Name it `InputRecorder.py` and insert the code found below:

```
from direct.showbase.DirectObject import DirectObject
from panda3d.core import *

class InputRecorder(DirectObject):
    def __init__(self):
        DirectObject.__init__(self)
        self.events = []
        self.setupEvents()

    def setupEvents(self):
        self.startTime = globalClock.getFrameTime()
        del self.events[:]
        self.accept("walk-start", self.recordEvent, ["walk-
start"])
        self.accept("walk-stop", self.recordEvent, ["walk-stop"])
        self.accept("reverse-start", self.recordEvent, ["reverse-
start"])
        self.accept("reverse-stop", self.recordEvent, ["reverse-
stop"])
        self.accept("walk", self.recordEvent, ["walk"])
        self.accept("reverse", self.recordEvent, ["reverse"])
        self.accept("turn", self.recordEvent, ["turn"])

    def replay(self):
        self.ignoreAll()
        self.acceptOnce("replay-done", self.setupEvents)
        last = 0
```

```
            for e in self.events:
                taskMgr.doMethodLater(e[0], self.createInput,
    "replay", extraArgs = [e[1], e[2]])
                last = e[0]
            taskMgr.doMethodLater(last + 1, messenger.send, "replay
    done", extraArgs = ["replay-done"])

        def recordEvent(self, name, rate = 0):
            self.events.append((globalClock.getFrameTime() - self.
    startTime, name, rate))

        def createInput(self, event, rate):
            if not event in ["walk", "reverse", "turn"]:
                messenger.send(event)
            else:
                messenger.send(event, [rate])
```

2. Open `Application.py` and add these two calls to the constructor:

```
self.rec = InputRecorder()
self.accept("r", self.startReplay)
```

3. Add these two methods to the `Application` class:

```
        def startReplay(self):
            self.acceptOnce("replay-done", self.replayDone)
            messenger.send("walk-stop")
            messenger.send("reverse-stop")
            self.panda.clearTransform()
            self.rec.replay()

        def replayDone(self):
            self.panda.clearTransform()
            messenger.send("walk-stop")
            messenger.send("reverse-stop")
```

4. Start the sample. Walk around a bit, then press the *R* key to see a replay of your actions.

How it works...

Our record and replay implementation is really simple. The `InputRecorder` class just adds additional event listeners for the input commands. But instead of moving an actor around the scene, it appends the command and its argument to a list. We also store the time the event occurred relative to the start time of the recording. This is enough for accurately reproducing player actions in the right order and with the correct timing.

When replaying, we first reset all transformations and stop playing animations. Then we queue up calls to the `createInput()` method, which is used to send movement commands, just as a normal input device would do. In fact, what we created here is a virtual game controller.

Finally, when the playing of the recording has finished, we reset the scene again and get ready to save another stream of user commands.

Reading audio data from a microphone

Microphones and audio processing have become a fixed part of game development, not only for music and singing games, but also for team based action and strategy titles, which require multiple players to coordinate their actions in order to succeed. It doesn't matter whether you want to make your game voice controlled, detect the pitch of someone singing or implement a voice chat, you will almost always need to get access to an audio device. In this short recipe, you will learn how to open an audio source for recording and do some simple signal processing on the received audio data.

Getting ready

Set up a new Panda3D Python project as shown in *Setting up the game structure* found in *Chapter 1* before going on with this recipe.

How to do it...

Complete these tasks to enable and handle input from a microphone:

1. Open `Application.py` and replace its contents with the following code:

```
from direct.showbase.ShowBase import ShowBase
from panda3d.core import *
import audioop

class Application(ShowBase):
    def __init__(self):
        ShowBase.__init__(self)
        self.addSmiley()
        self.addGround()
        self.setupMicrophone()
        self.cam.setPos(0, -50, 10)

    def setupMicrophone(self):
        for i in range(MicrophoneAudio.getNumOptions()):
            print i, MicrophoneAudio.getOption(i)
```

```
        if MicrophoneAudio.getNumOptions() > 0:
            index = raw_input("choose device: ")
            opt = MicrophoneAudio.getOption(0)
            self.cursor = opt.open()
            taskMgr.add(self.update, "update audio")

    def addSmiley(self):
        self.smiley = loader.loadModel("smiley")
        self.smiley.reparentTo(render)
        self.smiley.setZ(10)

    def addGround(self):
        cm = CardMaker("ground")
        cm.setFrame(-500, 500, -500, 500)
        ground = render.attachNewNode(cm.generate())
        ground.setColor(0.2, 0.4, 0.2)
        ground.lookAt(0, 0, -1)

    def update(self, task):
        if self.cursor.ready() >= 16:
            data = self.cursor.readSamples(self.cursor.ready())
            rms = audioop.rms(data, 2)
            minmax = audioop.minmax(data, 2)
            intensity = float(rms) / 32767.0
            self.win.setClearColor(Vec4(intensity, intensity,
intensity, 1))
            print rms, minmax

            currentZ = self.smiley.getZ()
            self.smiley.setZ(currentZ - 0.3 + intensity)

            if self.smiley.getZ() <= 1:
                self.smiley.setZ(1)

        return task.cont
```

2. Start the program. The window background color will get closer to white and the smiley will start to lift off the ground as you provide louder input:

How it works...

To open an audio recording device for reading data in Panda3D we have to retrieve a cursor object of the type `MovieAudioCursor`. For this, we choose a device option and open it. In Panda3D's `MicrophoneAudio` API terminology, an option describes a combination of input device, jack, channel, and sampling rate. First, we print a list of all available options. Then we create a console prompt that asks for the number of the device to use.

To read raw audio data from the recording device, we need to continuously poll the cursor, checking if enough samples have been buffered. To access the audio data we use the `readSamples()` method. This returns a string of audio bytes, which we can directly use for some simple audio processing.

Using the `audioop` module that is part of the Python programming libraries, we calculate the root mean square of the audio signal. This is used for getting the power of the signal, which means you will get lower values when whispering into the microphone and higher ones when screaming and shouting. We just use the root mean square to create a very simple visualization of input loudness, but we could also use it to encourage players of a karaoke game to sing louder or do some simple beat detection for audio visualizations by watching how this value changes over time.

For a more thorough analysis of the input data, we would need fast Fourier transforms, among other techniques. An efficient and easy to use implementation of fast Fourier transforms can be found in the `NumPy` library, for example, which can be downloaded for free from `numpy.scipy.org`.

Reading video data from a webcam

Using a live camera feed opens new and interesting possibilities for video games: Motion controlled games require players to get off the couch and use their whole bodies. Or why not add a video chat feature to enhance the presentation of player-to-player communication? Seeing your opponents face could even become a gameplay feature, for instance, an online poker game could greatly benefit from this. What about a game where players are taking turns in making stupid faces while their opponent tries not to smile or laugh at it? Detection of facial expressions works quite well and in the case of the last example, will detect even the slightest smirk!

Developing game ideas for camera-based video games is very interesting and great fun, especially when your game involves doing funny faces or flapping your arms frantically. But behind the pleasure of these games, there's always a technical side to it, which you will get to know over the course of this recipe. After you worked your way through it, you will be able to set up Panda3D to use a live video stream from a webcam and display it in your application.

Getting ready

To be able to work through this recipe, you need two things:

▸ First, a new project skeleton as described in *Chapter 1*.

▸ Second, you need to have a webcam connected to your computer.

How to do it...

Panda3D can read a video stream from a webcam if you follow these steps:

1. Open `Application.py` and replace its contents with the code that follows:

```
from direct.showbase.ShowBase import ShowBase
from panda3d.core import *
from panda3d.vision import *

class Application(ShowBase):
    def __init__(self):
        ShowBase.__init__(self)

        for i in range(WebcamVideo.getNumOptions()):
            print WebcamVideo.getOption(i)

        if WebcamVideo.getNumOptions() > 0:
            opt = WebcamVideo.getOption(0)
            self.cursor = opt.open()
            self.tex = Texture()
            self.cursor.setupTexture(self.tex)
```

```
            cm = CardMaker("plane")
            cm.setFrame(-1, 1, -1, 1)
            plane = render2d.attachNewNode(cm.generate())
            plane.setTexture(self.tex)

            scaleX = float(self.cursor.sizeX()) / float(self.tex.
getXSize())
            scaleY = float(self.cursor.sizeY()) / float(self.tex.
getYSize())
            plane.setTexScale(TextureStage.getDefault(),
Vec2(scaleX, scaleY))

            taskMgr.add(self.update, "update video")

    def update(self, task):
        if self.cursor.ready():
            self.cursor.fetchIntoTexture(0, self.tex, 0)
        return task.cont
```

2. Start the application. Your webcam should turn on and the live video feed should be displayed in the program window:

How it works...

If you already happened to have read the recipe on recording and using audio data found in this chapter, the code might seem very familiar—you choose an option, which is a combination of input device and recording resolution, and open a cursor to it that allows controlling and accessing the input data.

Additionally, you need to provide and setup a Texture object that will hold the recorded video images. Because Panda3D tries to use textures with edge lengths that are a power of two, you need to rescale the texture coordinates of the object the texture will be applied to. If you do not do this, you will see a stretched image that is surrounded by black bars, because your 640x480 video stream, for example, will be fitted into a texture that is 1024x512.

There's more...

This is a very basic sample. If you need to process the image data or do some analysis on it to detect motion, faces or colors, you should always think about using shaders, as they are the most efficient tool for the job. Take a look at *Chapter 4, Scene Effects and Shaders* if you want to know how to write and apply shader programs!

Reading input data from a network

In this recipe you will learn how to remotely control an actor by sending commands over a network. This is a very common usage scenario in AI simulations, for example. In many of these simulations one central server program is used for visualizing the current simulation state. Each of the simulated entities is processed on a dedicated computer that connects to the server to send commands for altering the state of the simulation.

The following instructions will teach you how to build such a setup using Panda3D. The client part of this application will send text strings to the server side. The server will then interpret these strings as movement commands for an actor placed in a simple scene.

Getting ready

To be able to complete this recipe, you need to set up a new project according to the steps presented in the *Chapter 1* article *Setting up the game structure*. Additionally, you need the `FollowCam` class from the recipe *Making the camera smoothly follow an object* found in *Chapter 2* as well as the `InputHandler` class described in *Implementing an abstraction layer for supporting multiple input methods*, which can be found in this chapter. Copy the files `FollowCam.py` and `InputHandler.py` to the `src` subdirectory of your project.

This recipe also assumes that you have worked your way through *Sending and receiving custom datagrams* in *Chapter 9, Networking*. Some of the code presented in the article will be reused and altered slightly in the following steps. If you haven't yet read said recipe, this might be the right time to do so.

This recipe consists of the following tasks:

1. Implement the classes responsible for sending and receiving in a new source file called `NetClasses.py`:

```python
from panda3d.core import *
from direct.distributed.PyDatagram import PyDatagram
from direct.distributed.PyDatagramIterator import
PyDatagramIterator
from random import choice

class NetCommon:
    def __init__(self, protocol):
        self.manager = ConnectionManager()
        self.reader = QueuedConnectionReader(self.manager, 0)
        self.writer = ConnectionWriter(self.manager, 0)
        self.protocol = protocol

        taskMgr.add(self.updateReader, "updateReader")

    def updateReader(self, task):
        if self.reader.dataAvailable():
            data = NetDatagram()
            self.reader.getData(data)
            reply = self.protocol.process(data)

            if reply != None:
                self.writer.send(reply, data.getConnection())

        return task.cont

class Server(NetCommon):
    def __init__(self, protocol, port):
        NetCommon.__init__(self, protocol)
        self.listener = QueuedConnectionListener(self.manager, 0)
        socket = self.manager.openTCPServerRendezvous(port, 100)
        self.listener.addConnection(socket)
        self.connections = []

        taskMgr.add(self.updateListener, "updateListener")

    def updateListener(self, task):
        if self.listener.newConnectionAvailable():
            connection = PointerToConnection()
```

```
                    if self.listener.getNewConnection(connection):
                        connection = connection.p()
                        self.connections.append(connection)
                        self.reader.addConnection(connection)
                        print "Server: New connection established."

            return task.cont

class Client(NetCommon):
    def __init__(self, protocol):
        NetCommon.__init__(self, protocol)

    def connect(self, host, port, timeout):
        self.connection = self.manager.openTCPClientConnection(hos
t, port, timeout)
        if self.connection:
            self.reader.addConnection(self.connection)
            print "Client: Connected to server."

    def send(self, datagram):
        if self.connection:
            self.writer.send(datagram, self.connection)

    def start(self):
        data = PyDatagram()
        data.addUint8(0)
        data.addString("hi")
        self.send(data)

class Protocol:
    def printMessage(self, title, msg):
        print "%s %s" % (title, msg)

    def buildReply(self, msgid, data):
        reply = PyDatagram()
        reply.addUint8(msgid)
        reply.addString(data)
        return reply

    def process(self, data):
        return None

class ServerProtocol(Protocol):
    def process(self, data):
```

```
            it = PyDatagramIterator(data)
            msgid = it.getUint8()

            if msgid == 0:
                pass
            elif msgid == 1:
                command = it.getString()
                self.printMessage("new command:", command)
                messenger.send(command)

            return self.buildReply(0, "ok")

    class ClientProtocol(Protocol):
        def __init__(self):
            self.lastCommand = globalClock.getFrameTime()
            self.commands = ["net-walk-start",
                             "net-walk-stop",
                             "net-left-start",
                             "net-left-stop",
                             "net-right-start",
                             "net-right-stop"]

        def process(self, data):
            time = globalClock.getFrameTime()
            if time - self.lastCommand > 0.5:
                self.lastCommand = time
                return self.buildReply(1, choice(self.commands))
            else:
                return self.buildReply(0, "nop")
```

2. Next, create another new source file called `NetworkHandler.py`. Implement the network input handler in the newly created file:

```
from InputHandler import InputHandler
from panda3d.core import *

class NetworkHandler(InputHandler):
    def __init__(self):
        InputHandler.__init__(self)

        self.accept("net-walk-start", self.beginWalk)
        self.accept("net-walk-stop", self.endWalk)
        self.accept("net-left-start", self.beginTurnLeft)
        self.accept("net-left-stop", self.endTurnLeft)
        self.accept("net-right-start", self.beginTurnRight)
```

```
        self.accept("net-right-stop", self.endTurnRight)

        taskMgr.add(self.updateInput, "update network input")

    def updateInput(self, task):
        self.dispatchMessages()
        return task.cont
```

3. Open `Application.py` and extend the `Application` class implementation:

```
from direct.showbase.ShowBase import ShowBase
from direct.actor.Actor import Actor
from panda3d.core import *
from FollowCam import FollowCam
from NetworkHandler import NetworkHandler
from NetClasses import Server, Client, ServerProtocol,
ClientProtocol

class Application(ShowBase):
    def __init__(self):
        ShowBase.__init__(self)
        self.setupScene()
        self.setupInput()
        self.setupNetwork()

    def setupScene(self):
        self.world = loader.loadModel("environment")
        self.world.reparentTo(render)
        self.world.setScale(0.5)
        self.world.setPos(-8, 80, 0)

        self.panda = Actor("panda", {"walk": "panda-walk"})
        self.panda.reparentTo(render)
        self.followCam = FollowCam(self.cam, self.panda)

    def setupInput(self):
        self.netInput = NetworkHandler()
        self.accept("walk-start", self.beginWalk)
        self.accept("walk-stop", self.endWalk)
        self.accept("reverse-start", self.beginReverse)
        self.accept("reverse-stop", self.endReverse)
        self.accept("walk", self.walk)
        self.accept("reverse", self.reverse)
        self.accept("turn", self.turn)
```

```
def setupNetwork(self):
    server = Server(ServerProtocol(), 9999)
    client = Client(ClientProtocol())
    client.connect("localhost", 9999, 3000)
    client.start()

def beginWalk(self):
    self.panda.setPlayRate(1.0, "walk")
    self.panda.loop("walk")

def endWalk(self):
    self.panda.stop()

def beginReverse(self):
    self.panda.setPlayRate(-1.0, "walk")
    self.panda.loop("walk")

def endReverse(self):
    self.panda.stop()

def walk(self, rate):
    self.panda.setY(self.panda, rate)

def reverse(self, rate):
    self.panda.setY(self.panda, rate)

def turn(self, rate):
    self.panda.setH(self.panda, rate)
```

4. Finally, press *F6* to launch the program. You should be able to see a panda wander around randomly in a simple background scene:

How it works...

We start this recipe by implementing our networking layer. This is mostly taken from Chapter 9, but not without a few notable alterations to the communication protocol.

In our custom network protocol, we distinguish between two general message types, indicated by a numerical ID sent along with every command string. A message ID of 0 indicates an internal command, while an ID of 1 stands for a movement command.

After the client establishes a connection, it sends the internal command `"hi"` to start the conversation between the two hosts. The server then sends the reply `"hi"` to signal it has successfully received a command. In fact, the server acknowledges every command it receives by sending this reply to request further data.

Every 0.5 seconds, the client sends a random command string out of the possible movement commands stored in `self.commands`. When the server receives such a command with message ID 1, it uses Panda3D's messaging system to create a new event named after the command. This is where the `NetworkHandler` class we implemented in step 2 comes into play.

`NetworkHandler` is derived from the `InputHandler` class to create a new input handling implementation for network commands. We implement this class to listen for the messages the server side protocol dispatches when it receives a new command from the client. Whenever a new movement command arrives, the `NetworkHandler` class translates it to the common input message format implemented previously in the recipe *Implementing an abstraction layer for supporting multiple input methods*.

This leaves us with the `Application` class. Here we set up the scene and the networking layer. Additionally, we implement methods for handling incoming input messages that make the panda move around the scene.

12
Packaging and Distribution

In this chapter, we will cover:

- ▸ Packing assets into multifiles
- ▸ Creating a redistributable game package
- ▸ Advanced package creation and hosting
- ▸ Embedding a game into a website
- ▸ Using website and plugin interoperability

Introduction

Besides the effort of developing an idea, getting the game design down to a point where it is great fun and actually producing all the code and assets we need, there's another thing we need to think about—how do we get our product into the hands of our customers? One way would of course be to just give them this huge pile of code, models, textures, sounds, and whatever else makes up our games, along with a manual for setting up the environment and dependencies. And while this is a tempting approach that spares us some work, we simply cannot do this to players who just want to play our games.

This is why we need to find a way to bundle up all the scripts and assets that make up our games and provide the end users with something along the lines of a button that says "click here to start playing".

If we make games available for download, we also want the file sizes to be small. While broadband internet connections may be fast, cheap, and widely available, costs for server traffic can easily get out of hand (and out of our budgets) if a million people happen to download our three and a half gigabytes of gaming awesomeness.

Illegal ripping and reuse of game assets does happen and is not in the best interest of game developers. Developers can make some assets free to copy and reuse, but that should be their choice. People creating nude patches or changing a game's behavior in an unintended way could cause us, as developers, some headaches. Therefore, protecting assets from misuse is an important part of game development and release.

The Panda3D SDK contains tools that provide solutions to these problems. In this chapter, we will see how we can make it easier for players to get and play our games. We will package our assets into container files. We will make our data harder to tamper with. We will make downloads faster by using data compression.

Packing assets into multifiles

If you take the time to browse through the folders of nearly any game that's installed on your hard drive, you will see lots of files with interesting extensions: `mpq`, `pk3`, `dat`, `upk`, and so on. What you most likely will not find are images, models, sounds, or scripts. But then you start the game and everything appears on the screen and runs perfectly fine—why is that?

As you may have already guessed, it has something to do with these strange files that are carrying even stranger name suffixes. These files are containers, hiding away the game resources from the end user. Basically, they are similar to `ZIP` or `RAR` archives. Most of them are using a proprietary file format that sometimes even resembles a small file system, just as it might be implemented in an operating system.

Besides the obfuscation of resources, such file containers provide at least two more very important advantages over distributing assets openly. The first one concerns the installation process: The setup program only has to copy a few large container files compared to transmitting hundreds or even thousands of small to medium sized files. This can speed up the process of copying files by a substantial amount.

The design of the game engine consuming these files is the other reason. Containers allow developers to store game assets in an optimized form and order that makes them easier and faster to load and process at runtime, possibly decreasing loading time and increasing the game's performance.

Panda3D provides the right tools and built-in features for creating and loading container files. In the terminology of this engine, they are called multifiles and the following steps will show you how to work with them.

Getting ready

This recipe extends upon the code created in *Loading models and actors* found in *Chapter 2, Creating and Building Scenes*. Please review said recipe before going on.

Additionally, you have to copy the files `panda-walk.egg.pz`, `panda.egg.pz`, and `teapot.egg.pz` from `C:\Panda3D-1.7.0\models` to the `models` subdirectory of your project directory tree.

How to do it...

Let's create a sample program:

1. Additional to the existing `import` statements at the top of `Application.py`, make sure to have the following lines:

   ```
   from panda3d.core import *
   import glob
   import os
   import os.path
   ```

2. Add the following lines of code to the constructor of the `Application` class directly after the call to `ShowBase.__init__(self)`:

   ```
   mf = Multifile()
   mf.openWrite(Filename("../models/models.mf"))

   for f in glob.iglob("../models/*.egg.pz"):
       filename = os.path.split(f)[1]
       mf.addSubfile(filename, Filename(f), 9)

   mf.repack()
   mf.close()

   fs = VirtualFileSystem.getGlobalPtr()
   fs.mount(Filename("../models/models.mf"), ".", VirtualFileSystem.
   MFReadOnly)
   ```

How it works...

The preceding code actually combines two steps that are normally not found within the same program.

The first step, which we would normally put inside a build script, is to build the multifile—to add files to the container. We are using a `Multifile` object to add so-called subfiles to the multifile. The `addSubfile()` method is the key point here. The first parameter is the name the added file will be accessible as inside the multifile. The second parameter is the full path to the file that is to be added. The third parameter sets the compression level.

The multifile libraries and tools of Panda3D are able to compress and decompress files contained in a multifile on the fly, as they are added at build time and loaded at runtime. This can help to keep the size of a game's distribution package small, and also provides a simple form of obfuscation. When working with multifiles, use 0 for no compression at all and 9 for the highest level of minimization. Choosing a higher compression level will keep package sizes small, but in exchange we must accept that creating these packages will take more time to finish.

Before we are done creating the multifile and close it, we need to `repack()` our container file. A multifile contains an index that stores the names and offsets of the subfiles. Repacking reorders this index, and makes sure all metadata and subfile content is in the proper place. We must not forget this step to ensure that the engine will be able to load data from the multifile.

The second part of working with multifiles happens in the last two lines shown in the previous code. Here we mount the contents of the multifile into the root folder of Panda3D's virtual file system, which makes it possible to transparently access all of the files found within the container.

There's more...

There are a few more things you can do with multifiles.

Updating a subfile

During development, you will repack your assets over and over again. The following method call will only add a subfile if it is different from the one already present in the multifile. This may help you to decrease the time needed to regenerate asset containers.

```
mf = Multifile()
mf.updateSubfile(internalName, Filename(fullPath), compressionLevel)
```

Extracting a subfile

Subfiles can also be extracted from a multifile like this:

```
mf = Multifile()
index = mf.findSubfile(internalName)
mf.extractSubfile(index, Filename(fullPath))
```

Encrypting subfiles

To protect your data, you can encrypt subfiles on a per-file basis. After calling the two following methods, all subsequent reads or writes will decrypt and encrypt subfiles respectively. Similar to using compression, encoding, and decoding your data using an encryption algorithm requires additional CPU resources. Also note that Panda3D uses the same key for encrypting as well as decrypting data. This means that the password required for accessing multifile data needs to be stored somewhere in your code, exposing it to possible reverse-engineering attacks. This kind of encryption should be seen as a time-consuming obstacle to be put in the way of attackers. It makes accessing the data harder, but not impossible.

```
mf = Multifile()
mf.setEncryptionFlag(True)
mf.setEncryptionPassword("arewesafenow?")
```

Creating multifiles on the command line

The Panda3D SDK also includes a command line tool for working with multifiles. The following line shows a possible way to invoke the program from the command prompt:

```
multify -c -z -9 -e -p pass -f models.mf panda.egg.pz panda-walk.egg.pz
teapot.egg.pz
```

This will create (-c) a new multifile called models.mf (-f), containing the subfiles panda. egg.pz, panda-walk.egg.pz and teapot.egg.pz. The subfiles will be compressed using the highest compression level (-z -9) and encrypted with the given password (-e -p pass). The multify tool also has several other options and flags which can be viewed using the command multify -h.

Note the .egg.pz file extension of the model files. These files are normal .egg files that were compressed using pzip. You can unpack the raw .egg data using the punzip tool.

Creating a redistributable game package

Time is a precious resource, even in people's spare time. If a TV show isn't compelling after seeing 3 seconds of it, we zap on to the next channel. If we don't like what we hear, we skip to another song when listening to music.

The same principles apply to video games. But not only do games have to be compelling and fun to keep players engaged—in the world of PC gaming we also need to provide an uncomplicated experience for installing and launching a game. If players needed to do lots of configuration work to get the game running, then that would drive off most of them from actually playing it rather quickly.

To prevent this from happening and to make launching our games as easy as possible, Panda3D gives us two things: The Panda3D Runtime and the Panda3D applet file that packs an entire game into one file. All players need to do is install the runtime and double-click the applet file.

This recipe will show you how to obtain the Panda3D Runtime and how to build a game package for easy redistribution of your games.

Getting ready

This recipe requires some runtime components to be present to work. Open your browser and download the Panda3D Runtime from the Panda3D website. The runtime download can be found at `www.panda3d.org/download.php?runtime`. Then go to `runtime.panda3d.org`, download the file `packp3d.p3d` and copy it to `C:\Panda3D\bin`.

You can use one of the samples found in this book or one of your personal projects as a starting base for this recipe. As long as it is built after the project setup described in *Setting up the game structure* found in *Chapter 1* you are set and ready to go.

How to do it...

You can create and launch a redistributable game package like this:

1. Open `main.py` and change its contents to this:

    ```
    from Application import Application

    gameApp = Application()
    gameApp.run()
    ```

2. Create a new batch file in the top-level directory of your project. Name it `deploy.bat`.

3. Edit `deploy.bat` and insert the commands found below:

    ```
    @echo off
    mkdir deploy
    xcopy /E /Y src\* deploy
    xcopy /E /Y models\* deploy
    xcopy /E /Y shaders\* deploy
    xcopy /E /Y sounds\* deploy
    packp3d -o pandagame.p3d -d deploy -r models
    rmdir /S /Q deploy
    ```

4. Invoke `deploy.bat` from a command prompt or by double-clicking it. This step might take a little time, as some additional components need to be downloaded.

5. Double-click the newly created `pandagame.p3d` file to launch your game. Before it starts, you will most likely see the following screen while additional data and assets are downloaded:

How it works...

To fulfill the requirements of the p3d game package format and the Panda3D Runtime, we first need to make a minimal change to main.py. Then we can go on to package our project. The packp3d expects all files, assets as well as scripts, to be present in one folder, which is why we copy all of our files to the temporary deploy directory.

Essentially, a p3d file is a special version of a multifile with a slightly different file header. While multifiles are mainly used for packaging game assets, p3d files contain all files needed to run a Panda3D based game. This includes assets as well as scripts and executables. Multifiles are just containers, but p3d files can be launched using the Panda3D runtime. Therefore they need to store some extra info to allow the engine to properly load and run p3d packages. For example, the version of Panda3D used to create the package, the application main file name as well as the names of referenced external packages are all included in a p3d file.

When you double-click the p3d file, the Panda3D runtime starts up and mounts the file. The engine then looks for a file called main.py and starts running the Python code found in it. If our main file has a different name, we can pass it to packp3d using the -m parameter.

To close off the discussion, we take a look at what might be the most important parameter of `packp3d`, which is `-r`. The initial Panda3D Runtime installation is very lightweight and does not contain all components of the engine. Instead, it relies on game packages to reference the various engine components. If a referenced package is not found in the local cache, or a newer version is available, it is downloaded from `runtime.panda3d.org`, which is the default package host.

This means that we have to use the `-r` parameter to add a reference for every package we use. Without these references Panda3D assumes that we are only using the packages included in the minimal runtime installer. So building a project using the default models means appending `-r models` to the command. If we use sound, we need to add `-r audio`. Using PhysX means an extra `-r physx` and so on.

Advanced package creation and hosting

In the previous recipe, *Creating a redistributable game package*, you learned about building one monolithic container file that stores all of a game's code and assets. Of course, this already made things simpler, as you only need to provide this one file and the information that the Panda3D Runtime needs to be installed to run.

In this recipe, you will take things one step further. Instead of just putting everything into one file, you will split your code and assets into two separate packages. You will be able to drop the requirement of having to copy all data into one directory and additionally, you will learn how to build these packages in a way that allows you to host them on the web using an HTTP server. This will allow you to easily distribute games and the data they require. Additionally, this will allow you to provide distinct packages containing game-specific data and others that are filled with common libraries and resources. This way, code and assets shared across multiple releases need to be downloaded only once, which helps in keeping client side loading times smaller as well as keeping server system loads and bandwidth costs low.

After finishing this recipe you will be able to control the packaging process in a more detailed way. This will allow you to further optimize the user experience and help you to save file hosting bandwidth and traffic because they will only be downloading what they need.

Getting ready

Additional to the prerequisites of the recipe *Creating a redistributable game package*, you need to download the file `ppackage.p3d` from `runtime.panda3d.org` and copy it into the `C:\Panda3D-1.7.0\bin` directory.

Panda3D expects packages referenced by the main `p3d` file to be hosted on a web server. Therefore you need to either set up a local web server or get some hosted webspace. There are many free HTTP servers like HFS, Cherokee, or IIS Express, for example, that all allow you to set up a simple web server very quickly.

How to do it...

Follow the steps below:

1. Create a new file called `deploy.pdef` in the top-level directory of your project.

2. Open `deploy.pdef` and enter the following code. Make sure to replace the URL with the one of your server:

```
from panda3d.core import *

packager.setHost("http://localhost:8000/")

class myresources(package):
    file(Filename("models/*"))
    file(Filename("shaders/*"))
    file(Filename("sounds/*"))

class pandagame(p3d):
    require("panda3d", "models", "myresources")
    config(display_name="My Game")
    dir("src")
    mainModule("main")
```

3. Open a command prompt window, navigate to your project's directory and enter this command:

   ppackage -i deploy deploy.pdef

4. The last command will create a new directory called `deploy`. Upload its entire contents to your server.

5. Double-click `pandagame.py`. The Panda3D runtime should start, download all necessary files, and then run your project. The following screen denotes the runtime not being able to reach the server:

How it works...

Instead of pointing a tool to a directory containing all of our data, we write a package definition file containing detailed information about the contents and name of each package. The syntax of a `.pdef` file is based on Python and even allows a subset of the Python language constructs, like importing modules or `if` conditionals. In a `.pdef` file, there are two classes you derive from to create either multifile packages or p3d applet containers. These two classes are `package` and `p3d`.

Within each of these classes, we use `file()` and `dir()` to add arbitrary files to a container file. What's nice about these two is that the packaging tool is able to detect model files in plain-text `.egg` format and automatically converts them into the more space and loading time efficient `.bam` format, for example.

In our sample we also set a configuration variable and define the main module of our p3d file using the self-explaining `config()` and `mainModule()` functions. Additionally, we must not forget to add a call to `require()` inside our .p3d definition. This references an external package—just like the running `packp3d` with the `-r` parameter flag.

There's more...

Before we are through with this recipe, there are just a couple of things you ought to know when working with packages.

Working with modules

In this recipe we only created a game package and one containing asset. One thing that's important to know additionally, though, is how to package Python modules. This enables us to create libraries of common classes and functions the user has to download only once, even though it might be used by multiple games.

There are two functions for working with modules: `module()` and `excludeModule()`. The `module()` function will add a Python module and all of its dependencies to a package. If we want to explicitly exclude a module from being included as a dependency, we add a call to `excludeModule()`. This is used in the scripts building the Panda3D core runtime packages to exclude the `PhysX` and `ODE` libraries to decrease the package size for example.

Creating patches

We created a new package using the `ppackage` tool in this recipe. But as it happens, games change slightly over time as bugs in assets and the codes are fixed later after the initial release.

When hosting packages on a server, Panda3D makes sure it always uses the latest version of all referenced applet and package files. But wouldn't it be a big waste of resources and time to download the whole package all over again because one little thing has changed? Definitely! And this is exactly what happens if we run `ppackage` for every patched release we make.

To overcome this problem and deliver updates more conveniently, Panda3D includes the `ppatcher` tool. Simply run the following command line after the initial release and after you are ready to distribute a new update (assuming our `ppackage` output is in a subdirectory called `deploy`):

```
ppatcher -i deploy
```

This creates all the necessary files for patching data on the client side to the newest version, only needing to transmit the data that has changed since the last version.

Embedding a game into a website

While providing a downloadable easy-to-run package of your game is a good step towards making users happy, we can take this to the next level. Why require players to ever leave our website? Why even bother them with downloading data to their hard disks where players, need to find the file again before they are able to double-click to launch?

Minor nuisances, we might say. But the truth is that people might have already lost the will to play a game after hitting the first few bumps in the road.

In this recipe, we take a look at how Panda3D allows us to embed games within websites. This allows us to make many things easier for potential players. Using the web plugin, we can create a website that just prompts players to press a button to launch the game without leaving the site, or even the browser. If the plugin isn't installed on a player's system, it's no problem either—we just forward her or him to the appropriate download page.

Online gaming websites have had great success with this operating model, so why shouldn't we, too?

Getting ready

This recipe assumes you have read and followed the recipe *Creating a redistributable game package*. Also be prepared to work with web technologies like JavaScript, HTML, and DOM.

The files `DetectPanda3D.js` and `RunPanda3D.js` are not part of the Panda3D SDK distribution and are only located in the source code package. Be sure to download the source code from `www.panda3d.org` to have the required files present on your system.

Adding to that, you will need a digital X.509 certificate in PEM format to sign your game package. You can (and should) retrieve a trusted certificate from many commercial certificate authorities for redistribution of your games over the web.

For testing purposes, you can create a self-signed certificate using OpenSSL. You can download OpenSSL from `gnuwin32.sourceforge.net/packages/openssl.htm`. Select the download link next to where it says **Complete package, except sources** as shown in the following screenshot. Save the file and install OpenSSL.

Download

Description	Download
• Complete package, except sources	Setup
• Sources	Setup

To generate a new test certificate, open a new command prompt and first create a new private key using the following command:

```
openssl genrsa 2048 > cacert.pem
```

Then, issue the following command to obtain a new certificate:

```
openssl req -config "C:\Program Files (x86)\GnuWin32\share\openssl.cnf"
-key cacert.pem -new -nodes -x509 -days 1095 >> cacert.pem
```

The OpenSSL program will ask a few questions about your location and company name. You don't need to answer them for internal use and can accept the default values by just pressing the *Enter* key. After finishing these steps, the certificate will be stored in a file called `cacert.pem` in the current working directory.

How to do it...

Embedding a game based on Panda3D in a website is done like this:

1. Copy your certificate file to the top-level directory of the project structure and rename it to `cacert.pem`.

2. Create a new directory called `web` inside the top-level directory of your project.

3. Copy the files `DetectPanda3D.js` and `RunPanda3D.js` from the `direct\src\directscripts` subdirectory of the source code package to the web directory of your project.

4. Inside the `web` directory, create a new file called `web.htm`. Open it in an editor and enter the following HTML code:

```html
<html>
    <script src="DetectPanda3D.js" language="javascript"></script>
    <script src="RunPanda3D.js" language="javascript"></script>
<body>
    <script language="javascript">
        detectPanda3D('noplugin.htm', false)
        P3D_RunContent('id', 'pandaPlugin', 'src', 'pandagame.
p3d', 'width', '800', 'height', '600')
    </script>
</body>
</html>
```

5. Add another HTML file to the web directory. Name it `noplugin.htm` and enter the following markup:

```html
<html>
<body>
    <p>Panda3D Web Plugin not found!</p>
    <p>Download it <a href="http://www.panda3d.org/download.
php?runtime">here</a>
</body>
</html>
```

6. Edit the `deploy.bat` file in your top-level project directory so it looks like this:

```
@echo off
mkdir deploy
xcopy /E /Y src\* deploy
xcopy /E /Y models\* deploy
xcopy /E /Y shaders\* deploy
xcopy /E /Y sounds\* deploy
multify -S cacert.pem -uf pandagame.p3d
xcopy /Y pandagame.p3d web\pandagame.p3d
rmdir /S /Q deploy
```

7. Open the `web.htm` file found inside the web subdirectory in a browser. After the Panda3D `plugin` has downloaded some additional data, you will see something similar to this:

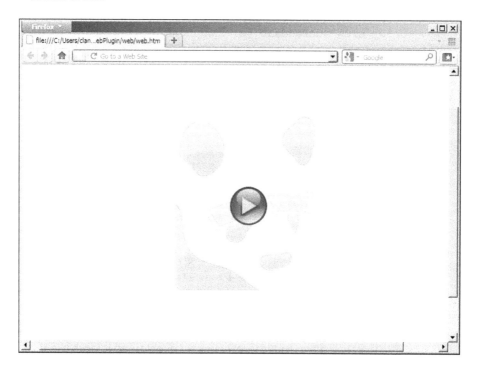

8. Press the play button to start the game running. If you are using a self-signed test certificate, the first time the program is started you will see the following message:

9. Click **View Certificate** to proceed. Next you will see this window:

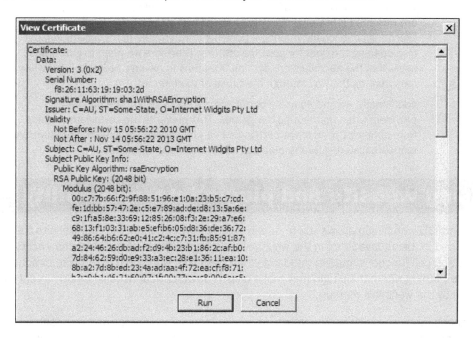

10. Your own test certificate can be considered as trustworthy, so you can press **Run** to allow your application to start.

How it works...

There are three important points to look at in this recipe. First, the detect Panda3D() function iterates over the list of installed browser plugins, trying to find an entry for the Panda3D runtime. If it can't be found, the function immediately redirects the browser to noplugin.htm, preventing the execution of any further JavaScript statement.

If detectPanda3D() was able to find the Panda3D Runtime, JavaScript execution goes on to P3D_RunContent(). This function takes care of placing the necessary <object> tags that make our application appear in the browser window, interpreting its parameters as key-value pairs used for configuring the plugin.

These scripts have one great advantage—detecting plugins and placing the correct objects in the document object model tree work slightly different across browsers. Luckily, the Panda3D developers have already handled this for us, taking a lot of tedious work off of our shoulders.

The web plugin of Panda3D accepts only signed packages and refuses to run any unsigned piece of code. This happens with good reason, as players are executing code locally, making it possible to run media-rich applications, but also opening the door for possible attacks. Therefore we need to guarantee users that the packages are coming from us and haven't been changed while they were on the way through the tubes of the Internet.

Additionally, we should use a certificate issued by one of the big trust providers when distributing our games. This prevents the certificate warning from popping up, as these certificates can be checked against their respective root certificates, guaranteeing our trustworthiness to the user.

Using website and plugin interoperability

The Panda3D web plugin allows you to deeply integrate your games with the website they are embedded in. Using JavaScript in the website, code from outside of the plugin can access values and call functions implemented in Python. This also works in the opposite direction, as code running within the plugin may make calls to JavaScript or access the document tree defined by the website's markup.

This opens many possibilities for interesting mashups between games and web technology. Automatically setting a player's name within your game based on login data, showing toast notifications when achievements are unlocked or posting status updates and screenshots to social networking sites using their JavaScript APIs. These are just a few of the many interesting things you could do using this feature of the Panda3D web plugin. But always keep in mind the security issues involved, especially with accessing personal information or login information!

Getting ready

This recipe carries on where the previous recipe *Embedding a game into a website* left off. Make sure you have a working version of the code produced in that recipe before going on.

Web technologies like HTML, JavaScript, and DOM will be used in this recipe. A basic level of knowledge in this area is assumed.

How to do it...

Let's add some interaction between the website and the Panda3D plugin:

1. Open the file `web\web.htm` in an editor and replace its contents with the code below:

```
<html>
    <script src="DetectPanda3D.js" language="javascript"></script>
    <script src="RunPanda3D.js" language="javascript"></script>
```

```html
<script language="javascript">
    function enableButtons()
    {
        var buttons = document.getElementsByTagName('input')
        for (var i = 0; i < buttons.length; i++)
            buttons[i].disabled = false
    }
</script>
<body>
    <script language="javascript">
        detectPanda3D('noplugin.htm', false)
        P3D_RunContent('id', 'pandaPlugin', 'src', 'pandagame.
p3d', 'width', '800', 'height', '600', 'onWindowOpen',
'enableButtons()')
    </script>
    <p>
        <input type="button" disabled="true" value="Wireframe"
onclick="pandaPlugin.main.base.toggleWireframe()">
        <input type="button" disabled="true" value="Get Value" onc
lick="alert(pandaPlugin.main.gameApp.foo)">
        <input type="button" disabled="true" value="Load
Smiley" onclick="pandaPlugin.main.loader.loadModel('smiley').
reparentTo(pandaPlugin.main.render)">
        <input type="button" disabled="true" value="Lights Out!"
onclick="pandaPlugin.main.gameApp.lightsOut()">
    </p>
</body>
</html>
```

2. Edit `src\Application.py` and add the following lines to the constructor of `Application`:

```python
self.foo = 42
base.appRunner.main.base = base
base.appRunner.main.render = render
base.appRunner.main.loader = loader
base.appRunner.main.gameApp = self
```

3. Also add this member method to `Application`:

```python
def lightsOut(self):
    base.appRunner.evalScript('document.body.style.
backgroundColor="#000"')
```

4. Open `deploy.bat` in your editor and change the line that runs the packp3d tool to this:

```
packp3d -c script_origin="**" -o pandagame.p3d -d deploy -r models
```

5. Run `deploy.bat`.

6. Open `web.htm` in your browser. The following buttons the Panda3D plugin will be enabled after the application has started successfully:

How it works...

Before we go on to discuss the communication between website and plugin, we need to first think a second about security. By default, JavaScript code is not allowed to call into the plugin, and the Python code running within it prevents arbitrary JavaScript from messing with our games. To explicitly enable this channel, we need to set the `script_origin` flag to the URL of the server that is going to call runtime functions from JavaScript code. In this sample, we set it to allow any host, but when making our games available to a broader public, we need to lock this down to a specific URL. For example, we could pass `scripts.example.com` to allow only scripts from this URL to access the runtime. We can also use wildcards for specifying these URLS: The rule `*.example.com` matches `a.example.com`, `b.example.com` but not `example.com`, while the rule `**.example.com` would match all of the aforementioned URLs.

The key component in enabling communication between the website, JavaScript, the Panda3D plugin and Python is `base.appRunner`. Using the `evalScript()` method of the `AppRunner` class, we can run arbitrary JavaScript code within the context of our website. This can really be anything allowed in JavaScript: A call to a function, a DOM tree manipulation or even a bigger string containing loops, calls, conditionals, and variables.

The other calling direction, which is from JavaScript into the plugin, also involves the `AppRunner` class. Here, any attribute attached to `base.appRunner.main` becomes visible to JavaScript code.

Lastly, the plugin provides the possibility to assign functions to a set of callbacks. This allows us to react to various events occurring during the runtime of the Panda3D plugin. In our case, we use the `onWindowOpen` event callback that is called right before the game actually starts running and produces the first frame.

There are several other events we can react to, like `onPluginLoad` after the plugin is loaded and initialized, `onDownloadComplete` after all dependencies are downloaded or `onReady` when the plugin is ready to launch our application. There are several more of these. You should see the official documentation of Panda3D on this topic, found at `www.panda3d.org/manual/index.php/Plugin_notify_callbacks`, to get a comprehensive list.

13
Connecting Panda3D with Content Creation Tools

In this chapter, we will cover:

- ▸ Setting up the Blender export plugin
- ▸ Exporting models from Blender
- ▸ Generating model files programmatically
- ▸ Using the "Pview" tool to preview models
- ▸ Compressing and converting model files using `pzip` and `egg2bam`

Introduction

When making video games we need to understand the meaning of the saying "Content is King". No matter how technically advanced our engine may be, all the ingenuity put into building all these great features is worth nothing without high quality content. Players are impressed by beautiful levels and nicely animated actors, not by feature lists, which is why we are highly dependant on artists creating 3D models for our games.

Model and animation artists are working with extremely feature-rich programs to put together and form the vertices, polygons, and textures that define the shape the look of game worlds and their virtual inhabitants. These programs all have their own proprietary data formats for storing mesh and animation data in memory and on disk. This is a problem for us because we need to get all this content loaded into the Panda3D engine and therefore, into our games.

In this chapter, we will see how to solve this problem by using a data export plugin that directly writes model files in a format that can be loaded by Panda3D. We will also look into the API for creating model files ourselves, so we can write our own converter if necessary. Lastly, we will pack and process the model data in order to store it in more memory- and bandwidth-saving data formats.

Setting up the Blender export plugin

Most of the digital content creation tools for making 3D meshes are very advanced pieces of software. Not only do they come packed with thousands of features, they cost thousands of dollars. This raises the entry barrier for everyone, but impacts less-funded developers more than well-funded ones. Luckily, there's an alternative to paying for an expensive modelling and animation tool, which does not involve robbing a bank.

Initially started as a proprietary product, Blender was bought and open-sourced by a community of enthusiasts when its original developer went out of business. Blender features advanced modeling and animation capabilities and has been used for various professional-grade film and game projects.

Besides abilities that enable artists to build stunning 3D meshes, Blender has a Python API for developing custom plugins. Many of these plugins add data import and export features, which made Blender a premium tool for converting 3D mesh data from one format into another.

In this recipe we set up a plugin called Chicken Exporter that was written for exporting models from Blender.

Getting ready

If Blender is not already installed on your system, you will first need to download and install it. Blender can be downloaded and used for free, just go to `www.blender.org/download/get-blender/` to get a copy of the program. Be sure to download a version prior to 2.5 because from this version on, Blender comes with a completely new version of its Python API that is not compatible with one found in previous versions. The download page should look similar to the following screenshot.

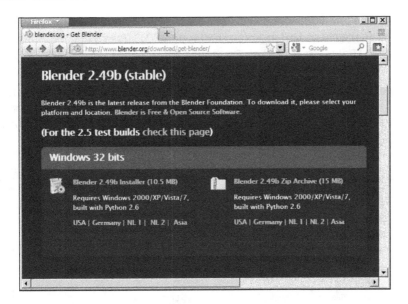

Download and run the installer. This recipe assumes you installed Blender in its default location. You will need to modify the file paths according to your settings if you made a different choice about the install location.

How to do it...

Configure Blender and Chicken Exporter with the following steps:

1. Go to `sourceforge.net/projects/chicken-export/files/`. Click the **Download Now!** button to retrieve the latest version of Chicken Exporter.

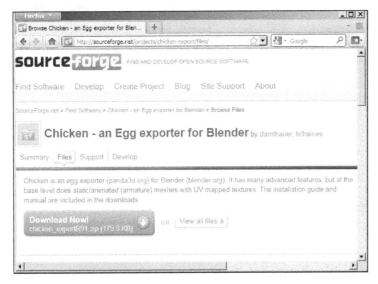

2. Unpack the downloaded archive. Copy the `bpydata` and `bpymodules` directories, as well as the file `chicken_exportR91.py` to `C:\Users\[YOUR USERNAME]\AppData\Roaming\Blender Foundation\Blender\.blender\scripts\`. Replace `[YOUR USERNAME]` with your login name.

3. Create a new environment variable called `PYTHONPATH` and set its value to `C:\Panda3D-1.7.0\python\python.exe;C:\Panda3D-1.7.0\python\DLLs;C:\Panda3D-1.7.0\python\Lib; C:\Panda3D-1.7.0\python\Lib\lib-tk`

4. Start Blender. Click **File | Export | Chicken R91 (.egg)**.

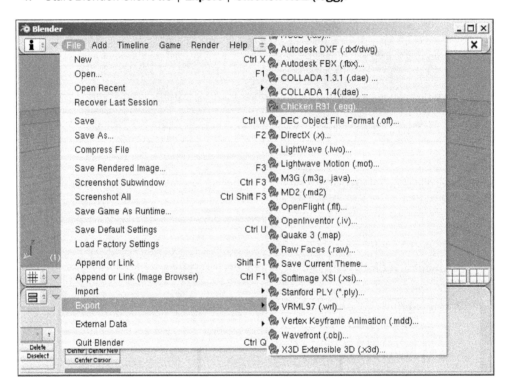

5. In the following screen, choose either **Auto** or **Manual**. When choosing **Manual**, you need to enter the installation path of the Panda3D SDK.

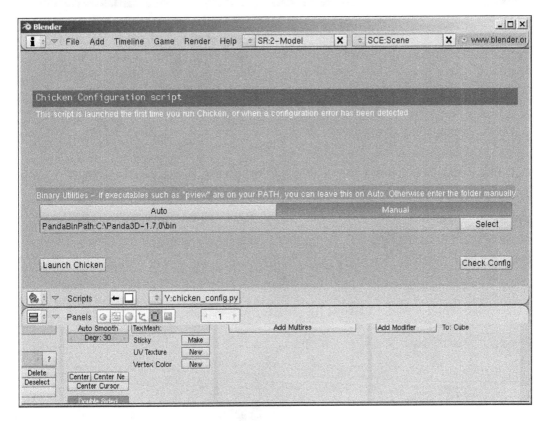

6. Click **Check Config** and then **Launch Chicken**.

How it works...

While installing, the plugin involves copying the right files to the right place, we need to take a closer look at the PYTHONPATH environment variable and how Blender works. Blender internally uses a minimal version of Python, which loads a set of scripts that define the user interface and its behavior. This embedded version of Python is also used for running any user-provided plugin scripts.

The only problem about Blender's embedded Python version is that it is a stripped-down version of the Python runtime. While this allows Blender to keep its initial download size small, this is a problem for us because some plugins like Chicken require functionality found in the standard libraries of the full Python distribution. To overcome this limitation, Blender automatically looks to see if the PYTHONPATH environment variable contains paths to a complete distribution of Python, which is then used instead of the built-in, slimmed-down version.

Exporting models from Blender

Digital content creation tools provide great features, and talented artists are able to create whatever they imagine. While these tools enable creators to make cool things, we need to think about the channel that leads from the tool used for creating the 3D geometry and animations to our engine. This is why we will step through the following tasks to learn how to use the Chicken Exporter plugin for Blender, so we are able to close the gap between the content creation tool and the Panda3D engine.

Getting ready

Exporting model data from Blender requires the Chicken Exporter plugin. Follow the instructions of the preceding recipe (*Setting up the Blender export plugin*) to get ready.

How to do it...

Follow these instructions to export a model from Blender:

1. Select all parts of the scene you wish to export.
2. Click **File | Export | Chicken R91 (.egg)**.

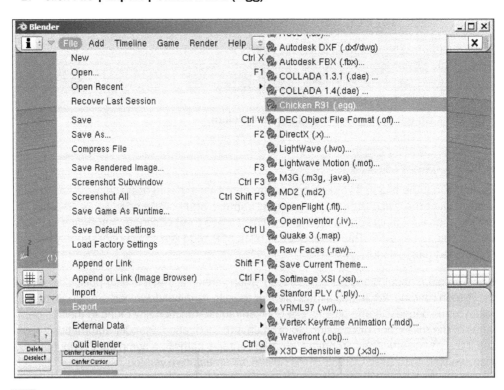

3. The last step opened the dialogue shown in the following screenshot. Enter the name of the exported file and click **Export**.

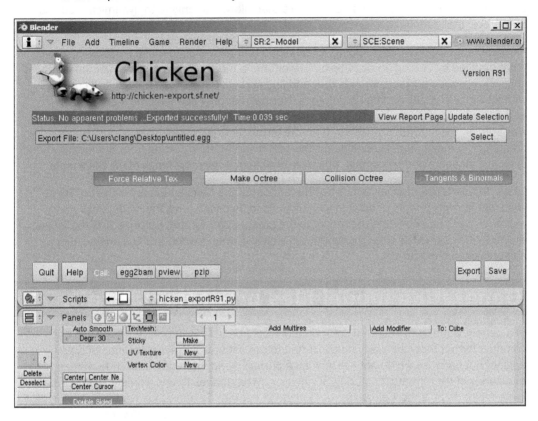

How it works...

The first thing we have to remember when using the Chicken Exporter is to select everything we want to export. The plugin does not export the current scene, but only the objects that were selected prior to launching the plugin. Although we are able to change our selection even after the plugin has been activated, we need to press the **Update Selection** button for Chicken Exporter to register our changes.

Besides the ability to update the selection of objects to export, Chicken Export has some more two-state buttons for toggling options that need some explanation. **Force Relative Tex** makes the plugin use relative paths for texture references, for example. So instead of specifying the path to these files starting from the file system root (C:\ on Windows or / on Unix based systems), file paths are used to describe the way from the directory that contains the model to the directory that contains the texture files.

Make Octree and **Collision Octree** enable optimization measures for bigger scenes. If these flags are active, geometry and collision shapes respectively, are split up and prepared to be stored in a hierarchical spatial data structure that allows the engine to dynamically cull parts of the level that cannot be seen by the player.

Panda3D supports normal mapping, a technique that allows us to make surfaces appear more detailed by putting an extra texture layer onto a model. This additional texture contains specially encoded surface normals that add fine surface details, like bumps and creases, without the use of any additional polygons. Normal mapping has become a standard technique in video games and if you want to learn more about it, there's plenty of material available on the internet if you search for the terms "normal mapping" and "dot3 bump mapping". To make models suitable for this technique when exporting from Blender, we need to export tangents and binormals, which we enable by activating **Tangents & Binormals**.

Lastly, there's a row of small buttons at the bottom of the Chicken Exporter screen. These two-state buttons enable or disable various tools to be called after the model data was exported. `egg2bam` converts the model to the binary `.bam` format, `pview` starts the Pview tool that lets us preview what the model will look like when loaded into the engine. `pzip` compresses the model file.

Generating model files programmatically

In a perfect world, every content creation tool would be able to import and export in one common format that can easily be converted to the native data representation of a game engine. But because we do not live in such a perfect world, there are literally hundreds to thousands of file formats for storing 3D meshes. What makes things worse is the fact that there might be no import plugin for our engine or content creation tool available, forcing us into writing our own converter, which is very often the case with brand new tools and file formats.

This recipe aims to be an exercise in writing our own custom file format conversion utility. We will be working on an arbitrary set of vertex data, converting it to Panda3D's internal format, and saving the data into a file.

Getting ready

This recipe extends the basic application skeleton described in *Setting up the game structure* found in Chapter 1. Please set up a new project according to these instructions before going on. Also, prepare a texture image in PNG format.

How to do it...

This recipe consists of these tasks:

1. Create a new subdirectory called `textures` in the project directory.

2. Rename your texture file to `texture.png` and copy it to the `textures` directory.

3. Open `Application.py` and add the following `import` statements:

    ```
    from panda3d.core import *
    from panda3d.egg import *
    ```

4. Extend the constructor of the `Application` class:

    ```
    class Application(ShowBase):
        def __init__(self):
            ShowBase.__init__(self)
            self.generateEgg()
            model = loader.loadModel("generated")
            model.reparentTo(render)

            dirLight = DirectionalLight("directional")
            dirNode = render.attachNewNode(dirLight)
            dirNode.setHpr(20, 20, 20)
            render.setLight(dirNode)
            self.cam.setPos(5, -5, -5)
            self.cam.lookAt(model)
    ```

5. Add the following method to `Application` class:

    ```
    def generateEgg(self):
        eggRoot = EggData()
        meshGroup = EggGroup("Mesh")
        vertexPool = EggVertexPool("Vertices")
        eggRoot.addChild(vertexPool)
        eggRoot.addChild(meshGroup)

        vertices = (Point3D(-1, 1, 1),
                    Point3D(-1, -1, 1),
                    Point3D(1, -1, 1),
                    Point3D(1, 1, 1),
                    Point3D(1, 1, -1),
                    Point3D(1, -1, -1),
                    Point3D(-1, -1, -1),
                    Point3D(-1, 1, -1))

        texcoords = (Point2D(0, 1),
                     Point2D(0, 0),
                     Point2D(1, 0),
                     Point2D(1, 1))
    ```

```
faces = ((0, 1, 2, 3),
         (4, 5, 6, 7),
         (7, 6, 1, 0),
         (3, 2, 5, 4),
         (7, 0, 3, 4),
         (1, 6, 5, 2))

texture = EggTexture("color", Filename("../textures/texture.
png"))

for face in faces:
    polygon = EggPolygon()
    meshGroup.addChild(polygon)
    for index, uv in zip(face, texcoords):
        vertex = vertexPool.makeNewVertex(vertices[index])
        vertex.setUv(uv)
        polygon.addVertex(vertex)

    polygon.addTexture(texture)
    polygon.recomputePolygonNormal()
    polygon.triangulateInPlace(True)

eggRoot.writeEgg(Filename("../models/generated.egg"))
```

6. Launch the program. You should see something comparable to the following screenshot:

How it works...

In the `generateEgg()` method, we can see a very common set of data to process. We have a vertex buffer, an index buffer for referencing vertices, and a set of texture coordinates as well as a texture image. All of which somehow need to go into an `.egg` file.

Panda3D's `.egg` files use a tree structure containing various nodes for geometry, textures, and materials, among others. The root of this tree is represented by the `EggData` class, to which other child nodes might be added. In our sample, we add a group node and a vertex pool.

The group node is used to store the polygons our model consists of, while all the vertices forming the polygons have to be part of a vertex pool. We can think of this data structure as a simple list of vertices. We can use multiple meshes and vertex pools to form a model, but all vertices used to build a mesh have to be part of the same vertex pool. In our sample we add the vertices that form our mesh to a single pool. Additionally, we assign each vertex a texture coordinate so Panda3D will be able to put a texture map onto the surface of our mesh.

We add a texture image to each of the newly created polygons. In our case, this is only one texture, but each subsequent call to `addTexture()` adds another texture layer to a polygon. We also calculate the polygon normal because we need that for lighting to work in Panda3D.

The algorithms and hardware involved in rasterized real-time rendering work most efficiently when processing triangles. In comparison to other geometrical forms, triangles are very simple and their properties are very well known. In addition, any polygonal surface can be split into triangles, which makes them a perfect format for describing arbitrary meshes. So to allow the graphics hardware to work most efficiently, we split the cube's six surface planes into twelve triangles.

Using the "Pview" tool to preview models

No matter which content creation tools our artists are using, we can be sure that these programs have different ways of displaying models than the Panda3D engine. This can be quite annoying for artists to work with, as they would have to export their work and wait for the game assets to be repackaged. Then they would have to start the game and load the model, just to check what it looks like in the game. This is not what we want to happen.

Instead, we want to have a little application that allows artists to quickly load a model so they can preview how Panda3D displays their work. Luckily, we do not need to write this program ourselves, as the Panda3D developers already implemented a little tool called `Pview` for this situation. This recipe will give you a short introduction to this tool.

How to do it...

Let's explore the features of the `Pview` tool:

1. Open a new command prompt window.

2. Type the following command and press the *Enter* key:

   ```
   pview -l panda panda-walk
   ```

3. Hold down the *left mouse button* and move the mouse to pan the panda around.

4. Push and hold the *right mouse button*, move the mouse forward and back to zoom in and out.

5. Hold down the *Alt* key on your keyboard while holding the *left mouse button* and moving the mouse to rotate the panda around its center point.

6. Center the Panda in the window by pressing the *C* key on your keyboard.

7. Press *W* once to turn on wireframe rendering. Press the key a second time to switch back to normal rendering.

8. Turn on basic lighting by hitting *L*.

9. Press the *COMMA* key multiple times to toggle through different background colors.

10. Open a new window. Press the *Shift* and *W* keys at the same time.

11. To close the newly opened window again, use the *Q* key.

12. Open animation controls using the *A* key:

13. Take a screenshot of the current window by pressing *F9*.

14. Press *Escape* to quit.

How it works...

While operating, the tool does not need any further explanation; we should take a quick look at the command line parameters that we used to start the program. The -l option makes Pview load the model data asynchronously, which means that the window appears immediately, and the model will be visible after a short loading delay. The first argument after this option is the model or actor to preview, which is mandatory. Optionally, as we do in this recipe, the second argument is the name of an .egg or .bam file containing animation data. Pview will load the first animation it finds contained within that .egg or .bam file and then begin playing the animation in a continuous loop.

Compressing and converting model files using pzip and egg2bam

When working with Panda3D, you will mainly encounter two kinds of files for storing models and actors. The one type of file has the extension .egg, while the other ends with a .bam filename suffix.q.

The .egg file format is intended to be a common intermediate and interchange file format. It was designed to be very easy to understand, to facilitate the development of format converters and export plugins for digital content creation tools. Files in .egg format are text-based and human-readable, which makes them easier to inspect and analyze. This also makes it possible for version tracking systems like Subversion, Perforce, or Git to efficiently store and track changes to the model data.

The big downside of the .egg model file format is file size. Storing this kind of data in a plain-text format is not very efficient and takes up a lot of storage space. Not only does this unnecessarily waste disk space, it also increases the time needed for loading geometry into the engine.

To keep file sizes smaller, .egg files can be compressed using pzip, as you will see in this recipe. This works fairly well but does not solve the problem of loading times, which brings us to the .bam file format.

Just like .egg files, .bam files are used for storing model and animation data. The difference between these two is the way the data is stored. While the .egg format is designed to be easily comprehensible for us humans, the .bam format is used to represent this data in a way that is friendlier to a computer and more specifically, to the Panda3D engine.

The .bam format encodes model data in a binary format that is closer to Panda3D's in-memory presentation of that data. This allows the engine to load models faster because fewer preprocessing steps are required for parsing the file format and filling data structures. Additionally, by this way, storing raw binary data is more space efficient, leading to smaller file sizes.

This recipe will show you how to compress .egg files to save disk space, and how to convert models from this intermediate format to the .bam format for efficient storage, loading, and distribution.

Getting ready

In this recipe you will work on an .egg model file. Of course you need such a model file to be able to work through the tasks. The steps of this recipe will assume the filename to be model.egg.

How to do it...

Use the following commands presented to compress and convert model files:

1. Open a command prompt and navigate to the directory containing your model file.

2. Type and execute the following command:

   ```
   pzip -9 model.egg
   ```

3. Convert the model to the .bam format using this command line:

   ```
   egg2bam -noabs -flatten 1 -combine-geoms 1 -txopz -ctex -mipmap -o
   model.bam model.egg.pz
   ```

How it works...

The pzip tool is used to compress .egg files. When invoking it the way we do in this recipe, the source file is compressed in place, generating the file model.egg.pz out of model.egg. If we want to keep the original file, we need to explicitly specify an output file name using the -o parameter. The pzip tool also takes an optional command line parameter for setting the compression level. While -9 sets the strongest compression, -8, -7, and so on—ranging down to -1—set subsequently weaker levels of compression. Less compression results in bigger file sizes, but less time will be needed for processing a file. Setting a higher compression level on the other hand will increase processing times but decrease file sizes.

When converting to the .bam format, there are a few more options we can pass to the egg2bam tool. With -noabs, we make sure the .egg file does not contain any absolute references to other models or textures. If any absolute file reference is found, the program aborts with an error. It generally is a good idea to use relative file references, because it makes it easier to relocate our model files, for example when we are installing them to a directory chosen by the user.

The next two options, -flatten 1 and -combine-geoms 1 apply some optimizations to the geometry and the hierarchy contained in the source file. While the first one enables simplification of the tree structure, the second of the two parameters instructs egg2bam to look for duplicate geometry groups and combine them into one.

Finally, we pass some options for how `egg2bam` should handle textures. The `-txopz` option causes the creation of texture object files. These files with a `.txo.pz` suffix store texture image data in a format that is already suitable for being loaded efficiently into the engine. Additionally, the file data is compressed to minimize storage requirements.

Using the `-ctex` flag enables lossy DXT compression to be applied to all of the model's textures. This kind of compression not only saves space, it can be decoded in hardware by most modern graphics cards. This makes it possible for texture data being stored inside the graphics adapter's memory in the compressed form, using up less texture memory. As a downside, this kind of compression will have a negative impact on the quality of our textures. If our textures are in a very high resolution however, the space saved by DXT compression is generally worth a minor loss in image quality.

Mipmapping is a commonly used level of detail technique where a set of textures is used instead of one single texture map. Each texture in the set corresponds to a mipmapping level. With each subsequent level, the texture is sampled down to half the size of the previous level. Depending on an object's distance from the camera, this allows us to choose a lower texture resolution, because it will only take a few pixels to draw a distant object. If objects are closer to the camera, mipmapping uses the higher resolution textures found in the set, as more details will be visible on a close object.

We can calculate the downsampled versions of the original texture using the `-mipmap` flag. This increases texture file size by 30% because of the additional texture detail levels being stored. But not having to generate them at load time may help to decrease loading times. Additionally, our runtime performance should become better, because mipmapping allows for more efficient rendering. We should however, always rely on profiling data to back our performance claims and check our games' performance metrics using the tools shown in *Chapter 10, Debugging and Performance.*

Index

Thank you for buying
Panda3D 1.7 Game Developer's Cookbook

About Packt Publishing

Packt, pronounced 'packed', published its first book "*Mastering phpMyAdmin for Effective MySQL Management*" in April 2004 and subsequently continued to specialize in publishing highly focused books on specific technologies and solutions.

Our books and publications share the experiences of your fellow IT professionals in adapting and customizing today's systems, applications, and frameworks. Our solution based books give you the knowledge and power to customize the software and technologies you're using to get the job done. Packt books are more specific and less general than the IT books you have seen in the past. Our unique business model allows us to bring you more focused information, giving you more of what you need to know, and less of what you don't.

Packt is a modern, yet unique publishing company, which focuses on producing quality, cutting-edge books for communities of developers, administrators, and newbies alike. For more information, please visit our website: www.packtpub.com.

About Packt Open Source

In 2010, Packt launched two new brands, Packt Open Source and Packt Enterprise, in order to continue its focus on specialization. This book is part of the Packt Open Source brand, home to books published on software built around Open Source licenses, and offering information to anybody from advanced developers to budding web designers. The Open Source brand also runs Packt's Open Source Royalty Scheme, by which Packt gives a royalty to each Open Source project about whose software a book is sold.

Writing for Packt

We welcome all inquiries from people who are interested in authoring. Book proposals should be sent to author@packtpub.com. If your book idea is still at an early stage and you would like to discuss it first before writing a formal book proposal, contact us; one of our commissioning editors will get in touch with you.

We're not just looking for published authors; if you have strong technical skills but no writing experience, our experienced editors can help you develop a writing career, or simply get some additional reward for your expertise.

Panda3D 1.6 Game Engine Beginner's Guide

ISBN: 978-1-84951-272-5   Paperback: 356 pages

Create your own computer game with this 3D rendering and game development framework

1. The first and only guide to building a finished game using Panda3D

2. Learn about tasks that can be used to handle changes over time

3. Respond to events like keyboard key presses, mouse clicks, and more

4. Take advantage of Panda3D's built-in shaders and filters to decorate objects with gloss, glow, and bump effects

Flash 10 Multiplayer Game Essentials

ISBN: 978-1-847196-60-6   Paperback: 336 pages

Create exciting real-time multiplayer games using Flash

1. A complete end-to-end guide for creating fully featured multiplayer games

2. The author's experience in the gaming industry enables him to share insights on multiplayer game development

3. Walk-though several real-time multiplayer game implementations

4. Packed with illustrations and code snippets with supporting explanations for ease of understanding

Please check **www.PacktPub.com** for information on our titles

XNA 4.0 Game Development by Example: Beginner's Guide

ISBN: 978-1-84969-066-9   Paperback: 428 pages

Create your own exciting games with Microsoft XNA 4.0

1. Dive headfirst into game creation with XNA

2. Four different styles of games comprising a puzzler, a space shooter, a multi-axis shoot 'em up, and a jump-and-run platformer

3. Games that gradually increase in complexity to cover a wide variety of game development techniques

4. Focuses entirely on developing games with the free version of XNA

Unity 3D Game Development by Example Beginner's Guide

ISBN: 978-1-84969-054-6   Paperback: 384 pages

A seat-of-your-pants manual for building fun, groovy little games quickly

1. Build fun games using the free Unity 3D game engine even if you've never coded before

2. Learn how to "skin" projects to make totally different games from the same file – more games, less effort!

3. Deploy your games to the Internet so that your friends and family can play them

4. Packed with ideas, inspiration, and advice for your own game design and development

Please check **www.PacktPub.com** for information on our titles

www.ingramcontent.com/pod-product-compliance
Lightning Source LLC
Chambersburg PA
CBHW062101050326
40690CB00016B/3163